Thanks and Acknowledgments

Thanks to my parents, Gene and Aurora Hough, for making our family's move to Turkey possible, and for believing that it made sense. Thanks to my wife Cari (Zarif Çiçeğim), and my daughters Grace, Sunny, and Babs. They heard about Ahmad ibn Hanbal, Gregory VII, the Papal Revolution, the Mihna, and other historical episodes more times than was kind.

Thanks also to several good Turkish friends, who should probably remain nameless here. In particular I thank the friend (and his family) who welcomed some bewildered and nervous foreigners in Istanbul into their home. Anyone moving to another country would be fortunate to find such a friend.

April 2016, BWH

Cover photo: Blaque W. Hough
Cover design: Alysia Menendez

Contents

Forward

Why yet *another* book discussing Islam? Because too many of the books and articles published, and too many blogs and websites, either bash Islam unfairly, or praise Islam uncritically. Because too many politicians, journalists, and political or public figures do the same thing. Because too much of our public discussion avoids identifying a real similarity or a real difference between Christian and Islamic background cultures when it isn't actively attempting to obscure it to secure peace in our time. Nobody wins when that's happening.

Timur Kuran, in *Islam & Mammon*, mentioned the low level of interest in discussing whether and how Islamic thought and questions of economics and development (his academic expertise) intersect. He points out correctly that scholars of either are rarely trained in both fields, and that they tend to avoid what they don't feel confident discussing; that "cultural relativism" inhibits comparisons which might instruct; and that discussion might enflame groups hostile to Muslims. He noted the possibility that his book might be abused,

> "But this is not a sufficient reason to avoid an honest analysis or to suppress troubling data. The principal victims of self-censorship could be the very peoples one is trying to protect. In any case, whatever the extent of current anti-Muslim prejudice, it is unlikely to disappear by ignoring potentially discomforting possibilities. On the contrary, a dispassionate analysis that dispels myths might serve as an antidote to religious prejudice."[1]

But even when our academics rise to the challenge and do great work, too often it never reaches an audience beyond university circles. There are many books and articles by learned professors discussing the themes of this book, but they're read by very few, and understood by even fewer. They are never read by those who need their information the most.

This is an attempt to collect and combine some of the work of great academic minds and place it before a busy public that doesn't have the time to plow through endless books and articles. It makes no claim to be an exhaustive and all-inclusive treatment of the many reasons Westerners may fail to understand Islam and Islamic societies, but instead focuses on the gravely neglected area of law. It is (hopefully) a dispassionate overview of why people from Christian and Islamic background cultures understand law and religion so differently – because they do.

Those different ideas of what law is, and what religion is, are at the bottom of the serious misunderstandings which the West has of Islamic cultures, and are equally at the bottom of the serious misunderstandings which Islamic cultures have of the West. Discussing law, religion, and their intersections, similarities, and differences is heavy going, so I've tried to put in enough of the general history of both Christianity and Islam to keep the story moving forward while these heavy topics unfold in their historical contexts.

Chapters 1 through 3 compare differences in the beginnings of Christianity and Islam and draw out some of the implications of those differences. Chapters 4 to 6 discuss the conversations within each of these traditions on authority of the state versus authority of the tradition, and the question of how decisions about knowledge and scholarship helped set both Christianity and Islam on different developmental paths.

The first six chapters are probably the most difficult, so Chapter 7 which reviews the transition to modern times may be a bit of a relief. Chapters 8 through 10 cover the shock to the Islamic world when the modern West invaded – in every sense of the term – and the varying reactions possible within an Islamic society. Those reactions were conditioned, shaped and guided by the prior development of Islam and Islamic doctrines. Without the background of the prior chapters, those reactions are so often misunderstood.

Finally, chapters 11 through 13 illustrate the social turmoil which many Islamic societies struggle to tame, and end on the hopeful note of a "reformation" by Muslims, for Muslims, within Islam.

But all of this demands engagement with topics which offend many people. Many people have such strong ideas about these issues they find it difficult to suspend judgment long enough to even hear an argument.

For example, religion is a major theme, as it must be. But I can imagine minds slamming shut already, knowing that the Christians have it right, or the Muslims do, or that some school or sect of either have it all figured out, or that neither of them do, and that their religions are pernicious nonsense, nothing but common psychological projections subconsciously designed to meet human needs, that do nothing but trouble the world and destroy lives.

It is also far too easy to insult the religion of whatever group isn't yours.

If you want to read a book knocking Muhammad for his marriage to Ayesha at a young age, insinuating that he was some kind of pedophile, or that Islam is only a religion of violence, then don't bother with this one.

If you'd like to read about the plots of the Western world to overthrow the heartlands of Islam, how missionaries were massed on the borders in Jordan, waiting to descend on Iraq for mass conversions to Christianity in the wake of American forces in the first Gulf War, don't read this book.

If you'd like to read another book pretending that Islam and Christianity are really the same, (since they both worship the same God, don't they?) stop now.

There is plenty of trash of this sort marketed to both Christians and Muslims, and there probably always will be.

This is the work of a generalist, working across academic disciplines. It is expected to provoke specialists to weeping and gnashing of teeth over many omissions, compressions, and simplifications. There may be gentle criticism of oft-told truths by both Christian and Islamic believers, but there is no hard source criticism of whether or not Jesus, Muhammad, or any other historical actor said or did (or didn't) a certain thing. I've avoided heavy footnoting, because I want this to be easy to read for the general reader, but I have included sources relied on, and which have influenced what I think, in the bibliography.

I want to avoid both academic obscurity and pandering to popular prejudice. Suspend, if you will, the question of the "rightness" of either or neither of these great historic monotheistic faiths. Instead, let's look at what Christians and Muslims over many centuries have *thought* the place of religion should be in the ordering of society. What both Christians and Muslims have done, and how they have thought and felt they must do it, may help us understand current events that shock, delight, or infuriate.

I realize I'm asking the impossible. If you've bothered to pick up this book, then you probably have some closely held thoughts and convictions on the subject matter. And if you perceive that I'm trying to attack what you hold dear, then the message I'm trying to communicate will have no hearer. My goal is modest and stunningly naive at the same time: I would like the people of two great civilizations to understand a little better why they too often don't understand one another. I would like people to talk about those differences which divide us, but also similarities which could help unite us, if we only understood them and talked about them openly.

This is not a history of either religion. There are already many on the market and I feel no need to contribute another. I am not comparing religious beliefs or doctrines, except incidentally. I will select certain historical episodes, and sometimes look at them in greater detail than is normal in a general history, or try to emphasize them in a different way to support my arguments.

That means that I am leaving out a great deal that is usually part of the narrative of either Islam or Christianity. That will irritate some readers who will wish to argue more on behalf of their own faith traditions. But remember, I am not directly discussing either - the focus here is limited to the confused intersections of law and religion within both Christianity and

Islam. That story is not often told, and it will make the beginnings of both Christianity and Islam particularly strange to some.

There is no discussion of Shi'a Islam, nor is there discussion of Protestant Christianity. There is no discussion of the mystic Sufi orders within Islam, nor the Christian mystics and enthusiasts. I'm avoiding discussion of "religious" topics like prayer, sin, fasting or religious obligations, focusing on the mainstream view of the interaction of law and religion within Islam and Christianity. That means sticking with Sunni Islam on one hand, and Catholic Christianity on the other.

People born and raised in Western societies have an idea of where the borders are between law and religion, and what both law and religion are to do in society. Those ideas are based on the struggle within society between Western (Catholic or Protestant – not Orthodox) Christianity and the forces of the State. Most Westerners don't even think about that struggle, but assume that where those borders lie now are where they ought to be, or are the way it always has been for Christians. That isn't so.

Similarly, people born and raised in an Islamic-majority society have their own ideas of where those borders are, and what the respective functions of law and religion in society are supposed to be, based upon their own history of conflict between the forces of religion and religious leaders, and the State. They too, often assume that where those borders lie now is the way it has always been for Muslims, or the way it ought to be in the future.

It should come as no surprise that the majority positions in both Christian-background and Muslim-background societies place the borders between law and religion in different places. But have they done that from the very beginning? Have there been significant historical turning points or decisions which shaped where the boundaries would be? How do those differences and historical turning points lead people to act in their societies today? Are these differences set in stone or may there be change?

What about when a Muslim thinks *his* assumptions about law and religion apply to a Western Christian? And what about when a Western Christian thinks *her* assumptions about law and religion are acceptable to (or even understood by) a Muslim? Do people in Islamic and Christian background societies even agree on what their own assumptions are? What happens when our assumptions collide through war, trade, colonization – or now the mass movement of refugees? What will that lead us to think about one another – or do to one another? Do either of our assumptions even make room for minority positions, or do they suppose only one answer to a particular question within either Christianity or Islam? Those are the general questions this book helps raise.

It doesn't matter in reading this book whether or not you have religious faith. These two great religions have helped construct social orders and we're stuck with what they've produced, like it or not. The question of whether the source of truth is inside both, outside both, either, or neither, of these traditions can go unanswered, so long as you'll admit the proposition that some things are true, and some things are not true. If you cannot accept that proposition, then you are left only with your choice of personal preference in these matters, and all of life.

If you admit that true things may be discovered through observation and reflection, then what matters is what you do with true things you discover. As Eugen Rosenstock-Huessy said of truth in *Out of Revolution: Autobiography of Western Man*: "Truth is divine and has been divinely revealed – *credo ut intelligam*. Truth is pure and can be scientifically stated – *cogito ergo sum*. Truth is vital and must be socially represented – *Respondeo etsi mutabor*."[2]

If this struggle to represent a bit more truth in our societies means that you must respond and change, then be open to change. If you think the observations and conclusions are too simple, too predictable, clichéd or just plain wrong, feel free to pitch this book into the nearest bin. But hold on to the idea of looking for the assumptions behind Islamic and Christian social orders to understand them. Accept that this work will be frustrating. Accept that a byproduct of a sincere attempt at understanding "the other" will be a questioning of your own conclusions, notions, and beliefs.

Let's jump in then, and look for things which might be true, and make some comparisons which might instruct. If we learn even a little about the different mainstream Islamic and Christian views of law and religion, then both Christians and Muslims will be closer to understanding why *they* do what *they* do, and maybe we'll all change for the better in response.

Respondeo etsi mutabor.

Chapter 1 - Christianity Begins

Christianity and Islam began very differently from one another. Examining their formation is vital to understanding why even today many Christians and Muslims think about the same subjects quite differently. But both are tempted to the same errors when discussing the beginnings: First, it is easy to project backward in history the developed thought and practice of today in either Christianity or Islam, and see it present in the beginning. Second, for the serious adherent of his or her faith, discussing only part of either Christianity or Islam and making no attempt to present the whole (glorious) picture is likely to trigger a defensive reaction.

So, Christians very serious about their faith must remember that this is only a limited attempt to understand some of Christianity's intersections with law and the constitutional order of society. Readers familiar with Christianity must do their best to forget everything they know, and try hard to imagine themselves as contemporaries of Jesus, looking on at his words and actions. For Christianity begins with Jesus Christ. That may seem arguable to some, so consider the case negatively: Without Jesus Christ, there is no Christianity. That seems clear enough.

Poet, novelist, playwright and theologian Charles Williams described the beginning of Christianity without the benefit of today's hindsight:

> "Historically, its beginning was clear enough. There had appeared in Palestine, during the government of the Princeps Augustus and his successor Tiberius, a certain being. This being was in the form of a man, a peripatetic teacher, a thaumaturgical orator. There were plenty of the sort about, springing up in the newly-established peace of the Empire, but this particular one had a higher

potential of power, and a much more distracting method. It had a very effective verbal style, notably in imprecation, together with a recurrent ambiguity of statement. It continually scored debating-points over its interlocutors. It agreed with everything on the one hand, and denounced everything on the other. For example, it said nothing against the Roman occupation; it urged obedience to the Jewish hierarchy; it proclaimed holiness to the Lord. But it was present at doubtfully holy feasts; it associated with rich men and loose women; it commented acerbly on the habits of the hierarchy; and while encouraging everyone to pay their debts, it radiated a general disapproval, or at least doubt, of every kind of property. It talked of love in terms of hell, and of hell in terms of perfection. And finally it talked at the top of its piercing voice about itself and its own unequalled importance. It said that it was the best and worst thing that ever had happened or ever could happen to man. It said it could control anything and yet had to submit to everything. It said its Father in Heaven would do anything it wished, but that for itself it would do nothing but what its Father in Heaven wished. And it promised that when it had disappeared, it would cause some other Power to illumine, confirm, and direct that small group of stupefied and helpless followers whom it deigned, with the sound of the rush of a sublime tenderness, to call its friends."[3]

So, what were those "stupefied and helpless" men and women to make of all this? What were they to do in their everyday lives? What was their group identity, if they even had one? They didn't even have a name! What was their proper relationship with the surrounding society, with the religious leadership in Jerusalem (they were all Jews, of course), and with the state, dominated by Rome? What were they to make of a statement like "…give back to Caesar what belongs to Caesar - and to God what belongs to God."?[4]

A Westerner would most likely argue that those men and women should have recognized that Jesus was explaining that in life there are two spheres of authority in the world, one which is secular and involves politics, government, law, and power here and now, and another sphere which is spiritual and involves matters of faith and belief, right and moral conduct now, and then an afterlife. But those first Jewish believers were not the beneficiaries of nearly two thousand years of history of the Christian faith. As Williams noted, they had to cope with that "recurrent ambiguity of statement".

Christianity began to define what it was, and what it believed, under three dominant cultural influences, those of the Jewish religion, the Roman law, and Greek culture. Historians of Christianity realize that each of these cultural strains had an influence upon the development of this new faith, especially when that faith was so loose, or ill-defined, as it was. Was Christianity part of these cultural strains, against them, subject to them, or somehow above them?

Jewish Religion

Several groups existed within the Jewish religion at the time of Jesus. One of the largest, the Pharisees, was a party often wrongly associated with strict rule following and hypocrisy (although sometimes that was true). Some of the great Pharisees, such as Hillel, who died in 10 CE, made statements strikingly similar to those Jesus made, and just as aspirational in quality: "What is hateful to you, do not to your neighbour: that is the whole Torah, while the rest is the commentary thereof; go and learn it."[5] There have been arguments that Jesus was himself a Pharisee, given the similarity of statements. The other major party was the Sadducee group, about which the scholars don't know much. It is usually portrayed as an upper class segment of Jewish society with a Hellenic culture.

In addition to the two mainstream parties, who both seemed content enough under Roman rule, there were various types of radicals living outside the cities, or on the desert edge. Some focused on elaborate religious rituals and teachings of an end time. Some were more resistant to Roman rule, and wanted an uprising and a restored Jewish kingdom there and then – and not too much later, they would try for it, provoking Roman destruction of Jerusalem and deportation of many Jews. Significant numbers of Jews also lived all about the Mediterranean, mostly in the large cities, where they tended toward the well-to-do, and often had both Hellenic culture and Greek language.

The temple of the Jews was still in Jerusalem – or more accurately, the second temple, built by Herod (dedicated in 18 BCE – probably not really finished until the 60s CE) after the destruction of the original temple by the Babylonians in 587 BCE. As a symbol and center of ritual it was still important, but the center of gravity within the Jewish religion had begun to shift by then, to the local synagogue.

The synagogue, a building for worship, assembly, and study, originated at a time obscure to us, although some would argue it may have been as far back as Moses. We know with much more certainty that the institution of the synagogue received a great impetus in the Babylonian captivity. When the Jewish upper classes were deported by the Babylonians, and the temple was destroyed, the need of an institution for teaching and preserving the religious life of the Jews became sharply apparent, especially in the absence of a temple where sacrifices could be made, and a symbol of the people's religion could be seen.

When some exiles were allowed to return to Jerusalem and begin their rebuilding of the city, synagogue building was part of the reconstruction of Jewish life. Even though Herod began building a great temple again, synagogues were also built in the lands of Israel and abroad. In fact, "foreign" Jews, according to tradition, even had their own synagogues in Jerusalem at the time of Jesus. The practice of religion became de-centralized through the institution of the synagogue wherever there was a significant enough population of Jews to fund a building program.

It naturally follows, given the absence of the temple, presence of the synagogue and emphasis upon teaching that the center of Judaism would begin to shift toward the intellectual endeavors of collection, writing, and teaching. The collection called the Talmud is several thousand pages dealing with law, customary practices, and the accumulated oral traditions and learning of Judaism. Usually the Jerusalem and Babylonian collections, around 200 CE and 500 CE respectively, and of those two, more often the Babylonian, are what Talmud means. Learning and mastery of these complex and voluminous materials was, and is, the work of a lifetime.

Wherever the center of gravity of the Jewish religion, or Judaism, of the day might have been located, there was without doubt a strong tradition of worship and holy scriptures at the time of Jesus, and a robust tradition and system of education into the knowledge and rituals for the young. The literature relating tales of famous ancestors like David and Solomon, the religious lessons to be drawn from their lives, songs and poems, prophetic warnings, legal texts, synagogues and liturgy – all of these were part of a rich religious practice in the society into which Jesus was born and in which his followers lived.

Greek Culture

Greek culture, the culture of the Hellenes, was a transnational culture. It included a trade language in wide use to facilitate commerce, and a culture lived in the many cities throughout the Middle East organized on Greek cultural lines, despite how the surrounding countryside might speak and live. "The name Hellene no longer suggests a race but an intelligence, and the title Hellene is applied rather to those who share our culture than to those who share our blood."[6] By the time of Christ, that Hellenic culture had roots hundreds of years deep, rooted in many different places.

The Greeks spread themselves out and colonized a great deal – into the Black Sea, in Sicily, in Italy, to what is now Marseilles in France, and even further West. The colonies typically kept a strong allegiance to the mother-state, but depending on local pressures, could find themselves fighting other Greeks quite easily. Colonization also meant bumping up against other practices and peoples. Adopting and adapting things taken from other cultures while remaining identifiably Greek was something Greek culture did well – and was forced to do, through contact with strong enemies from the East like the Persians.

In Greek religion there was historically a multiplicity of gods, competing with, loving, aiding or thwarting humanity, sometimes for what seems the most arbitrary of reasons. Ritual and sacrifice as legal and religious categories existed, mystery-religions from the East were practiced, and there was a general sense that the gods approved good behavior, but there was no single authoritative voice of god. Neither was there a central organization like a Church, nor one sacred book. There were priests of different gods and shrines, but no priesthood interpreting the law of god like that of the Jews.

Along with the old gods, and by this time winning the competition for followers with them, there was "an exceptionally strong emphasis on men's self-realization in this world."[7] Philosophy, in other words. "But the Greek approach is quite distinctive. Its rationality does not share the prejudices of an underlying world-view. On the contrary, Greek rationality began to operate in opposition to the Greek spiritual tradition...the Greek philosophers of nature did not take Olympic mythology very seriously."[8]

For example, Anaximander thought that everything came from the "boundless", and that the visible world could be explained in terms of orderly universal processes, eventually being absorbed back into the boundless[9]. Anaximenes postulated that everything is made of air, which operates like the boundless by changing form and qualities.[10] Xenophanes made the critical observation that people from Thrace showed their gods looking like Thracians, black Africans, like black Africans, and stated that if cows and horses had hands, then they would make their gods look like cows and horses![11] But yet somehow, there was a unique divine intelligence which governed everything.

The old pre-Socratic philosophers show us that what Greek culture expected was that even despite the gods, man could, using reason, discover the nature of the universe and how it was assembled. Their scientists though, never really put together observation and theory as we do in modern times – even when they did trouble to observe instead of theorize. We might summarize with "Man is the measure of all things" as Protagoras said around 450 BC.[12]

Laws similarly could be discovered by reason, not by revelation from the gods, and reason could apply law to society. Plato thought that law would not even be necessary if people received the right training and were properly socialized. His *Laws* opened with a discussion about the advisability of forbidding everything that is potentially harmful: Should alcohol be prohibited? The conclusion was that it would be better to train the citizens to drink only in an appropriate manner.[13] Because of the strong educational function of laws, they should have preambles explaining why each law was necessary.

The strong tradition of Greek poetry and drama hardly bears mention, as it is printed and performed to this day, but must be remembered as yet another of the tools of the intellect which helped to unite Greek culture. All of these cultural activities were intended to produce a sense of community on several levels – the broadest symbolized by Olympic games for all Hellenes.

But under this level of a shared common culture there was conflict, involving single states, or leagues of allied city-states, or other leagues existing for defense on a more temporary basis. The community at the local level was quite stratified – the demos was made up of only the citizens of a respectable strata, not foreigners, or slaves, or the poor. History shows continual tensions between oligarchic, dictatorial, and democratic forms of government in the Greek states.

The 499-449 BC wars with Persia didn't even produce a political or legal unity in the face of an enemy from the East, although they did produce a stronger cultural unity in the face of Persian invasions. A short time later, Alexander the Great finally brought about a large, more or less unified Greek Empire, and campaigned on into the East, as far as Western India, between 334 and his death in 323 BC. As he went, Alexander planted Greek cities, numerous Alexandrias among them, outposts of Greek culture amid surrounding cultures. Upon his death, the empire fragmented and was divided between his more successful generals, but the Greek cultural veneer in the kingdoms, deeper in the cities, stayed.[14]

It was Alexander who gave Greek culture on a wider basis to the Middle East where Jesus lived and Christianity started. In 146 BC the expanding Romans overthrew Greece as a power. But the Roman upper class admired Greek culture, and imported well-educated slaves as teachers in many subjects. In Greece itself and further East around the end of the Mediterranean, they essentially left Greek culture alone. Many histories note the great number of surviving inscriptions on buildings which still appeared in Greek during and after this period. Greek culture stayed, so long as it was content to exist peacefully under Roman law.

Roman Law and Order

Roman law and order was the most recent addition to the three categories of religion, culture, and law that shaped the life into which Jesus was born. At the time of Jesus' birth, Rome was an Empire, ruled by an Emperor – Augustus, who had become Emperor in 17 B.C. Prior to that time Rome had had some sort of Republican government, which had degenerated as the wealthier classes fought for primacy, and passed through a period where strong men like Julius had fought with others for power. Rome had been expanding steadily for several hundred years, westward as far as Spain, eastward around the East end of the Mediterranean, and straight South across the Mediterranean to the coastlands of Northern Africa.

Some of this expansion had involved bitter and prolonged military campaigns – don't forget the long struggle with Carthage, and the stories of the Carthaginian general Hannibal, struggling across the snow and ice of the Alps with his elephants for a counter-blow against Rome. Some had been easier, where power was weaker, or grown decrepit, and there was even the odd case of the king in what is today central-western Turkey who gave his kingdom to Rome in his Will, since he had no other heir he preferred.

All of this expansion had brought a great number of different ethnic groups, religious persuasions, languages, and cultures, under the control of the Empire. Rome had to decide how to govern and manage these different forces pulling in all sorts of directions. In response, Rome implemented a legal and political order during the Empire that could be compared to a fishnet – loose enough to let little things slip through, but something that would catch the big problems.

Rome was willing to be quite pragmatic: Laws weren't precisely the same everywhere. They could vary from province to province. Cities could have their own councils and officials, regulating their own affairs and making their own limited local law, even conducting affairs in the local language instead of Latin. This is difficult to understand today, when we're accustomed to ideas like a nation having one set of laws, applied equally to everyone, regardless of race, sex, or national origin.

Rome went further in allowing different laws than merely allowing cities to make some of their own. Laws could be different depending on who you were, not merely on whether you were inside the boundaries of the Empire. Citizenship determined the law that applied to you – think of the panic of the Roman officer when St. Paul informed him that he had ordered Paul (a citizen) to be beaten.[15] Slave, free person, or noble, and sub-ranks within those classes measured by the size of one's fortune, all entitled one to different treatment at law.

During Roman history, the class of citizens gradually expanded to take in more people. The purchase of citizenship was allowed. Finally all residents of the Empire were declared citizens, and law applied more equally to all.

Religion and the regulation of religion was included in this legal order. Eastern mystery religions, Greek philosophy, Jewish monotheism, the traditional panoply of gods, whose names changed from Latin to Greek (Jupiter to Zeus, Juno to Hera, etc.) as one moved farther East from Rome, all were allowed. The Romans didn't really care what religion a person practiced, so long as they didn't create problems with public order. This is consistent with a pluralistic legal order, with city self-rule, changes in emphasis in law from province to province, and different rights and remedies for different classes and citizens.

This may sound like a recipe for chaos. It was not. A weave in the net of social order this loose allowed for the ebb and flow of little problems, for local quirks and enthusiasms. If there was a problem big enough to get caught in the net and pull it, or threaten to tear it, then Rome reacted ferociously. The famed Roman roads weren't built for tourism or primarily for trade, but to move the army from one place to another quickly. If rebellion or disorder threatened, the roads were used, and the military killed until order was restored.

These three strands of law, culture, and religion are exemplified by Herod I (Herod the Great), who lived around 74 BCE to 4 CE. By birth and ancestry an ethnic Aramean (Arab), he accepted Judaism (to some extent) but was at the same time a client king of Rome, and a sympathizer and participant in Hellenic culture.

Finding a Way Forward – the Struggle for Identity

In this mix of competing and blending conditions, the early Christians began to feel their way forward. "They had not the language; they had not the ideas; they had to discover everything. They had only one fact, and that was that *it had happened.* Messias had come, and been killed, and risen; and they had been dead 'in trespasses and sin,' and now they were *not.*"[16]

Convinced that *it had happened,* the immediate problems facing Christians were organizing the substance of these events into a coherent order, working out any religious doctrine or social program that the life of Jesus implied or demanded, and then communicating the doctrine and program to different cultures in ways they could understand.

The very first issue of the new Christian community was its own identity. Were Christians (and they hadn't even been given this name yet) Jews or something different? Certainly the immediate followers of Jesus were Jewish, and they still went to the temple.[17] There is no doubt that Christianity borrowed heavily from that religious culture, "for the Christians took out of the synagogue with them the devotions, scriptures, liturgical music, hours of prayer, and feast days, as well as the sermon type of scriptural exegesis, the moral code, and above all the concept of sacrifices and oblation that had characterized jewish worship."[18]

And yet Acts chapter four shows almost immediate conflict with the Jewish religious leaders. The early followers were explaining to other Jews why Jesus ought to be followed, loudly and publicly. This threatened the established religious order, so that it had to ask whether these men should be silenced or punished. Conflict didn't exist because it was clear that a new religion was competing for the top spot in the religious marketplace, but because it looked like a threat of displacement of the established religious leaders and order within their own religion.

Belief in this new way spread very quickly beyond Jews alone. The biblical book of Acts gives a laundry list of ethnicities from all around the Mediterranean, North African coastlands, and the Middle East, verging on Central Asia, all of whom heard and believed this new religion.[19] A familiar story involves Peter, an early follower of Jesus. In a dream he was commanded to kill and eat from a selection of ritually unclean animals. This was repeated until he got the point, that nothing God had made was unclean, and so therefore his scruples about associating with non-Jews could be done away with.[20]

This was another part of the struggle for identity. Religion and ethnicity had always been strongly paired for the Jews. Was this new way of believing in God independent of ethnic background, or must new believers take on Jewish cultural norms like circumcision, or not eating certain foods? Peter chose to enlarge his cultural identity, but faced with arguments from other new believers in Antioch, relapsed into familiar religious requirements. Paul argued in opposition to him, and the struggle went on.

Paul Johnson, in his popular *History of Christianity*, titles a chapter "The Rise and Rescue of the Jesus Sect" arguing that with a strong Jewish ethnic and cultural identity and the similarities to what Hillel and other Jewish religious leaders had said, this new group could have easily been reabsorbed within Judaism, and a new religion might have died in birth. He credits Paul with the recasting of the message of Jesus into a more universal form. Think of Paul speaking before the Greek philosophers of Athens, pointing out the unknown God to which the Athenians had erected a statue, alluding to the poet Epimenides of Cnossos, and the *Phainomena* of Aratus.[21] Perhaps as some argue, Christianity really does begin with Paul.[22] If not, then it soon started a slow process of religious and cultural divergence from Judaism.

Around the end of the first century, Ignatius, one of the first bishops of Antioch, wrote letters condemning non-Jewish believers who adopted Jewish practices in their religion. There was supposed to be a difference of identity. The problem didn't go away. Over two hundred years later in 348, Cyrial, the Patriarch of Jerusalem remarked in a sermon that there were actually people who worshiped Jesus Christ, yet refused to be called Christians, insisting that they were Jews.[23] This fear of losing religious identity as a result of similar patterns of belief and behavior, especially on the popular level, was shared by Christians and Jews.

The famed John Chrysostom gave a series of sermons in Antioch on the same topic in 386. He thought that a preoccupation with Jewish ritual and observance, even synagogue and festival attendance, were dangerous for Christians.[24] Strange blends of Jew and Christian, like the Ebionites, were caught in the middle in the struggle for differentiation and identity, and disappeared into either one or the other of the religions, as their borders drew further apart. Identity as followers of a new religion didn't come only from several hundred years of internal argument, though, but from outside forces as well.

Christianity spread initially within the Roman Empire, though it speedily moved beyond imperial borders to the East. Maps showing the spread of Christianity in its first few hundred years through the whole Empire may be a little misleading since Christianity tended to find more adherents in the cities than in the countryside. The new faith included significant numbers of wealthy, cultured, upper-class city people, not only the poor and oppressed, as some assume.

Given the multiplicity of Gods and religions throughout the Roman Empire, why would just another religion out of the East matter? The answer lies in the assertion that this was not "a" God, but "THE" God which was being talked about; that this God was not of one culture and people, but readily transcultural; and that this God was universally applicable to all humans. That was a potential threat to the state, which relied on religions as support for established state order, but couldn't tolerate a rival. Rome began to pay attention to Christians.

Emperor Nero had blamed Christians for the fires in Rome around 64 CE, and had them captured and killed. An identifiable enemy onto which popular anger may be deflected is always useful to a government. The Roman Emperor Nerva, around 98 CE, recognized that Christians were something different from Judaism, by exempting the Christians from the tax paid annually by Jews. Within the space of roughly thirty years, Rome recognized a Christian identity in both positive and negative ways for Christians as a group.

The Roman State – Ally or Enemy?

For a long time, imperial treatment wavered between extremes. Christians argued, reasoned, wrote books and carried on religious services for generations within the empire without significant problems. But sometimes Christians were suppressed by Rome, but not everywhere, and not always. Some Emperors regarded the Christians as more of a threat than others, and the persecution would grow more intense. A change in Emperors might bring relaxation of persecution, or even approval. A religion growing as quickly as Christianity could be either an ally, or an enemy, of the empire, and the imperial power wasn't sure yet how to classify Christianity.

As the empire grew weaker in the West, and the stable East looked more attractive, the question of the Christians, and whether to recognize them negatively or positively, grew sharper. The practice of having co-Emperors to rule an empire which seemed too big for one Emperor alone became common. The Emperor also tended to move. Thinking of the Emperor as seated in Rome during the period of time up to about the year three hundred is misleading. Co-Emperors, their courts, and armies, all moved to shore up the empire where weakness appeared. If only there were some other significant source of stability, power, and control within society to rally around for the peace of all!

The Emperor Trajan Decius tried to unify the Empire in 249 by reviving the old Roman religion and ordering universal compliance. He made a law that everyone in the Empire must sacrifice, pouring out wine while uttering a short religious formula. This was to be done before local officials, and records of obedience or disobedience were required. A universal religious rule was something new to Roman law.[25] The problem was that it just didn't work. The Roman upper classes had not been taking the traditional Greco-Roman gods seriously for quite some time, and the locals with their own beliefs and traditions were no more likely to respect them. After the fierce

Decian persecution of disobedient Christians died down, Christians lived more or less at peace in the Roman Empire, and their own religion with its claims of universal applicability kept growing.

Yet another issue of identity was the argument over the identity of Jesus himself. This subject is known as Christology and was one which consumed enormous amounts of energy and time from the theologians of the Christian faith. Theology at its root means the study of god, and since Christ had been so maddeningly vague about himself at times it is natural that concerned and intelligent members of the faith, educated in Roman and Greek traditions, should try to work out exactly who or what Christ was.

Opinions varied, quite often along regional and cultural lines, which is critically important. Some said Jesus was entirely human, others, that he was entirely divine. Some tried to split the difference and define his composition of two natures – god and man – united in one body, or was that present at the same time in one body, or was that fused in one body? Then there was the problem of the relationship between Jesus and God. These views are usually labelled with the names of their most vigorous exponents, for example, Athanasius for the proposition that God the Father and Jesus are eternally one and same, Arius for the proposition that they were similar, but the Father was greater.

These debates were not only theological, nor held in a vacuum, and it is a grave error of Christian history to treat them so. These debates were held in the context of an Empire at risk of spinning apart, and the desperate desire of Emperors and co-Emperors to hold it all together. So, the Emperors became involved, and their involvement shaped the debate just as much or more as the arguments of ecclesiastics. After all, if Christians could quit arguing about the nature of Christ on regional and ethnic grounds, but had an identity – one single identity – wouldn't this be better for a strong and united Roman Empire?

Constantine, while still co-Emperor in the West, was drawn into the debates. During the Diocletian persecution (303 to roughly 305, as long as 313 in the East), probably the fiercest empire-wide assault on Christians, made possible by the Decian law requiring universal worship[26] many terrified Christians in North Africa had denied their faith. Once the persecution ended, the question of what to do about those who had renounced their faith, and now wanted to take it up again (for some, along with their lucrative church offices too) was raised. Were they still Christians fit to serve?

Donatus, for whom this Donatist Controversy is named, was a bishop elected by popular acclaim as a Christian fit to serve, since the then-current bishop had buckled under the persecution. Constantine called a church council at Rome in 313 to decide this, claiming that his respect for the Church wouldn't allow him to let division and schism continue. It decided against the Donatists. The Donatists appealed, and in another council in Arles in 314 lost again. The Arles council was presided over by Constantine, who supported the decision that Donatus was wrong and his position a heresy, declaring that the decision of the bishops in council was that of God.

In his role as Judge of the highest Court, Constantine also acted as a Judge to settle some of the further disputes in 316. When Donatists refused to leave office, Constantine also acted as chief executive, exiling some, confiscating properties, but backing off a bit when this didn't bring success, writing again in 321 to the bishops that God would, in effect, solve the problem.

Constantine had long recognized the powerful unifying social force of Christianity. In 311, with his co-Emperors Galerius and Maximinus Daia, he declared that Christians ought to pray for the success and integrity of the State. In 312/313, now down to only one co-Emperor, Licinius, the well-known Edict of Milan (or Edict of Toleration) was published:

> "When I, Constantine Augustus, as well as I Licinius Augustus fortunately met near Mediolanurn (Milan), and were considering everything that pertained to the public welfare and security, we thought -, among other things

which we saw would be for the good of many, those regulations pertaining to the reverence of the Divinity ought certainly to be made first, so that we might grant to the Christians and others full authority to observe that religion which each preferred; whence any Divinity whatsoever in the seat of the heavens may be propitious and kindly disposed to us and all who are placed under our rule..."[27]

Christianity Becomes Part of The Establishment

As Constantine re-oriented the Empire to the East, defeating Licinius just across the Bosphorus from the old Greek village of Byzantion, which he built into the imperial center of Byzantium, he went further than settling disputes to unify the Church, and further than religious toleration and freedom. He sought to bind Christianity firmly to the empire to create a cohesive society.

His tool to bind the Empire and Christianity together was law, or rather, a series of laws favoring and establishing Christianity. In 313 a law was passed exempting clergy from municipal service obligations, an expensive and time consuming burden on the upper classes. Naturally, the better sorts flocked to join the religious hierarchy, and in 329 Constantine had to pass another law restricting entrance to the clergy lest too much talent and money drain away from the State![28]

In 321 we find laws stating that people were free to leave bequests in their Wills to the church; and that Christians couldn't be forced to make traditional sacrifices. In that same year, the "venerable day of the Sun" was recognized as a day of rest, and Christians promptly re-set their day of worship from the traditional Jewish day (Saturday) to Sunday. Tax exemptions for clerics in trade to support themselves (so long as they didn't earn too much) were also approved.

Not every law distributed favor and benefits to bring the clergy into imperial patronage, a soft control by the state. Some laws seem actuated by a good religious intent, like the law of

319 against murdering slaves, or the rule that branding the face of criminals was not allowed, since the face reflected God, and hence branding was to be on the feet. Some laws, such as the law stating that no repression of non-Christians was to take place, even seem open minded or liberal by modern Western standards.

Constantine was a patron, in the good old Roman sense, not of individuals or small groups, but of the Christians and their Church as a whole. State revenue helped to support the Church, along with endowments of land, and a great number of basilicas were constructed. He returned properties seized during earlier persecutions, and as already mentioned, constructed a system of favorable tax exemptions. Christians could even receive preference for appointments to government posts.

The other half of the patron-client relationship responded by giving Constantine what he wanted – stability in the Empire. The partnership in the social order is illustrated by the church council in Nicaea, in 325, called by the Emperor. He showed by his call to convene that he had the right to require that a question of doctrine be decided. What's more, that question must be answered conclusively, and, in a way agreeable to Constantine – he expelled a few hold-out bishops from the council, and criticized others.[29] While agreeing with the council's result, Constantine felt free to disregard finer points, recalling Arius from exile, and ordering Athanasius be sent to the city of Trier.

Constantine was in effect the head of the Church, although his powers might be ill-defined. There is no definitive answer to whether or not Constantine was really a Christian. Some point out that Constantine wasn't baptized until just before he died in the Spring of 337, but late baptisms were a common practice of the time. Others point out his continued tolerance of the traditional Greco-Roman religious institutions and practices, or point out that his coins and imperial mottos make him look like an adherent of the Sol Invictus group. In counter-argument, the many imperial laws supporting and establishing the church may be mentioned – surely a non-Christian wouldn't have made those?

Whether Constantine was or wasn't a Christian is a way of asking the question: Did the Church use the Empire, or did the Empire use the Church? Probably a little of both. But deciding that question is beside the point. The point is that without noticing it, something had happened to Christianity. Christianity, born under Jewish religion, Greek culture, and Roman law, was well on its way to becoming Christianity, itself the Greco-Roman religious, cultural, and legal establishment.

Return for a moment to the council of Nicaea and the triumphant entrance of Constantine. Eusebius, bishop of Caesarea Maritima in Palestine, reported Constantine's entrance and appearance in glowing terms, about as close as a Christian could come to making out Constantine himself as a god. Eusebius was one of Constantine's advisors, and a tutor within the imperial household, though how influential he was at the time is not clear.

Eusebius explains one of the East Roman (Byzantine), rationales for the place of the Emperor and Church in the social order. This Neoplatonic explanation is that visible objects were imitations or reflections of divine originals (Platonic ideals). Thus, the Roman empire was the human counterpart of a divine, perfect political system, the Kingdom of God. And, as the kingdom of God was eternal; the empire was to last as long as the world. Since God was an absolute monarch; the monarchy of the emperor was limited only by his responsibilities to God. God would support the emperor as long as the emperor did what God wanted.

Gilbert Dagron, in his *Emperor and Priest – The Imperial Office in Byzantium*, wrote that the Church made Constantine a saint (after him there were no others), to raise his status to a point where following his example would be impossible, preserving some Church power from the state. While in theory God was over all, in practice the emperor was over all. While there are times in Byzantine history when the Emperor removed a Patriarch of the Church, there are no stories of a Patriarch removing an Emperor.

The other major justification of involvement of the Church in the political order involved the biblical figure of Melchizedek, a shadowy figure who is called "King and Priest in Salem" in the biblical text.

> "This historical Melchizedek who had abolished the Law and inaugurated by anticipation the time of Grace, this uncircumcised person whose right to make the Jews pay tithe had been recognised, this king come directly, like Constantine the Great, from paganism to the religion of Christ – who else could he be than a sovereign of the Christianised Roman empire? He was said to be without geneaology or descendants, and imperial legitimacy was not transmitted hereditarily; even when the crown fell to the son, it was by association and not by filiation, by virtue of a choice supposedly made by God. Priesthood of the order of Melchizedek was not, like priesthood of the order of Aaron, a function, bound up with membership of the tribe of Levi in Judaism or with clerical status in Christianity, but an indelible character, conferred directly by God on the 'just king' for a great historical mission. The emperor was not a specialist in sacred things, or of the clergy, but he was invested with a superior priesthood."[30]

The strong practical legal and theoretical basis for the intertwining of church and state continued after Nicaea. For example, laws passed from 331-334 closed down pagan temples throughout the empire. But then there was the curious case of the Emperor Julian, known as Julian the Apostate. Julian was raised as a Christian (Eusebius was one of his tutors), but threw faith aside in adulthood. As Emperor (361-363) he didn't persecute Christians, but revived the traditional blood sacrifices. He sacrificed so many animals that some locals on his journey through southern Turkey derisively called him butcher boy. Julian made it clear that the prior Church-State teaming was at an end.

His actions had an unintended effect. While he might only have been trying to bring a stronger religious plurality into society, (he supported the Donatists in North Africa) he sparked fear in the Christian community. Old people could remember the last of the great persecutions. Julian's actions revived that fear, with the difference that this time the Christian community was strong enough to become persecutors themselves after Julian's death. This fear and the growing pressure within the Church to conform to a uniform and orthodox set of beliefs, led to the mob beating and death of the pagan philosopher Hypatia in Alexandria because of her alleged interference in Church politics.[31]

A high (or low) point in the tangled identity of Empire and Church was reached in 380, with Theodosius I and his *constitutio Cunctos Populos:*

> "It is Our will that all the peoples who are ruled by the administration of Our Clemency shall practice that religion which the divine Peter the Apostle transmitted to the Romans... according to the apostolic discipline and the evangelic doctrine, we shall believe in the single Deity of the Father, the Son, and the Holy Spirit, under the concept of equal majesty and of the Holy Trinity. We command that those persons who follow this rule shall embrace the name of Catholic Christians. The rest, however, whom we adjudge demented and insane, shall sustain the infamy of heretical dogmas, their meeting places shall not receive the name of churches, and they shall be smitten first by divine vengeance and secondly by the retribution of Our own initiative..."[32]

The Emperor defined faith, stated the proper name of the faith, and promised vengeance on any who disagreed. Heresy wasn't only a religious problem, it was a criminal act against the State. The criminal code defined further prohibited acts – associating with heretics, believing a heresy, having any heretical writings around, teaching heresy or holding a heretical church service, etc.

Further Church councils in 381 and 383 didn't solve all the problems of orthodoxy, so Theodosius I slowly began to change his views (his Western co-emperor held an Arian-demiurge concept, and Ambrose was against forced conversions). But, in 387 he started to crack down again using the machinery of State justice. So did later Emperors. After all, the "stability of the state depends upon the religion by which we honour God" as Theodosius II wrote later in 431.[33]

In 390 Valentinian criminalized the study and learning of astrology. In 391, Theodosius closed all the pagan temples and outlawed pagan worship. In 407/8 pagan celebrations were outlawed, and bishops were allowed to exercise their power to prevent them. Sometimes cases against these outlaws were heard in courts presided over by bishops, and sometimes the histories even show bishops in command of imperial soldiers.

Conclusion

Christianity in roughly its first 350 years had come a long way. From a new religion floundering to distinguish itself from its Jewish parent, struggling to adapt to the Greek culture, and facing sporadic persecution from the Roman state and legal order of the day, official Christianity had discarded the Aramaic of the Jews and adopted Greek and Latin. It had adapted Jewish religious content and liturgical practices to its own uses while differentiating itself from the Jews. It had copied the organization and hierarchy of the Roman Empire, and finally become part of the Roman legal order with power of its own.

Christianity had found an identity, but not the only identity it could have had, nor an identity that was inevitable given the words of Jesus. For future generations, the most momentous part of that adopted identity was the place of Christianity in the constitutional order – the relation of religion to law and power in society. A more full discussion must wait until after the beginnings of Islam in the next chapter.

Chapter 2 - Islam Begins

Sometime after December 609, when the Angel Gabriel first appeared to him and commanded him to recite what was revealed, Muhammad recited that "...I am the first of the Muslims."[34] It is easier to identify a beginning for Islam than it is for Christianity. If one person alone is not enough, then Islam began when Khadija, his wife, accepted the message he brought. Then, Muhammad's cousin and son in law, Ali, submitted to God[35], for that is what the root word from which Islam is derived means – submission to God, as any Arabic dictionary makes clear.

First, for clarity: A culture is Islamic, or we may speak of what Islam demands of an adherent, but it is an individual human being who submits to God and becomes a Muslim, a member of the *ummah*, or community of Muslims. So, with Khadija and Ali, and the small group that began to form around Muhammad, a community of Muslims began to grow in Mecca.

And here I must caution the Muslim reader, as were Christians in the last chapter, not to read into the beginnings of Islam the mature and highly complex Islamic social and legal structure of today, nor to be upset that the fullness of Islam is not explained in a traditional re-telling. The concentration here is on the relationship of Islam to law and the constitutional structure of society.

The Birth of Islam within Arabic Culture

The Mecca of that time does not seem to have been either an unduly wealthy or poor city. Its merchants dealt in spices, but so did those who used the easier Red Sea route which bypassed Mecca. The Byzantines used that route when trading for spices, and for trade with the fellow Christian kingdom of Ethiopia. It was undoubtedly easier to transport spices by ship than by unloading and making an arduous trek northward on foot with a camel caravan. The Byzantines knew this, and had established customs stations to tax traffic in the Red Sea. The back road of camel caravan to the north might have been used to avoid Byzantine tolls, giving Mecca an economic boost.

Overall, the trading activity some traditional sources tell us about was likely at a lower level than represented when it comes to spices, or was carried on with other, cheaper, goods. Also, Mecca was likely not as important a pilgrimage destination for worshippers of traditional tribal gods as some histories indicate, either.[36] The surviving Arabic sources of the time mention several other cities as destinations, but not Mecca.

This is not to disparage the traditional story told of the origins of Islam. Instead, trying to be more realistic about trade and pilgrimages is intended to make an important point about Muhammad's message that spices, wealth, and temples may obscure: Islam did not succeed because it had great wealth to lure followers, nor because in Mecca it already had control of an important destination for religiously observant Arabs. It succeeded in attracting a swiftly growing number of Muslims because it was a message with tremendously strong and beneficial social implications, that proved itself quickly.

Arabian culture of the time was organized upon a strong tribal basis, dictated to some extent by the difficult and arid environment where those tribes lived. Arabian polytheistic tribal religions were also quite strong.[37] This is a difficult area to investigate today, since the vast majority of Arabs would identify themselves as Muslims, and don't particularly want to hear about, or investigate, pre-Islamic Arabian religious practices. Those beliefs and practices are labeled as belonging to the *jahilyah*, or "time of ignorance" prior to Muhammad.

Nonetheless, the basic idea was of a god who served as the patron or protector of the tribe that was organized around its leader, and lived according to the tradition (rules) of that leader. To the extent the god supported the tribe the god was retained, but could be discarded if enough misfortune befell the tribe. There is one story about a tribe who had made an image of their god from clarified butter and dates. When the god failed to protect, and the people were hungry, in desperation they

Page 24

devoured their god. It's difficult to imagine a more conclusive repudiation of a god than that!

There is no doubt that there were Arab Christians in the peninsula, as well as Jews. Arabs sometimes travelled to Syria to visit the Christian St. Simeon Stylites. The Arabs had even been exposed to the ideals of Hellenism. From the East, the Zoroastrian religion made its influence felt, because the Sassanians (Persians) were present in the Eastern parts of the peninsula, like Oman. They traded, carried on mining, and sought influence in the tribes elsewhere. The religious writings, practices, and ideas of all these varied groups were available to the Arabs of Muhammad's time.

Before the Byzantines, the Romans had known of Arabia and Arabs, and had a line of little fortresses extending along the inland caravan route from Syria down to the Gulf of Aqaba. The Romans sought leather goods for their armies from the Arabs, but never had much of a presence in the peninsula.[38] By the time of Muhammad's birth, Rome had dwindled in the West, and the power of the Eastern Romans, or Byzantines, was exercised in the region from Constantinople, sometimes in cooperation with the Ethiopian kings, who in 525 had taken control over Yemen, and installed puppet kings in power.

The power of Byzantium had been sorely strained in a contest with the Persian Sassanian Empire, situated in today's Iran and Iraq, during the century prior to Muhammad's birth. These two dominant powers of the day had tried to recruit Arab tribes as proxies in their own struggles. Their religious establishments had proselytized in the areas under their control. They were more or less exhausted by the time Muhammad was born, leaving the Arabian Peninsula as an area of jostling tribes. But in this region on the sidelines of the Byzantine-Sassanian struggle, the ideas and religions of the people of those empires were still circulating, even if the armies were gone.

Muhammad's actions should be viewed against a background of competition in religion, both among the many gods and tribes of the Arabs, and to a lesser extent with those promoted by or identified with foreign empires.[39] Despite the presence of Christians and Jews, Arab tribal ideas of religion and culture were dominant, so Muhammad was able to express a message sent in Arabic specifically to Arabs, as the Koran states[40], in the way best suited to Arabian society. It is not accurate to use a term like nationalism, but undoubtedly Muhammad knew of these other religions and may have felt the need to have a stronger and better idea of god to unite Arabic people. Failure of the Byzantine and Persian religious traditions in the peninsula also may be due to the fact that they were identified with warring empires, which sought to rule or use the Arabs.

Muhammad was not the only Arab to propose strong religious ideas, ideas that could even transcend the tribe. Other leaders were making similar attempts. For example, Musaylima was reputed to perform minor miracles, and he suggested prayers similar to those of Muhammad, as well as prohibitions of pork and wine. But Musaylima lost, and his tribe eventually embraced Islam, so that to this day he is referred to as a liar or "the liar" in traditional Islamic history.[41] But before he lost, and before Mecca became a city for Muslims, there was still a struggle to be undergone by the *ummah*.

When Muhammad began to talk about the revelations he had received, and tell people that they must submit to Allah, this caused conflict with the existing order within Mecca. Muhammad did not meet resistance in Mecca because the people were terribly ignorant, or especially wicked, but because the idea of worshipping Allah as he proposed went against the established religion and order of the tribe. Just why should the tribe listen to this upstart? What Muhammad was doing in Meccan eyes was to create disruption within Mecca.

The small group of Muslims gathered around Muhammad eventually annoyed the leadership of Mecca so much that with Muhammad's approval a small group left for Ethiopia, where they were welcomed and allowed to settle. Things didn't get better, so others felt it necessary to make a strategic withdrawal from Mecca to the nearby city of Medina. Finally, Muhammad himself left for Medina with the last few followers. This move to Medina is known to Islamic history as the *hijra* – the cutting off, or cutting of ties. Homes, and heavy or immovable wealth were left, and Muslims struggled for the safety of Medina before a pursuing force could catch and fight them. There is nothing like shared adversity to unite a people and make a community – an *ummah*.

A New Community

The word *ummah* is used in a variety of ways in the Koran. Certainly it is used when referring to the body of Muslims, but also when referring to other peoples who have a prophet or a religious tradition of their own. The term was used of pre-Islamic Arabs. The *ummah* has been said to be like a tribe, but one based on religion, not ethnicity.[42] Some early uses of the term make the *ummah* sound like an ethnic tribe, and later like a religious tribe. Eventually the term came to be used exclusively for the Muslim *ummah*. Similarly, the term Muslim, that at its root means a person who believes in and submits to God, also became further defined in time to be limited to only those who followed the revelation of God given by Muhammad.[43]

How was this *ummah*, newly arrived in Medina, to set itself apart from other communities who might also be called *ummahs*? Of course there is the content of the Koran – but remember – the Koran at this time had not yet been completely revealed to Muhammad. The *hijra* to Medina took place in 622, and Muhammad lived and received revelations until 632. "From the first the religious message proclaimed by Muhammad had been addressed to a *qawm* or *umma*, a 'tribe' or 'community', that is, to a body politic of the type familiar to the Arabs."[44] It naturally followed that self-definition of this small band of believers and relations with outsiders, should be subject to a formal agreement, so under Muhammad's leadership Al-Wathiqa, commonly called the Constitution of Medina, was written.

Al-Wathiqa is properly a treaty or contract (most accurately a series of those, numbering anywhere from two to eight, depending upon the scholar commenting[45], dating back to 622, as reported to us by Arab historians of the successive centuries). The agreement was made between the Muslims from Mecca and the other people of Medina who believed, and with the non-Muslims and Jews resident in Medina. This included members of several different tribes, and sub-tribes, or client tribes who sought the protection and friendship of more powerful tribes.

It contained assertions like sovereignty, meaning that the Islamic community had the right to do whatever it wanted within its own territory. It declared that Muslims were a united community (*ummah*), to the exclusion of all others. Al-Wathiqa continued with headings, or rules for 'Independence', 'Diversity', 'Conduct, or the Rules of War', 'Loyalty', 'Fighting Poverty', 'Fighting Injustice', 'Fighting Corruption and Bondage', 'The Right to Rebellion or Revolution', 'Search, or Striving, for Peace', 'Freedom of Religion', 'Believing in Capital Punishment', 'The Right of Minorities', 'The Rule of Law', 'Sanctuary', 'Immigration', 'Privacy Right', 'Security and Defense', 'Respect for International Law', and 'The Supremacy of *Al-Shari'ah*' for Muslims. It deals with prisoners of war and ransoms paid. The rights and the status of *dhimmi* (protected non-Muslim people) were established.[46]

It would be a great mistake to be confused by the word constitution into thinking of Al-Wathiqa as something like a modern constitution. A modern constitution generally defines the structure of government and the way people are to relate to the state (rights and duties). It sets out the most basic level of law, on which all other laws of the nation will be built. It typically provides for law making and enforcement through the legislative, executive and judicial functions or branches of government. It is the basic legal document of the state. Al-Wathiqa is different though, because it is the constituting document of a community, not a state.

The basic policing function of how people are to live is placed in the social community. The members of that *ummah* are responsible to see that those functions are carried out. To do that, the state may be constructed by the *ummah*. "...Islam is unique among the great civilizations in the extent to which the state has ceased to embody public norms..."[47] The state may change, it may even come and go, but the community remains. The basic and local level of family and community governance is sometimes called community pressure in our own day, though that simplifies this foundational fact of Islamic society too much.

Becoming a Muslim then, meant not only submission to God, with prayer and other rituals, but also accepting a new, and well defined, status as a member of a community. It meant stepping into a web of relationships and defined rights and duties. One of those duties was fighting, both in defense of the *ummah*, and on the offense against those Arabs who refused Islam. Initially, Muhammad made alliances with neighboring tribes, but as the Muslims grew stronger, Muhammad began to demand belief in God and of his status as prophet, though alliances with non-Muslims were still made.[48] By the time he died, Muhammad had united nearly all of the Arabian Peninsula. The competing tribes had been given a greater unity and centralization of power than they had ever known in the past.

Muhammad's personal authority in this was central, if not always clear. Muhammad was the man through whom the law of God was revealed in the Koran. He was accepted as a messenger or prophet from God, and more. The Koranic term *rasul* is said to include authority and responsibility stronger than that of a prophet only.[49] We know also that Muhammad acted as a traditional arbitrator or judge between members of the community, an accepted role in Arabic society for a leader like him. Where authority within the *ummah* was centralized like this in one man, and that man also gave the *ummah* the body of rules that organized it, there was an obvious risk upon his death.

Death of the Prophet and the Succession of Leadership

Muhammad died in 632, and the first test of the new community was upon it. Would the community break up since he was gone, or continue? Muhammad had no sons who survived into adulthood, so the traditional tribal choice of successor wasn't possible. There was a dramatic scene in the Mosque where Muhammad's companion Umar was giving a speech declaring that Muhammad had not really died, but would reappear after a time as Moses had. Abu Bakr interrupted him to declare "O men, if anyone worships Muhammad, Muhammad is dead: if anyone worships God, God is alive, immortal.' Then he recited this verse: 'Muhammad is nothing but an apostle. Apostles have passed away before him. Can it be that if he were to die or be killed you would turn back on your heels? He who turns back does no harm to God and God will reward the grateful'."[50]

Umar nominated Abu Bakr as the new leader, though several other companions of high status had a harder time turning away from accepted practice and thought the choice should have been Ali, the cousin and son-in-law of Muhammad. As Abu Bakr assumed power, tribal restiveness continued. Some refused to pay the *zakat*, the tax of the *ummah*, others wanted to withdraw all together and re-form their own communities. Abu Bakr responded with military force to re-unite the tribes. Certainly that formed a stronger unity, as did Abu Bakr's expulsion of Jews and Christians from the Arabian Peninsula.[51]

> "Had Abu Bakr allowed these departures, Islam would surely have gone in a very different direction. It might have evolved into a set of practices and beliefs that people embraced individually. But Abu Bakr responded to the crisis by declaring secession to be treason. The Prophet had said, 'No compulsion in religion,' and Abu Bakr did not deny that principle. People were free to accept or reject Islam as they pleased; but once they

were in, he asserted, they were in for good. In response to a political crisis, Abu Bakr established a religious principle that haunts Islam to this day – the equation of apostasy with treason. Braided into this policy was the theological concept that the indissoluble singleness of God must be reflected in the indissoluble singleness of the Umma. With this decision Abu Bakr even more definitively confirmed Islam as a social project and not just a belief system. A Muslim community was not just a *kind* of community, of which there could be any number, but a *particular* community, of which there could be only one."[52]

Growth of an Empire

Once the wayward tribes were brought back in to the *ummah* and the Arab Peninsula united, Arabic armies advanced North into Syria, East into Mesopotamia, Iran, and Central Asia, and West across the top of North Africa, driving back Byzantines and Persians before them. The success of the armies brought lands, houses, great riches, and new problems. The struggle to solve those problems would come to a height roughly two hundred years later under the Abbasid dynasty in Baghdad in the mid-800s, so it is necessary to ask what these problems were.

One of the new problems was that of ethnicity. Non-Muslims were initially the majority of the population in Syria, Iraq, Iran and Egypt, and there were far too many of them to expel, as from the Arabian Peninsula. The process of conversion of subject peoples was long and very uneven, especially since some of them were explicitly recognized as protected minorities with the *dhimmi* status. Pagans survived in Syria for hundreds of years after the conquest – their last temple in Harran was reported to have closed in the 1100s.[53] Some Christian groups even kept growing after the conquests, though eventually pressure from the *jizya* tax and other inducements (and sometimes threats) were applied, causing many to convert.

Besides supporting the Islamic scholars arguing against Zorastrians and Manichees, Caliph al-Mahdi (d. 791) and some of his successors later persecuted those believers in other religions.[54]

Leaving aside the issue of conversion of subject peoples, the question raised was how these foreign people were to be governed in other respects. "The political organization which the first Caliphs had created was essentially a military organization for the purposes of expansion and enjoyment of the fruits of conquest, and was furnished with no administrative organs for other purposes."[55] The Arabs who had first joined with the *ummah* under Muhammad were naturally the primary beneficiaries of the new wealth. They benefitted from Umar's establishment of a *diwan*. "The *diwan* was essentially a list of those who were entitled to a share in the booty acquired during the course of military campaigns and distributed by the state; rank within it depended not on tribal identity, but on *sabiqa*, "precedence" according to one's contributions to the new polity."[56]

Arabic customary law provided what seemed like a simple answer to the problem of subject peoples not included in the social order, and who couldn't share the wealth: Make them Arabs! So, for some time these non-Arabs were required to become *mawla*, or clients, and accept a sort of client-tribe status to Arabic tribes.[57] That status was attained by marriage, childbirth, or adoption (even adult adoption), or affiliation as an ally, but didn't always immediately result in a tribal identification. A *hadith* of the Prophet was produced in support, which stated that "[c]lients, allies and sons of tribeswomen (by men from outside the tribe) are part of the tribe."[58] While non-Arabs slowly began to share the wealth, that progress seemed too slow to some.

As the new capital was established in Damascus, Umayyad leaders struggled to cope with the problem of state organization. Borrowing imperial administrative procedures of the old Persian Sassanian empire, while helpful, wasn't enough in an empire which wasn't solely Arab any longer. "The

Umayyad Caliphate, in its successive phases, represented a series of compromises - of interim arrangements which preserved the unity of the Islamic polity, at the cost of establishing a predominance of the Arab aristocracy and an imperial system that gradually borrowed more and more of the structure and methods of the defeated empires."[59]

The Umayyad caliph al-Malik (ruled 724 to 743) tried to cope with the grumblings of the *mawali*, the non-Arab Muslims who had been left behind in the rush for success, and to remove their disabilities. The demand for laws and traditions that could include the new population of the empire without treating them as inferior drove the attempt to remedy the Arab-centeredness of government by examining the state institutions of the conquered Persians.[60] As the Abbasid dynasty took control the capitol moved from Damascus to Baghdad, and this trend continued.

Disabilities of *mawali* kept being removed, and "a new multi-national ruling elite emerged, of officials, soldiers, landowners, merchants and men of religion. Their common characteristic was Islam, which replaced Arabism as the first-class citizenship of the Empire."[61] Even caliphs could have foreign mothers. If an identity as a Muslim, or member of Islamic society now began to rise at the expense of the older understanding of being Arabic, then the leadership of the society was just as critical an issue as it had been immediately after Muhammad's death, especially as his contemporaries began to die of old age. The caliphs were not tribal leaders, but leaders of the *ummah*, and their role needed to be defined. The status of the Koran, and what other rules existed for the *ummah*, was also part of the question of leadership. Let's go back again to just after the Prophet's death.

Abu Bakr had been appointed by Muhammad to lead the Friday prayers in his place, and he was now nominated as caliph, but "the word *khalifa* as applied to Abu-Bakr was vague; but this vagueness was an asset, since the meaning of the word was able to develop as the office itself grew in importance and changed its character."[62] As errant tribes re-submitted to Islam, and Islam expanded out of the Arabian Peninsula, defining the role of the leader became more important. Matters of state like war, trade, and diplomacy must be decided, and the internal life and worship of the community guided, in all of which Muhammad had been central. Whether those leadership roles were to be diffused or remain centered in one man was the issue for the *ummah* after the determination that it wouldn't break up.

It is here in the history of the three "rightly guided" caliphs after Muhammad where the historical sources are weighted differently, depending on one's Sunni or Shi'a identity. "[I]f *khalifa* meant 'deputy of God' from the start, then the Shiites can hardly be altogether wrong in their claim that the legitimate head of state…inherited both the religious and the political power of the Prophet."[63] It was clear that the status of caliph meant more than ruler of state only, and even after the power of the caliph declined in Sunni Islam, "it was held that he validated the legal and social system based on the revealed law. What distinguished the caliphs from Muhammad was their lack of the office of prophet and their inability to receive further revelations."[64]

Consultation by the caliph with the leading men of the community was expected, and necessary as the Islamic empire quickly expanded. By 642, only ten years after the death of Muhammad, Arab armies had defeated opposition and extended the rule of Islam to Iraq, Iran, Syria and Egypt. The leading men would make sure that the ruler didn't depart too far from the historical path of their ancestors, as Arabic tribal leaders had always done. The caliphal office still included the judging of disputes, but groups of judges began to develop, as the empire was simply too large to allow the personal involvement which Muhammad had been able to have.

Disputes over the Succession of Leadership

After Abu Bakr, Umar succeeded as caliph, then Uthman. On Uthman's murder in 656, Ali at last got his chance to serve as the fourth caliph. Although a companion like the first three and moreover a relative, he wasn't generally accepted.

Uthman's death and subsequent rebellions against Ali are the beginning of the first *fitna*, or civil war, within the Islamic community. It lasted roughly five years and ended after Ali's death at Kufa in Iraq with the founding of the Umayyad dynasty in Damascus.

The nature of the *fitna* is of great importance, because:

> "…what looks to us like a choice between political rivals was in fact a religious one in early Islam. To give allegiance to an imam was to affiliate oneself to a guide who might or might not be the true representative of God; it was to choose one's umma. The fact that Ali and Muawiya may well have had identical beliefs in no way means that contemporaries were faced with a purely political dilemma. There was only one true imam and one true umma, so that whoever made the wrong choice would find himself outside the community where no amount of religious observance would save him from a Jahili death."[65]

The Umayyad dynasty founded by Muawiya claimed Uthman as the first of their line, and pointed out that he had been properly chosen by a *shura* (council). Selection by council, not by narrow family line alone, was necessary to proper Sunni Islamic rule.

The arguments during the *fitna* had also encouraged the growth of a group of scholars who could give opinions on the law of the *ummah*. After Muhammad's death, some rebellious tribes had found a proper legal footing for their actions in the claim that their leaders had prophetic authority like Muhammad's.[66] It was clear after several caliphs though, that nobody claimed prophetic authority like Muhammad any longer. The only alternative (other than repression) to charismatic leadership of the *ummah* by one man was for leaders to unite around a body of knowledge given in the Koran, and in the decisions made by Muhammad during his life. So it was necessary to study, and "[h]istorical investigation, Quranic exegesis, and the administration of law merely formed different aspects of an activity whose real focus was quite naturally the historical prophet..."[67]

Rise of the Scholars and Why They Were Necessary

The origins and rise of the scholars is obscure. There was most likely a progression of some nature from the *mufti*, a figure giving legal rulings, necessary as soon as a definitive ruling on what Muhhamad had meant or decided in some area, arose, going on to the several different types of scholars or scholarly functions classical Islam would have.[68] Whether the scholars were initially judges assisting the caliph in his judicial function, jurisprudents giving opinions on the meaning of the Koran or traditions of Muhammad, or both, is not clear. By the year 700 or thereabouts, quasi-formal teaching was given in big cities in the empire, and by about 750 groups of scholars are identifiable.

This work of the scholars, intentionally or not, eroded the powers of the early caliphs. Since beside the Koran a great number of *hadiths* existed, scholars were necessary to explain them, and the caliph couldn't do so unless he was a scholar himself. Since the *hadiths* were so great in number, and often specific on their subject matter, they were a source of law which the caliph found it difficult to ignore, or interpret his way around. Sometimes *hadiths* were discovered (or made) in competition with, and for, the power of the caliph.[69] The *hadiths* also supported each other. Fitting the *hadiths* together into a coherent framework of Islamic law meant that commenting or criticizing one *hadith* in particular affected others, and they in turn affected the interpretation of the original *hadith*.

The Abbasid dynasty overthrew the Umayyads in 750 and ruled until their defeat by the Mongols in 1258. Their caliphs used the same rhetoric regarding their status as the Umayyads. The claimed that they were deputies or trustees of God, imams of guidance, imams of justice, rightly guided, the best of creation after the prophet – almost prophets themselves, chosen by God, etc. The caliphal task was guidance and light, it was like rain, a source of healing, refuge against error, God's rope, or the pillar of Islam, necessary to escape fire on judgment day. [70]

But claiming high-sounding titles is one thing, and having the authority from the past to back up those claimed titles is another. By this period, the *hadiths* were recognized as an independent source of law, alongside the Koran itself. They were regarded as so important that one scholar of the time is recorded as being alarmed that the caliph was not intervening to ensure that the collections and works of the scholars were in agreement with one another's.[71]

But the scholars were not so strong that they could exercise all of the law and do without a caliph. Appointments to lucrative judgeships were made by the caliph, or an official of his court. "If a man wanted to obtain the post of judge, he must be careful not to offend those who wielded political authority; there appear to have been usually more candidates for posts than there were posts."[72] But to be considered for a judgeship, the scholars in their schools had to approve the legal knowledge of the aspiring judge. Abbasid caliphs recognized the legitimacy of the schools, but at the same time brought pressure to bear in the main cities to try to secure some uniformity in knowledge.[73]

The scholars and the caliphs co-existed in a delicate balance to govern Islamic society. Both were necessary to ensure that the *ummah* remained on course. The caliph or ruler ruled according to the law of God - the *shari'a* – that in turn was developed and explained by the scholars of the *ulama*. That did not mean the scholars as a group were rulers themselves, but that there was a balance of power between the caliph and the scholars. The ruler promised to obey God's law, as explained to him by the *ulama*. The scholars promised in return to support and uphold the Caliph as a legitimate ruler, ruling as God would have him rule. Neither could do the job alone.

This structure provided a balance of powers. Once accepted as a scholar, rank and prestige was at least in part dependent upon the caliph. On the other hand, the caliph could enforce his will through military might in a selfish or abusive way, but this would be immediately known to the scholars. They could decide that the caliph had abused God's law, that he had not fulfilled his function of commanding the right and forbidding the wrong properly. If that decision was made, then the scholars met the problem of any judicial system: It is a judicial body, not an executive body. As a general rule, there is no police, army, or quasi-army under the command of a non-executive official. How then could a judgment of improper caliphal action be enforced by the scholars?

The caliph, if not designated by his predecessor (since there was no automatic succession), was appointed by those with "binding and loosing" power.[74] This group was made up of senior scholars. They promised allegiance to the caliph if he followed the law. The implication was that if they decided he was not following the law, their allegiance ended. Scholars remaining silent, or offering lukewarm support to the government would be noticed immediately by the populace at large, and disobedience could be expected. If the scholars were particularly aggrieved and acted more aggressively, they could even depose the caliph, propose a new claimant to that power, or prevent the nominated claimant from assuming control.

The growth of the power of the scholars and their contest with caliphal authority, sometimes obvious, sometimes hidden, was gradual, and lasted through the Umayyad (661 to750) into the Abbasid period, where it reached a critical point in combination with other social factors. For now, we must briefly turn to law, another primary occupation of the scholars, something that their collection and categorization of *hadiths* supported, and also something that involvement in a constitutional balance in government with the caliphs demanded. The importance of the scholars and the law though, goes beyond only power exercised in conjunction with or in competition with caliphs, but extends to law as a powerful social unifier and definer, especially in the presence of all those new non-Muslim subjects.

The scene between Umar and Abu Bakr in the Mosque may be interpreted as a rejection of the possibility of worship of a man, and refocus of the energies of the *ummah* upon the revealed doctrines and rules of God after the lawgiver died. The community would stay together, since the message remained after the death of the messenger. The ideas of Islam in forming the *ummah* could also be a powerful social unifying force, if they were recognized as applying not only to Arabs, but to Muslims first, with ethnicity following. That is precisely what the struggle with ethnicity helped confirm, as had the earlier expulsion of Jews and Christians from the Arabian Peninsula.

Uthman had fixed a definite text of the Koran and published it in 651, but the Koran alone was not enough to give guidance to the *ummah* after the death of Muhammad. A fringe group called the Kharijites in the late 600s claimed that the text of the Koran alone ought to be read to order life in the *ummah*, and disparaged the use and importance of tradition, but their argument was never accepted by even a substantial minority within the Islamic world. There were areas where the Koran was silent, where decisions were needed. The answer was to turn to what Muhammad had done when faced with the same or similar issues.

It was imperative then, for scholars to collect and record the traditions, the *sunna*, of Muhammad, including writing biographies of him. This was not a radical step for the *ummah*, since Muhammad had made decisions and established principles for the *ummah* not found in the Koran when he was still alive. Arabic culture also demanded a sense of continuity in the laws and way of life of the ancestors. The methods of one of the earliest scholars of law at Medina, 'Urwa b. as-Zubair, who died in 716, fit that description. He was a relative of the prophet, and very well-connected within the early *ummah*. His letters to the Caliph Abd al-Malik may be the first Islamic historical writing. He was well acquainted with traditions and sayings, and passed them on to his own pupils orally.[75]

Knowing the substance of the Koran, and the *sunna* of the Prophet, (even if that were only the minimum necessary for daily life), was necessary for any member of the *ummah*. That knowledge was required by the revelation of Islam, and had been made explicit by Muhammad. "The value set upon education in Islam is indicated by certain hadith sayings which, though they may have no claim to rank as authentic, yet undoubtedly reflect the educational ideas of Islam in its early days, and may be taken as representing the prevailing views of the first generations. Thus it is handed down as a saying of the Prophet himself, that 'A father can confer upon his child no more valuable gift than a good education [citation omitted]."[76]

It wasn't only the knowledge necessary to be a member of the *ummah*, or the exigencies of a large empire which drove scholarship, but also competition with newly encountered religious systems. "Islam is a religion based on knowledge – and not on love as is for example Christianity – a knowledge in which the intellect (al'aql) itself plays the positive role of leading man to the Divine."[77] Since Islam claimed to supersede the religious figures and ideas which had come before it, it was compelled to examine the intellectual products of the earlier ages, and either distinguish them away, assimilate them as part of the unity of knowledge of Islam, or reject them as dangerously incorrect.

The Abbasid Empire included not only Shi'a Muslims, but Zoroastrians, Manichees, Christians of several types, Jews, and pagans of all varieties in the countryside.[78] Christians and Jews were familiar, and were clearly *dhimmi* as "people of the book" mentioned in the Koran, a status extended also to Zoroastrians, but not to another new faith, Manichaeism. New faiths "presented an intellectual challenge to them [Muslim scholars] because it was new to them in a sense that Christianity and Judaism were not." So the government and scholars of Islam had to adapt or respond to these groups. The problem was that traditions and *sunna* were not enough, since there were no traditions about problems that hadn't been encountered before.

In order to compete against the new religions, Islamic scholars needed a familiarity with both the arguments and the intellectual techniques of their adversaries. Translation of their works and borrowing logic tools helped, and so did new methods of philosophical inquiry. A group of scholars called the Mu'tazilites (the 'seceders' or 'neutrals'), began to develop these new intellectual tools within the Islamic tradition. "The Mu'tazila were the predominant early theologians, and nearly all of them were born and lived in 'Iraq or Iran; many were *mawali*, converts or sons of converts."[79] While all this made some more conservative scholars anxious, the Mu'tazilites were tolerated since "in those days the Mu'tazila were missionaries of Islam against the eastern religions."[80]

The Abbasids also appeared to be borrowing what they liked and needed for imperial administration from Persian practice, not asking first whether or not those ideas met the demands of Islam. Some of the scholars were quite put out by this. The dangers of contamination to Islamic thought from adoption of Sassanid governing procedures and rules had to be avoided if possible. The "Hanafi chief *qadi* Abu Yusuf, who in the preface to his Kitab al-Kharaj, addressed to Harun al-Rashid, explicitly bases the principles of a truly Islamic government exclusively upon the sunna of the Patriarchal Caliphs and 'Umar b. 'Abd al-'Aziz, and implicitly protests against the prevailing cult of the Sasanid tradition" was one of the few to protest against this caliphal practice.[81] Some scholars began to concentrate even more on the collection and transmission of traditions.

The body of knowledge itself required travel and correspondence, so that scholars could learn from one another. This had the effect of uniting culture, and making men of disparate backgrounds similar to one another.[82] In the new lands where non-Arab converts lived, the term *mawla* appears to fall into disuse by the time of the Abbasid dynasty. If Islam could demonstrate, as it had, the ability to move beyond Arab culture alone, yet retain a (sometimes precarious) unity, the need to distinguish Arab from non-Arab was less, but the need for law to define and unite culture was greater.

A Sketch of Islamic Law

In its widest sense, *sunna* was the history of the community of Islam, and its traditions. Concepts like a way of life, behavior, example, customs and customary practices, things Muhammad did, or allowed by silence or inaction, are all contained within *sunna*. If understood like pre-Islamic Arabic cultural practices, Al-Wathiqa could be *sunna*, as a contract made by Muhammad and the community. Even the Koran itself could be at a stretch conceptualized as *sunna*, part of the history and tradition of Muslims and of Islam which began with Muhammad. Of course, most Muslims would object to the Koran being placed within that class, arguing that as it claims, the Koran was revealed through the angel, from God, to Muhammad.

Hadith is a narrower term often used interchangeably with *sunna*, although they are different. A *hadith* shows what Muhammad taught, and said, in respect to a certain subject. These may be contained within the *sunna*, but it isn't necessarily true that all of the subject matter of *sunna* will have a specific *hadith* supporting it. *Hadiths* (the plural is properly *ahadith*) consist also of a chain of proofs, rather like the idea of provenance in art. This provenance is designed to show that the *hadith* is reliable, and may be traced back to someone who actually witnessed the teaching, speech, or action taken by Muhammad (or to some of the earliest caliphs, who gave *hadiths* which are still accepted).

The chain of proofs was necessary for the authority of a *hadith*. That chain determined the weight to be given to a *hadith*, such as very little when there was suspicion that a current leader had simply made it up to meet needs of the moment. Modern critical scholarship has shown that some *hadiths* are simply made up from whole cloth. On the other hand, a *hadith* with an impeccable provenance could not be ignored (at least in theory) when reaching a decision. Others have been rejected in the past by different scholars, schools of law, or branches of Islam like the Sunni or Shi'a.

Sorting and collecting the *hadiths* was one of the primary occupations of the more conservative scholars within Islam as it began to grow. By the late 800s, the collections of *hadith* in Sunni Islam were more or less fixed in the collections made by al-Bukhari, who died in 870, and Muslim, who died in 875, though there were also other collections. Defining rules for the chain of proofs was an important adjunct. Some sort of objective mechanism was required for sorting out *hadiths* since the scholars had to find a way to fit even objectionable *hadiths* into the whole of Islamic law if determined to be sound.

It is wittily said that the Koran needs the *sunna* more than the *sunna* needs the Koran, and there is great truth to this saying – a saying incidentally, not of a modern Western scholar, but by the Syrian jurist Awza'i, who died in 774.[83] Most Islamic scholars consider the *hadiths* as essential in order to understand and clarify the Koran. Given the nature of *hadiths*, the Koran isn't really used to understand *hadiths*, but the other way round. *Hadith* are also used after the Koran as sources of legal substance, and for support and explanation for laws made.

The phrase "Islamic law" is often used interchangeably with *shari'a* or the phrase *"shari'a* law", all sometimes characterized as strict religious law mandating cutting off of hands and other harsh punishments. That isn't accurate. Harsh punishment may be part of a subset of the *shari'a*, but the term itself is a wide umbrella, derived from a root meaning "the way" or "the way down to water."[84] Given the brutal climate in which many Arabs have lived in the peninsula, the "way down to water" can be understood more simply as the way to life. *Shari'a* then, is something which gives life, and is the right way in which a Muslim should believe and live. Outside the *shari'a*, as out in the desert away from the water, lies death.

It is obvious at this point what a central place in life Islamic law held, so a brief sketch of its qualities as much of Sunni Islam recognizes them is necessary, even though this gets ahead of the historical narrative by several centuries. *Shari'a* law developed not from general principles, but from specific rules laid down either in the Koran or *sunna*. Those rules were developed over many centuries, and the scholars overlaid them with general principles in an attempt to explain them. *Shari'a* also appears with words like *fiqh*, the jurisprudence or philosophy of law, necessary to build the categories into which the scholars could organize the law.

The word *qanun* is also used within Islamic law, and means law made positively by a ruler to govern the cases where the Koran and traditions were silent. The word *qanun* itself is a direct borrowing from Greek texts of a legal word and concept, because such a type of ruler-made law didn't exist within Islam originally. Sources of law then, were the Koran and *sunna*, the caliph, or later sultan, for some matters of law such as market rules or court ceremonial rules, the political process for matters which we'd classify today as international law, and the enormous mass of legal commentaries, cases, books of philosophy and jurisprudence, and the actual practice of law itself.

Finding what the law actually was on a point in question could involve a long process, and different strains of Islamic thought didn't necessarily recognize all the steps in the process as valid, or might weight them differently, so what follows is a crude generalization. The first step in the legal process was to find a text which answered the question. If the Koran was clear, then the matter was settled. If the answer didn't appear there, then *sunna* (primarily *hadith*) was the next step. Finding an answer in the *sunna* could involve difficult analysis of conflicting *hadiths*, and ranking *hadiths* in order of importance, and required an impressive mastery of the voluminous *hadith* collections and commentaries on the law.

The Koran and the *hadiths* couldn't answer every question, and if there were a gap in the substance they supplied, then *qiyās* (analogy) was the next tool at the disposal of the jurisconsult or judge. A known textual point was taken for departure, and then hadiths were compared with that, to render a new result. A common *illa*, roughly cause, was sought in both textual rule and *sunna* in order to make the analogy.[85]

The customs of the *ummah* itself also crept into the law. They were not recognized as an independent source of Islamic law until the modern era, but during the early and classical years of Islamic law custom nonetheless was used. One way was simply to include custom under the heading of *sunna*, perhaps even to do a little pious fiction writing and write a *hadith* incorporating it, or to label it a matter of consensus. Custom also came into law through the practice of judicial personal preference (*istihsan or istişlah*)[86], which modern Western law might include under the heading of judicial discretion. A Judge hearing a case could choose whether to apply a secondary source of law, such as *fatwas* (legal rulings given in response to a question posed to a judge). A Judge might use legal fictions (*hiyal*), ways to reach a desired end goal. Or, the judge could use the legal doctrine of *darūra* (necessity), usually a way to explain that a legal rule must be relaxed to obtain a correct result.[87]

Finally, *ijmā'* (consensus), could be appealed to for an answer, and this was understood variously as either the consensus among scholars, or the consensus of the Islamic world as a whole. The rationale for allowing this is Muhammad's statement that the *ummah* could never agree upon an error.[88]

One last step in legal analysis was *ijtihad*, independent reasoning to the best of one's ability and strength, in order to reach a result. This was supposed to be undertaken only by the best scholars, exerting their utmost academic skills. It is a matter of controversy today, since "the doors of *ijtihad* closed" after several hundred years (or did they?), as a result of later developments.

This great work of defining what the Islamic law consisted of began in a rapidly expanding Islamic empire, still strongly Arabic in character, though that would change in the future as cultures and peoples were assimilated into Islamic life. The Koran was given to Arabs, so it reflects the Arabic cultural and literary traditions that predate it. Pre-Islamic Arab tribes placed a high value on the skillful use of language and poetry.

"Tribal contests were fought out as much, or more, in the taunts of their respective poets as on the field of battle, and so deeply rooted was the custom that even Muhammad, although in general hostile to the influence of the poets, himself conformed to it in his later years at Medina."[89] Scholars note the stylization of the Koran, using language and formulas similar to the old poets, but also, as the *ummah* moved back from Medina to Mecca, more concrete content like normative or legal rules.

As something with both original content, and traditional Arabic language patterns, the Koran is considered by many to be the primary literary monument of the Islamic world. It is in a class of its own within Arabic literature, and it was subsequently followed in style both directly and indirectly, especially in law and commentaries. It is said so often as to be a truism, but it is difficult to make a good translation of the Koran into other languages. The "ambiguities and shades of meaning which the old poetry often had are here also, so [the Koran] suffers greatly in translation."[90]

Correctly understanding the Koran was important since it was and is one of the basic sources of Islamic law. Therefore, philology and lexicography were the first "Islamic sciences" to begin developing[91], in order to judge authenticity of *hadiths*, and to give meaning to the *sunna* of Muhammad. This included the refining of grammar rules, where Persian culture made an important contribution. The Persians were heirs to an arguably older and more developed literary tradition, and could claim with perhaps a touch of snobbishness that their efforts were required to give the more uncultured Arabs of the time a proper grammar.

Summary and Conclusion

Islam had come a long way from the first Muslim, Muhammad, who was Islam's central character. The Koran he revealed, his acts as ruler, the biographies written about him and his *sunna*, and the Arabic cultural context within which this all took place, are the basis upon which the earliest Muslims organized their community, their *ummah.*

Islam began not within a society, or under the power of a state that might persecute it, but as a society containing a rudimentary state mechanism, a mechanism which could grow as the *ummah* felt it had the need. It expanded quickly, not within a state, but as the guiding principles *of* a state, causing Islam's first internal struggles. Those struggles were not to define the nature of Muhammad, for everyone agreed he was a man. Rather, they were to define how Muhammad's successor was to be chosen, the place of Arab identity versus a wider Islamic identity, how law was to be found and understood, and whether caliph or scholars would take the lead in developing law within society.

Law swiftly became complex to try to meet the challenges of an expanding empire. The nature of Islamic law, closely embedded in Arabic culture that looked back to the Koran and Muhammad's *sunna,* demanded a group of educated men with highly specialized knowledge. They were not priests set apart by religious office with religious knowledge. Rather, they were recognized by their merit as scholars of a wide body of knowledge containing what the modern West understands as both religion and law. After all, the Arabic word "*din*", which is usually translated in English as "religion", has a secondary translation of "law".[92]

Whether that *din* was to be understood primarily by looking at the traditions of Muhammad, or whether there was a role for reason, and just how that role might be limited, was a question which began to be asked with some urgency under the Abbasids. It would be the basis of a critical struggle and crisis for Islam.

Chapter 3 – Similarities and Differences in the Beginnings

Is there any use in making comparisons between the beginnings of Christianity and Islam? The answer is yes if the use of the comparisons is a positive and productive one. Comparison of differences is often used as a cudgel with which to clobber those of differing practices and beliefs. At other times comparison of similarities is used as a salve for all sores, equating practices and beliefs while ignoring very real differences. That may be more dangerous and harmful in the long term than comparing in order to show that your side is in the right.

A lack of dialogue leaves room for wrong assumptions to be made, for misunderstandings to be prolonged, for errors to go uncorrected, and for fear and anger to grow. There is no guarantee that a better understanding of each other will make either Christians or Muslims like one another, or even want to begin liking one another, but it can at least allow the possibility for men and women of good will in both of these traditions to try to hate each other *less*. That is reason enough to examine where Christians and Muslims differ from and resemble each other.

Any method of comparison contains assumptions. Here it is assumed that: Both of these religious systems (the substance of faith and practice, the persons, institutions, creeds and traditions accepted by most adherents of either) contain truth. Neither one contains all truth to the exclusion of allowing truth to exist in any other tradition. Either may at times do better or worse at expressing in their actions what the substance of the respective belief actually is. Each may or may not have enough truth to be a reliable guide to life in the here-and-now, as well as the hereafter. But there *is* truth, some call to transcendence that much modern academic study does not recognize. Even if it were not so, the assumption must remain since the true believer certainly thinks there is truth in his or her tradition!

No comparison methodology for these systems has been chosen in advance. Choosing a methodology at the beginning means that the range of possible outcomes has already been defined before the matter is studied. Without a methodology, bias will, or may, creep in. Certainly it may. Bias must also creep in as a consequence of the assumptions and methodologies of even the most carefully constructed study (and even precisely because of the careful construction), so the reader is left in no different position.

Finally, comparisons are limited to those that bear on the place of religion in society, and the intersection of law and religion. That means that many issues of faith and practice that interest or anger people are simply ignored as not relevant to the inquiry, and in any case, are covered well in many other places.

The Place of Religion in Pre-Industrial Societies

The first similarity between these two religious systems is one so basic it usually passes unnoticed. The place they held in society was shaped by the fact that they both began in pre-industrial times. In pre-industrial times, the power of the state, and government, was in some ways similar to that in our own times – there was little or no hesitation to forcibly extract taxes from the populace, young men were drafted into the army whether they wanted it or not, and those who disagreed went to jail, were exiled, or killed. But the difference from modern times is that the power of the pre-industrial state, strong as it was, was limited in application. There was simply no ability to manage the life of the population in all its small details and disputes, nor to supply the many and varied local services modern states furnish to virtually all of their citizens, things like police forces, medical care, garbage removal, even other social services as basic is justice.[93]

Those functions were not yet the exclusive functions of the state, but were carried on by alternate social groups, such as the family, tribe or kin group, or religious association. For example, the idea of the *paterfamilias* is an ancient and widespread legal notion.[94] The head of the family had legal, financial, and even judicial-like powers over the family members. Widening that scope of authority a bit, the local village council, or kin group, was next. Only offenses and questions that rose to the kingdom or national level would be handled anywhere other than on the local level, by some sort of national authority. Religion was often one of those authorities.

The state organization of that era has been called a capstone government. It sat on top of the variety of local institutions, attempting to balance them against one another, or even against the state, to maintain order. Religion, as (usually) more widespread than family or kin groupings, was a natural ally, or enemy, to the state. The question was which it would be. In this light, the real offense of the early Christians against the Roman state was the potential for power which they held if united in their beliefs. They could easily be too powerful as a group for the state to control.[95]

Both Christianity and Islam had a potential for power to organize their respective societies widely in this time of the pre-industrial state, and both of them did. They went about it differently, due to the different conditions of their birth, and this is the first significant difference between the two to compare.

Christianity began to organize the life of its adherents from outside the accepted order of the Roman Empire. It was a tolerated religious system within society, and sometimes its followers were persecuted by the state, for roughly the first three hundred years of its existence. Seeing the power that Christianity had to give cohesion to a threatened empire, Constantine adopted it and made it part of the official structure of empire. Christianity and what it believed showed in its first few centuries that it could thus be outside the state-governed structure of society, or in opposition to it, or part of it. The

Christian religion and the law were different things, though they could unite.

Islam in contrast began as a unity. The idea of an opposition or struggle of opposing forces within society was not part of Islamic society. You were either in the *ummah*, or not. The ideas of Islam were what formed society. Islamic society, as it spread rapidly in its first few centuries, constructed the state to serve the needs of Islamic society. Islam did not struggle with an external Roman state like Christianity did. Think back to the Constitution of Medina, which regulated international relations.

Islam and Christianity in pre-industrial times shared another similarity. Modern religion is often limited to narrow areas of worship or morality, but the religion of pre-industrial times was more pervasive in the life of the mind of a typical person. Religion could offer explanations of life's good and bad events which would be explained in differrent ways in modern societies. God sent rains upon the land in pre-industrial times. Falling barometers and relative humidity were felt by experience, but the language and knowledge to express the fact and the cause of rain scientifically did not yet exist.[96] This doesn't even touch yet the issue of rules for daily living, which we'll come to later.

It is fair to say that both of these pre-industrial era religious systems exercised, and expected to exercise, a great deal more power over the lives and thoughts of everyday people than modern Western societies are accustomed to expect. This physical, intellectual, and spiritual authority was exercised by a variety of different types of professional religious persons. There are both differences and similarities between these servants of Christianity and Islam which bear examination, as both bodies of men (and that's a similarity) carried out the wide exercise of power expected of them in pre-industrial times.

A Hierarchy – or None?

It is more confusing than helpful to read in books and articles discussing Islam and Christianity a statement to the effect that Islam doesn't have priests like the Christian Church, and therefore lacks the hierarchical nature of Christianity.[97] This is about as helpful and illuminating as stating that Christianity doesn't have imams. There are differences - an imam does not dispense sacraments to the people like a priest. Sacraments are holy things, and someone dispensing holy things must be holy, so there is some sort of setting apart between the priest and the rest of society. Imams marry, and so did Christian priests in the beginning, though in the West a rule of celibacy would come to be adopted in the Middle Ages, and that is often raised as a difference.

These surface differences too often obscure more important underlying similarities. In both, a hierarchy certainly does exist, and existed from very early times. In both religious systems, there was a system of selection for those who would act as priests or imams. In Christianity, the selection process was rooted in a tradition of authority – a higher office holder appointed a lower, but in order to do so that higher office holder had to hold a place in a chain of authority stretching back to the beginning. This is why, for example, both Antiochean Orthodox and Catholic Christians will trace back to Peter as the first leader with authority to appoint others.

In Islam, the selection process was initially rooted in authority – the rightly guided caliphs directly following Mohammad undoubtedly had this. Shortly after, Islam was engaged in its first struggle to define itself by law in a wider world, and with the question of authority of the caliph to define Islamic society. The need for and importance of the scholars increased and the power of the caliphs began to diminish. As will be fully discussed later, the scholars were self-appointed, and earned their places by merit and the recognition of this merit by their peers. A place within the religious structure was earned, not conferred.

In both these traditions there is an interplay between knowledge required of an officiant, and authority. A degree of knowledge was required within the Islamic tradition, but only those already recognized as authorities could recognize the sufficient knowledge of the aspiring young man. Knowledge alone was not enough. Acceptance by those already confirmed in their status was also required. In Christianity, a priest or bishop with enough political or social connections to be appointed, who might be wonderfully ignorant, was nonetheless required to discharge his office in accordance with the knowledge of the Church as a whole.

This interplay of knowledge and authority leads back to hierarchy, and it is often pointed out that the hierarchy within Islam was either non-existent, or quite flat when it began. There was one caliph, and he and everyone else were members of the *ummah*. With the rise of the scholars, the authority of the caliph was somewhat diffused. But all scholars were not created equal. Their innate abilities and hard work set them apart from one another. The weight to be given the collection of *hadith*, or commentaries on law, of one scholar versus another was something well known within the scholarly community. The hierarchy was present, but it was a hierarchy mostly of the intellect.

The hierarchy within early Christianity, especially after it began to borrow from Roman imperial ideas either consciously or subconsciously, was much easier to discern. Authority was fixed in geographic districts, or was given over certain other groups of religious officers, or extended to only certain acts within the Church. Christian hierarchy may be easier to discern, but it is similar to Islam in that someone in the hierarchy in either of these religious systems would have the authority to give an answer to a question of how an adherent of the faith was to live. Not everyone in either tradition could give that answer. On this issue, the only difference between Christianity and Islam is in how the hierarchy was constructed, not on whether or not it existed.

A hierarchy, whether of offices granted from a long tradition of authority, or whether earned or advanced in by intellect and effort, was necessary to both of these religious systems. Prestige, power, and financial reward were quickly available in varying mixes to those pursuing the vocation of holiness. If available, self interest demanded that these scarce goods be somehow preserved for the select group, not spread to everyone in society. Preservation meant limiting entrance of new aspirants, whether that be done by way of formal appointment or testing of intellectual powers.

Balancing the Here-and-Now with the Hereafter

Beside the similarity of power exercised by a limited body of holy men, Islam and Christianity had in common in their beginnings the attempt to answer the two questions of the more sophisticated religions: How shall I live in the here-and-now; and, how do I reach God in the hereafter? Both Christianity and Islam struggle between the poles of trusting God for the life of the soul after death and doing a sufficient number of good works here and now to ensure one's place in the hereafter. That is a very difficult question for adherents of both faiths, and is beside the point of this discussion, though obviously of highest importance. What is more to the point of the intersection of law and religion in society is the answer to the question of how to live here-and-now, and what weight Christianity or Islam place on that versus the hereafter.

The idea of life and how it ought to be lived was not (conceptually) very different within early Islam and early Christianity. Both communities evolved a set of rules about living life that adherents were expected, or required, to follow. If followed, then a perfect, or moral, life was attained. The set of rules in each ranged far and wide in regulation of human conduct, from prayers, to marriage, to sexual life, to crimes, and financial matters.

The devil truly is in the details as he is reported to be. Comparing the rules then, as now, leads to confusion, accusations, and anger. A value, such as truthfulness, might be demanded by both Islam and Christianity. But, if a Christian expected to see that behavior modeled in society in a certain way when he looked at an Islamic society, and did not see it, then the temptation was to declare that Islam didn't have the value. Many similar social values were present in both religious systems, but were just shown in different ways.

Sometimes though, values present in both traditions had different ranks on the scale of most to least important. This is a matter which is rarely discussed, but a rank and ranking process for values is present in all systems of values, religious and otherwise. Different emphases and weighting meant that the shape of religious and communal life was different. For example, Christianity in late Roman culture ranked values of asceticism highly, while Islam did not. The difference in ranking of values could have unintended effects:

> "The chief attraction of Islam was that it was practical; it did not demand seemingly superhuman efforts. . . The Christian East on the eve of the Islamic conquest had forgotten the limitations of human nature. Many members of the Church desired to imitate the angels; hence the mass movements towards the sexless life of monks and nuns; hence the exodus from towns and villages into the desert; hence the feats of self-mortification which showed the extent to which men could subdue their bodies at the dictates of the spirit. Some of these Eastern ascetics slept only in a standing position, others immured themselves in dark cells or lived on pillars, or ate only herbs, and even those not more than once a week. Islam stopped all these excesses. It swept away the exaggerated fear of sex, discarded asceticism, banished the fear of hell for those who failed to reach perfection, quenched theological enquiry. . . Islam was like the sand of the desert. . . It created a sense of solidarity and brotherhood which had been lost among the contending Christians."[98]

Finally, perhaps some values were not present in both or either of these religious systems, a possibility that cannot be discarded.

Other Similarities and Differences

Conflict is also something both Islam and Christianity have had in common from their very beginnings. One of Islam's earliest struggles was to define whether caliphs ought to be chosen by the *ummah*, or whether they must be relatives of the prophet Mohammad, producing the enduring Sunni – Shi'a split. Christianity struggled over whether Christians were Jews or something else, over the culture Christianity was or would be part of, and over the nature of Christ himself. Islam did not initially have such struggles, as to be an Arab was to be a Muslim, a single identity of culture and faith, and Muhammad was a Prophet, but a man.

There are many other similarities in both religious systems, such as both formal and informal prayers, holy books, and religious writers who tended to improve the stories of saints or histories of the faith: "The ninth-century belle-lettrist Ibn Qutayba quoted the Prophet's companion Hudhayfa ibn al-Yaman as blithely acknowledging that: 'We are Arab people; when we report, we predate and postdate, we add and we subtract at will, but we do not mean to lie.'"[99] Anyone who has read a pious Christian hagiographer ought to smile with the familiarity of that statement. The writers of both of these holy books didn't share modern presumptions of scientific history.

The holy books of Islam and Christianity themselves share issues like the ordering of their parts, neither being in chronological order, so the reader of either is advised to do some research so that the materials may be read in chronological order, therefore illuminating the text and arguments of either. Both share difficulties with translations. Is a Koran not in Arabic a Koran? The standard answer is no, and that it is in fact an interpretation, and that to truly understand the book it must be heard, and read, in Arabic.

Christianity is more liberal in its point of view on translation, not insisting that a student read the Bible in Aramaic or Greek. There is a truly astonishing and bewildering variety of translations and paraphrases from which a student may choose. And here again, some will grow quite insistent, if not angry, that a particular translation (King James Version, for instance) is the only correct translation.

But those are beside the point. I am skipping over many subjects, and loosely labeling some as similarities when they could bear a closer look. Let me give one example to illustrate the danger of easy identification of similarities. Some will make a great deal of the fact that Christ dying, and rising again, as asserted by Christianity, is really nothing new in the history of religion. They'll point to several instances where gods have died, and come back to life, in the Spring of the year, just as Christ did. The god dying and rising again for his people is a commonplace, really no big deal, so Christianity has nothing to be particularly worked up about, runs this argument.[100]

That, as some scholars of comparative religion will say, is looking at the outside of the bowl, when we ought to be looking at what's *inside* the bowl.[101] Yes, the god dies and comes back to life, and Jesus dies and comes back to life, but what does this mean? There lies the difference: To Christianity, a one-time event that somehow in a mystery changes, or has the potential to change, believers from what they were, into something new; while to another religion of the ancient near east, that death and rebirth is only an annual fertility rite, renewing the earth and sustenance.[102]

The Greatest Difference – Law or Religion?

Let us look inside the bowl for what is one of the central differences between Islam and Christianity from their beginnings. Where was the weight in the system: On rules for the here and now, or hopes for the life hereafter? There is in each a varying application and understanding of norms and aspirations. To put it in modern terms, this question is whether they look primarily to us like "law" or look primarily like "religion".

A norm at its simplest is a given standard of behavior that must be met, at the risk of some penalty if not met. An aspiration is a goal to be striven toward, with the hope that it will someday be reached. It is usually more vague and ill-defined than a norm. Norms may be of assistance in reaching an aspirational goal: A norm like not driving faster than 55 miles per hour on the road bears the financial penalty of a police officer's traffic ticket for disobeying, and is designed to meet the aspirational goal of keeping drivers safe on the road.

Norms and aspirations can be found in both of the places the modern West labels "law" and "religion". They can also be found in the beginnings of both Christianity and Islam. Remember, as pointed out above, that the values given, whether set out as norms or aspirations, may be in different rank orders of importance within Christianity and Islam – ascetic behavior might be ranked more highly than routine human life. The subject matter of the mix of norms and aspirations in each is much different, and comes directly from the different ways both Christianity and Islam began.

Christianity began outside the constitutional order of the Roman Empire. Therefore, it didn't provide norms for things like international relations. The Roman state made those rules, as well as many of the important rules governing life in Palestine. As Charles Williams noted, Jesus "said nothing against the Roman occupation."[103] Instead, he often spoke of something called the kingdom of God, that seemed to be both something in this world, and also something in the world to come, or perhaps both. The interested reader should make a search for this in the Gospels of Jesus and make of these references what he or she can.

Christianity began with a very limited set of norms relating to the state and the individual. "Christ made no attempt to participate in the political activities of the roman empire, nor even in the local jewish hegemony of Palestine. He left behind him no legacy of political theorizing."[104] He actively refused power: "Jesus, who could see they were about to come and take him by force and make him king, escaped back to the hills by himself."[105] Christianity had no state to administer. But yet some rules did evolve over the first few hundred years of Christianity. "Early Church constitutions, such as the *Didache* (c. 120) and *Didascalia Apostolorum* (c. 250), set forth internal rules for Church organization and affairs, clerical life, ecclesiastical discipline, charity, education, family, and property relations."[106]

In contrast, the headings in the Constitution of Medina, Al-Wathiqa, are those of a state conducting international relations with other states, like 'Conduct, or the Rules of War', 'Security and Defense', or 'Respect for International Law',[107] Similarly, Islam from the beginning contains norms relating to the state, but also in relation to the individual within society, like 'Loyalty', 'The Right to Rebellion or Revolution', 'Search, or Striving, for Peace', 'Freedom of Religion', 'Believing in Capital Punishment', 'The Right of Minorities', 'The Rule of Law', 'Sanctuary', 'Immigration', or the 'Privacy Right.'[108] The Constitution for the *ummah* in Medina was a matter of international law and norms, with and between the other tribes in Medina. It described relationships between the *ummah* and the state it constructed, and the internal relationships of that community, down to things as fundamental as death and inheritance.

Islam records many different *hadiths* of Muhammad deciding questions of inheritance, and the Koran itself contains several specific passages as well, including sura 4:11:

> "God charges you, concerning your children: to the male the like of the portion of two females, and if they be women above two, then for them two-thirds of what he leaves, but if she be one then to her a half; and to his parents to each one of the two the sixth of what he leaves, if he has children; but if he has no children, and

his heirs are his parents, a third to his mother, or, if he has brothers, to his mother a sixth, after any bequest he may bequeath, or any debt. Your fathers and your sons -- you know not which out of them is nearer in profit to you. So God apportions; surely God is All-knowing, All-wise."[109]

In contrast, the Gospels lack substantive norms of inheritance, and show Jesus seeming to duck the chance to provide them. The Bible at Luke 12:13 relates the story of a man who spoke up during a public speech by Jesus, asking that Jesus make his brother divide the inheritance with him. Evidently the first brother had gotten a little greedy, and hadn't given the second brother the share to which the law entitled him, hence the demand on Jesus. "'My friend' he replied, 'who appointed me your judge, or the arbitrator of your claims?'"

The words of Jesus as recorded in the Bible give very few norms, but a great deal of disturbingly aspirational language. In fact, Jesus seemed to positively delight in flipping norms on their heads, and turning them into aspirations. Take for example, the well-known story of "The Good Samaritan", an unfortunate editorial mislabeling which is very misleading without the set-up for *why* Jesus told the story. If you are not familiar with it, see Luke 10:25-37. The background is a "lawyer" asking Jesus questions about what is necessary to inherit eternal life. Jesus answered by pointing the man back to his own holy law, so the lawyer cited a passage ending with the prescription that he must love his neighbor as himself. "But the man was anxious to justify himself and said to Jesus, 'And who is my neighbor?'." The actual story of the Good Samaritan is the reply to that question.

The question is looking for a norm – a standard of behavior. After all, if the man can find out a good definition for what a neighbor is, then he can go ahead with the difficult business of loving that neighbor as himself. Jesus answers by telling the story of an injured man ignored by several passers-by, until finally the Samaritan stops to help the man. He closes by asking the lawyer which one of the travelers proved to be a neighbor to the poor injured man. The lawyer of course answers "'The one who took pity on him.'" "Jesus said to him, 'Go, and do the same yourself.'"[110] Do you see what happened there? The question asked sought a norm which would limit and define behavior – *who is my neighbor?* The answer given is *to whom can you be a neighbor?* Not normative, but aspirational. That sort of answer has disturbing implications.

Comparing the Koran and the New Testament yields different proportions of text on legal subjects. Nowhere in the New Testament are there extended passages on the legalities of marriage, or succession of property on death, as in the Koran.[111] Both faiths had norms and aspirations for their followers from the beginning. Christianity seems to have started with a stronger weighting toward the aspirational, and Islam with a stronger weighting toward the normative. But either Christianity or Islam may choose to emphasize the norms, or the aspirations. Many Muslims in favor of reform argue that normative verses of the Koran have been emphasized wrongly over the aspirational, as later material will show. Christianity and Islam have from their beginnings made different claims about the relationship between the state and law, society, and religious teachings and leaders.

Cultural Differences and Cultural Borrowing

Identity is another difference between Christianity and Islam in their beginnings. For Islam, early identity was quite easy. The earliest Muslims, nearly all ethnic Arabs, were Muslims if they were followers of Mohammad and his message of God, if they'd left Mecca for Medina on the *hijra*, and if they recognized their place in the *ummah* of Islam formed by that journey and the Constitution of Medina. That Constitution made explicit boundaries between those who were part of the new faith community, and those who were not. There were easily discerned norms in this area of identity.

It is unclear whether the first Christians realized they were Christians, as distinct from Jews. The book of Acts reports things like the believers in Jesus going to the Jewish temple, and assembling there.[112] If they truly were different, why were they there? Or was their new message something which was part of the Jewish religion? In early Christianity, there was no *hijra*. There is no document like Al-Wathiqa which sets distinctions between those who are believers, and those who are not. The distinctions are much more vague and difficult to define in a normative way.

Cultural backgrounds also illustrate the differences in identity of adherents between these religions. While Christianity certainly looked Jewish and borrowed from Jewish holy writings and liturgies, it also showed an almost immediate transcultural movement. There is a very interesting episode where Peter gave a sermon to a crowd, all of whom heard him in a variety of languages. The list of languages and peoples includes: "Parthians, Medes and Elamites; residents of Mesopotamia, Judea and Cappadocia, Pontus and Asia, Phrygia and Pamphylia, Egypt and the parts of Libya near Cyrene; visitors from Rome (both Jews and converts to Judaism); Cretans and Arabs."[113]

Paul, who has already been shown speaking in Athens and casually dropping Greek cultural allusions, also showed familiarity with Roman law and its categories in several illustrations in his New Testament writings.[114] Philo of Alexandria, a Hellenized Jew, was arguably an influence upon Paul, and upon John, to whom is attributed the Gospel of the same name. Similarities between Philo and John have been commented upon, as well as differences. There is no doubt that Philo's bridging attempt between the Jewish corpus and Greek philosophy influenced other writers of the early Christian Church.[115] "[T]he early Christian intellectuals naturally followed his lead in attempting to accommodate the teachings of Plato and the stoics to the doctrines of their religion."[116]

In fact, borrowing the tools of Greek culture may have been necessary for the successful spread of Christianity. "The

Greek culture was an intellectual machine for the elucidation and transformation of religious ideas. You put in a theological concept and it emerged in a highly sophisticated form, communicable to the entire civilized world."[117] After Constantine and the rise to dominance of the Byzantine culture in Christianity, the language of the religion and the Church became Greek, and Latin, Latin more so in the West as imperial power crumbled in that area. That cultural adoption alienated the Mesopotamian and Arabian-area Christians with their vibrant Syriac tradition, which was suppressed and disfavored by Byzantium.[118]

In contrast, the Koran revealed through Mohammad states that it is "an Arabic Koran" in sura 12.2, which sura 46:11 says is "in an Arabic tongue." It was revealed to and discussed with Arabs, by an Arab leader. Islam expanded quickly, but the language of Muslims was Arabic. The greatest initial challenge of cultural identity was with the Persian language and culture, which supplied the growing Islamic empire with ideas and language (e.g., for procedures at court) that were lacking in the Arabic language and culture. The greatest test of cultural identity of Islam and its relationships with other cultures was to come in the Abbasid dynasty, discussed later.

Early Islam borrowed what was necessary, and placed it in areas of need in the context of a dominant Arabic culture. As mentioned, early Muslim converts were understood to be clients, sponsored in a sense by a specific Arabic tribe, although as the empire expanded to the west, this practice was abandoned as too unwieldy. Islam from its first days had a comprehensive idea and blueprint of society in the *ummah*. It did not need to adapt itself to a larger culture to spread and grow as Christianity did using Greek culture. It *was* the culture.

Finally, while early Christianity had to struggle to differentiate itself from the Jews, a process of several hundred years duration, Islam had no problem with differentiation. Even beside the cultural factors above, Islam made it clear from the beginning that Muslims were different from those around them. Tools and institutions for doing so beside the mosque, the prayers, and the legal rules of Islamic life for the Muslims inside the *ummah* were directed at those who had made the choice to stay outside. They included the *jizya*, a tax required of those who did not convert to Islam, and the status of *dhimmi*, a contractual protection afforded by Islam as a whole to members of minority religions within the Islamic empire.[119]

Identity also mattered in economics. For the early Christians, economic matters don't seem to be an issue of identity. Within the economic order of the Roman Empire, some Christians carried on working, buying and selling. Some chose to give away their riches. Expansion of the faith does not appear to have been systematically coupled to the economic order, until Constantine began to explicitly favor the Church, as mentioned.

Islam on the other hand disadvantaged non-Muslims through the *jizya*. More importantly, Islamic society operated on the assumption that territory and goods gained by conquest were to be shared out, according to the list of precedence made by the leaders.[120] Islamic society had an economic model which assumed expansion by Muslims and benefit by Muslims from the expansion. This economic arrangement was not necessary to the Islamic state, but it did accompany it in fact. A state which depended upon expansion for revenue was in a precarious position, as the Ottomans would later realize to their sorrow.

There are sharp differences in the social program (or lack thereof) within early Christianity and early Islam. Islam had a charter that defined relations with those outside the *ummah*, and had rules for how the *ummah* would relate within itself. Christianity had a vague idea of the "kingdom of God", within currents of Greek, Roman, and Jewish culture. The Islamic social program was society. In Islam the idea of the *ummah*, and its solidarity was always central. "From the first the religious message proclaimed by Muhammad had been addressed to a *qawm* or *umma*, a 'tribe' or 'community', that is, to a body politic of the type familiar to the Arabs."[121]

In the area of law, one of the conditions under which early Christianity began was Roman law. The Christians didn't make law, but were forced to accommodate themselves to the legal regime which existed. If Christian law could be said to exist, then it was a matter of church procedure and discipline, matters for individual believers, essentially private in nature within the Roman state. But that was only up until the time of Constantine and the transformation of Christianity to become a part of the legal and constitutional order.

Al-Wathiqa, on the other hand, established an Islamic society and legal order that in turn constructed a state to implement those things imparted in the Koran and the traditions of Mohammad, and "state affairs were not a distraction from spirituality but the stuff of religion itself."[122] Muslims very consciously made law, and a law which was exclusive, from the beginnings of Islam.

This difference in the legal order has further implications. For the early Christian, choice of faith was allowable under Roman law that recognized a pluralistic religious marketplace. The choice was essentially a private matter, with which the state was not concerned, so long as the state was obeyed. Not so in Islam, where the status of Muslim or non-Muslim was a public act, with immediate implications in public law, such as tribal clientage, *jizya*, or *dhimmi* status. Early Christian belief was in essence a private act which *could* have public consequences, but not *necessarily*, as in Islam.

Summary and Conclusions

National identity and religious identity started as different things in Christianity. One could be a Roman citizen and a Christian, Roman citizen but non-Christian, non-Roman citizen Christian or non-Roman non-Christian, all within the Roman Empire. From the beginnings of Islam those two identities were identical. A Muslim was a full member of the Islamic empire. Non-Muslims within the empire as *dhimmis* were permitted to retain their chosen religions, but were not full members of society in the sense that a Muslim would be. Of course these issues of identity could change. In the Middle Ages Christian societies assumed Christianity by their inhabitants and disadvantaged non-Christians, particularly Jews. At that time and for hundreds of years subsequently, Jews were on the whole treated better in Islamic societies than Christian.[123]

It is fair to recognize different spheres of authority for matters of state and matters of faith within early Christianity. These two became very close to being one after Constantine within the Byzantine Empire, and would be a matter of contention in the West during the end of the classical area and into the Middle Ages, as will be seen. Again, not so with Islam, since Muslim faith and matters of state were a unity from the beginning.

For the Christian then, a legitimate difference with the state didn't mean a constitutional crisis (even under Byzantium), although it might mean persecution by the state, or even allow room for victory over the state. In Islam, a difference between state and faith meant either that the ruler was illegitimate in not encouraging the good and forbidding the bad, or that the individual or group in question had placed themselves outside Islamic society, in distinction or opposition to it, as will be discussed.

Finally, speculation about God and the content of the faith has shaped the way in which society could be formed, even from the beginnings of Islam and Christianity. Christianity asserted that the "word" of God was a person – Jesus. Islam asserted that the "word" of God was the Koran. "For Christians, the revelation is that of a person, and the basic theological question in the early centuries was that of the relationship of this Person with God; for Muslims, the revelation is a Book, and the problem of the status of the Book is therefore fundamental."[124]

Where were the limits in speculating about the nature of God for Christians, and the relationship of Jesus to God? The answer could only be that time and theological study would reveal those limits. Even a cursory look at the speculations of Christianity in its first several centuries show some pretty wild ideas, and the gradual growth of an orthodoxy that would assert that limits must exist.

The limits within Islam from the beginning seem easier to discern, and by their nature more legal. The scholars were necessary for a proper understanding of what God had said in the Koran, and what Mohammad had meant by silence, words, and acts. Even setting aside what ambitions they might have to power, the nature of Islam calls for their existence, and sets limits upon their activities. Speculation that ranged too widely in Islam was at that time a question not yet answered, one that by the legal and juristic nature of the Islamic society was slower to arise, but the question would arise – and be answered – in only a few short centuries.

The outlines of allowable speculation from the beginning did not disallow Christians the opportunity to speculate about law. They could develop law and legal systems as part of their faith, and even to try to apply legal rules to society as a whole, but the Christian root texts do not demand it. The Islamic root texts, the Koran, the biographies of Muhammad, and the *sunna*, do demand an Islamic law, but maybe not so defined as strict schools of Islamic law make it out to be today.

The constitutional order – the place of religion within society – is more easily capable of change within the Christian tradition than within the Islamic tradition (at least in theory). From the beginning Christianity showed a more obvious differentiation between itself and the state, as it progressed from tolerated, to persecuted, to ally. Within the first three hundred years of Christianity, the three options between state and faith of neutrality, enmity, and friendship had all been tried.

Within the first few hundred years of Islamic development, we do not see a similar flexibility in defining the constitutional order. The first struggles in Islam, involving definition of the caliphate, and the rise of the scholars, are all set in the context of only one of the three possible relationships between state and religion, that of ally, if not unity. Islam *was* the constitutional order, and arrangements in that order only took place inside the *ummah* of Islam.

Differences in Christianity and Islam as they began produced very different assumptions about the place of each in society. Their abilities to lead or guide were quite different. The possibilities of a persuasive role for religious thought against a forceful (even coercive) role were different. Christianity was in this sense so ill-defined that it could take on a number of roles, ending in this time period with a combination of authority with the Byzantine state that wasn't that different from early Islam.

Whether later challenges arising within their societies could change these roles is the next question. For neither Islam nor Christianity stayed in their earliest forms. Both grew, and changed, through new struggles to which we must turn next.

Chapter 4 - The Papal Revolution

Christianity by the early 300s had become an official religion, part of the constitutional order presided over by the Emperor Constantine. Constantine was defined in both ancient Jewish and modern Greek terms as mysteriously both priest and king, so it was natural that he would call and preside over the great church council at Nicaea in 325. Nobles flocked to take positions in a church that began to take on a hierarchy and organization modeled on imperial lines. The new center of the empire, Constantinople, soon boasted great churches built with imperial patronage. The language of the church was increasingly Greek, or in the West, Latin.

Greco-Roman culture had embedded itself firmly in the church, or perhaps the other way round. This Christianized Roman Empire in the Eastern half of the old Roman Empire is usually called Byzantium, especially as it became different from the Western half of the empire. Eastern half may be misleading, since the East had the most population, the best resources, and strongest and most stable economy.[125] The reorientation of imperial energy to the East and movement of the capital left old Rome behind, and that helped bring change.

Rome wasn't intentionally surrendered to invaders, but gradually it and the rest of the Western half of the empire became ungovernable from Constantinople. Decay and fragmentation in the West started a process which led to the turning point in European History that some call the papal revolution.[126] The way the West changed, and how both Christianity and the new states of Western Europe responded to it, laid the foundation on which the modern assumptions of Western society and Western Christianity stand.

It is a complex and tangled story starting with the collapse of government and society in the West, involving new roles and competition for social leadership by kings and church.

The order of the church, with popes, priests, and monks, is involved. The question of rules and order in the heavens, and this world, and both, is part of it. Corrupt, greedy, and scheming priests and nobles play their part, as do those who badly wanted reform and holiness. The substance of law, roles of lawgivers and rebirth of Roman law in the new universities are involved. All of these factors must be woven together to complete a tapestry of conflict, for it was out of conflict that what we think of as the modern Western order began to emerge.

The Fall of the Western Roman Empire

What better place for a story of conflict to begin than with German barbarians storming south from their gloomy forests. The Fall of Rome is sometimes romanticized as an earthshaking tragedy of fires and destruction brought by those hairy German barbarians, with looting and the usual accompaniments. I remember, from reading Gibbon's *The Decline and Fall of the Roman Empire* many years ago, a frantic succession of Emperors, none of whom were able to hold the Empire together, as they fell to palace coups, in battle, or to old fashioned murder. These were all part of the Fall - no sudden event but a gradual disintegration of Roman society for a variety of reasons in the area from Italy extending West to England.

Sometimes the barbarian Germanic tribes, under pressure from those behind them, moved South and West with the permission, and in alliance, with Rome. For example, there is a long history of commercial, diplomatic and military alliances between Germanic chieftans and Roman authorities along the Danube River.[127] Archaeological evidence and records of land ownership and place names in Southern France for instance, show that the invaders didn't always destroy the accepted ways of life, but even bought land in the usual way, with the normal legal formalities, and settled down to farming.[128] Sometimes they did actually invade and conquer, and simply overwhelmed the ability of government to control them by their sheer numbers.[129] The movement of Germanic peoples into imperial territory was sometimes violent, sometimes peaceful, and differed greatly from place to place.[130] It provoked and sustained change in the Western half of the empire that was already in decline.

The stability of the economy in the West had been faltering for some time. Struggles between the co-emperors of the Romans, and defense against invaders all during the 300s had hit the peasantry hard, both through enforced military service and increased tax burdens.[131] The peasants could escape these burdens by moving away, so Constantine tried to stabilize farming, food supply, and the tax revenues of government by tying those tenants to the land, a bond which was shortly to become hereditary.[132] Similar legislation made trade guild memberships hereditary, and froze the class of *curials*, the merchants, small industrialists and landowners responsible for ordering society.[133] These measures had the unintended effect of making governance more local, rather than empire-wide, especially when Rome had finally fallen.

Different historians provide even more reasons for the decline of Rome, and a variety of dates for the fall of Rome. Perhaps it took place in 376 with a vigorous infusion of new Gothic blood from the north. Maybe it was 395 with the death of Theodosius I, the last emperor ruling (at least in theory) a unified empire. Perhaps Rome ended when it was looted by Alaric and the Goths in 410, or when it was sacked a second time in 455. Some will place the fall as late as 476, when the last emperor in the west, Romulus, was thrown out by Odoacer, a German invader who promptly seated himself in Rome.

Regardless of when the fall of Rome can be dated, civil government decayed over those years so that it was no longer possible to stop invasions. It was no longer able to collect taxes, or supply its population with the services those taxes bought. There wasn't even enough civil authority left to stand up to Constantinople when the Emperor wanted something the locals did not. The years from roughly 500 – 900 were the "most turbulent and misery-laden that Europe has ever experienced."[134]

Turbulence and misery forced remnants of the old Roman nobility, who had joined the church and held high office, into action. The bishops of the church did exercise authority in areas where the modern mind expects the state to act, like regulation and suppression of non-approved, non-Christian religious practices, but they did so under imperial approval and sometimes with explicit imperial law authorizing them to act on behalf of the empire.[135] At least in the East it worked that way, but in the West the Emperor was far away.

Lacking imperial authority and a working government, bishops of the Western church had to act. Ambrose of Milan (340-397) provides an example. "Ambrose's aristocratic origins and friends, his previous experience as an imperial governor, and his own courage and personality enabled him to deal with the imperial state more successfully than had any previous Christian bishop."[136] A few generations later, Pope Leo I (Leo the Great) rode out from Rome to meet Atilla in 452 as he lead his Huns Westward, and persuaded Atilla to spare the city.[137] The reality is that Leo was only one of three ambassadors sent by the Romans to Atilla, but he was important enough in city affairs to be included. A bishop in the West "might become truly the *pater populi* or *pater civitatis,* but in the east the emperor's officials remained fully responsible for the maintenance of law and order."[138]

The new kings of the West though, expected to rule their own kingdoms. If bishops in the West tended to take on the kings tasks at need, then the kings equally expected to take part in the tasks of the church. Traditional rules and practice within the Germanic cultures of the West often combined the roles of tribal leader/tribal priest in the same person. If not combined, they were likely allied very closely, since "the Germanic rulers remained the supreme religious heads of their respective peoples, appointing bishops and dictating liturgical and other religious matters."[139]

Competition for Leadership Produces Conflict

The degeneration of the empire and rise of both kings and bishops to fill that power vacuum soon produced competition for leadership, and conflict over it. The conflict drove men in and outside the church to form new theories about the place of kings and religion in the social order. Those theories would be cited to support the actions of either, but first the practical and local matters around which conflict centered must be discussed. Often the issue was the identity of the person who ought to be bishop or priest. It is described in several different ways, or presents several different aspects: investiture, or simony, or what is called the proprietary system.

Appointments, or investiture of clergy by rulers was an expected part of life in the earliest of the Germanic tribes moving into Europe, as we've seen. It was also accepted in the empire - Ambrose may be an example of the state appointing the person it wanted in order that imperial policy would be carried through. His governorship in Gaul made him "one of the half-dozen most important civilians in the empire."[140] He made the transition from layman to bishop in an amazing eight days. As kingdoms expanded into the Merovingian and Carolingian societies of Western Europe, this expectation didn't change.

The problem for the church and advantage for the king with investiture is obvious: Where do the loyalties of the appointee lie? Could the bishop be expected to obey the local lord who had appointed him, or the pope far away, or the emperor, even further away? Were the local bishops part of the struggle between kings? While Theodore of Marseille was bishop, power in the city was shared between two kings, but in 575 when king Sigibert died, his successor began to fight with the other king, Childebert. Theodore was arrested and accused of plotting treason. The charge wasn't upheld but the damage was done. Local clergy and population rallied against him, and though he managed to hold on to his see, he remained under shadow and threat of further arrest for the rest of his career.[141]

What have been called proprietary churches were a related part of this problem. These were churches actually built, endowed, maintained, and owned by a king or local lord, who might define the services to be offered, good works to be performed, and even the rule of life to be adopted by the clergy.[142] In addition to the appointment of the priest or bishop the king chose, this ownership system allowed tithes to be diverted for local use and benefit, and decentralized control over the churches. It was too easy for a local lord or king to use proprietorship as a tool to extend power or raise revenue, although some no doubt had pious motives.[143]

The fact that bishops were often from the old Roman nobility, or upper classes related to the ruling lords and kings, only complicated matters more. If lords could inherit lands and estates, then why not bishops their offices? There seems to have been acceptance in society of the idea of the right kind of person being able to inherit church office.[144] And if an aspiring office holder wasn't necessarily the right type, there was always the possibility of buying an office in the church for money – the practice of simony. The selling of spiritual gifts or status for money was recognized and condemned as far back as the New Testament writings.[145] The church recognized the obvious problem with simony, and extended the definition further than a matter of mere money, to the influence in spiritual matters that could also be found in word or deed.[146]

But conflict in practical matters was not only caused by kings' and lords' actions toward the church; it was also caused by the church's actions that trespassed into the areas the kings claimed as theirs. In the West, the newly arrived tribes were often outnumbered by a romanized population, and if they settled in quietly and bought land, there was no need to disturb established Roman rules. Some were refugees, or were not well organized, and wanted to adopt Roman laws, or mix their own traditional rules with Roman law.

The educated men of the church were the members of society best suited to write new laws and help organize society. Roman law was what they knew, so they borrowed from Roman law and transmitted it back to the leaders of Western Europe in changed forms, in which the Christian substantive context steadily grew in importance.[147] The Theodosian Code was used in both the East and the West. In the West it was foundational in forming Alaric II's 506 *Lex Romana Visigothorum* (Breviary of Alaric). Bodies of law like the Burgundian Code of the year 500 (more or less) and Theodoric the Great's *Edictum* (around 508) as well, blended customary law with Roman and Christian elements.

Influence on substantive legal matters by the Church can be traced out in areas of the law like heightened penalties for an assault upon a priest or bishop[148] or rules regarding marriage and divorce that had changed in the Theodosian Code, and from there made their way into Western bodies of law. "In these legal codes, and the whole complex business of cultural interchange which lay behind them, we see the Church exerting its influence at the most formative and sensitive point in the whole body politic of the new Germanic societies – their basic customary law."[149]

But kings didn't leave law-making up to the church, nor could they. Law-making, as well as the issues of investiture, proprietorship of churches, simony, and other matters of the right ordering of society, all illustrate the intertwining of Christianity and rulership in Western Europe. Charlemagne "legislated on education, on roads and trade, on justice and military service as might be expected. But with equal freedom he issued decrees touching theology, the liturgy, and monastic reform. His father Pepin had cooperated with the papacy in fighting the pagan and in pushing church reform. Charlemagne did not cooperate so much as dictate. He did not follow the lead of the pope; he ignored or led him. He appointed bishops and abbots, convened synods to discuss doctrine and liturgy, and even lectured the pope on his failure to introduce the Filioque clause..."[150]

Drawing some examples from England a few centuries later, the Church felt free to criticize rulers. Bede's Ecclesiastical History is said to have been intended partly as a mirror for kings – a moral guide for rulers. Sometime around 750 King Aethelbald of Mercia received a letter of criticism from St Boniface, and in 786 visiting legates of Pope Hadrian I arrived in England. One went to Northumbria and, "with the king present, held a council of ecclesiastics and laymen. They listened as the matters for correction were read out, including the instruction that kings and princes should give just judgements and obey their bishops. Finally, they swore to abide by what they had heard."[151]

Some have no doubt noticed that in this discussion of competition between church and kings, examples have skipped about over several hundred years, as well as geographically throughout Western Europe. That should help to underline that the arguments, and resolution, were far from uniform in either time or place. A strong king or pope might exercise a great deal of power, but upon death and accession of a new man, the power could shift dramatically. The issues that caused conflict were more or less a constant, but the heat of the controversy rose and fell depending upon personalities of rulers in either church or state, and the degree of support they might expect from their subordinates.

Competition and Theorizing about Power

Rulers of both church and state also articulated theories to support their claims for primacy of leadership in Western society. Gelasius I, pope from 492 to 496, was a strong proponent of papal power, asserting it over all of the Church, despite the opposition of the Emperor and Eastern Bishops, and gave a famous formulation for which he has long been remembered: "The spiritual and temporal powers are entrusted to two different orders, each drawing its authority from God, each supreme in its own sphere and independent within its own sphere from the others."[152] His order, since it had to ultimately give account to God, had the higher responsibility and authority.

That formulation hardly solved the problems of Western Europe. It asserted two spheres of authority, but didn't define either, or where the borders between the spheres might lie, or whether they might be allowed to overlap at times, or for specific reasons. That made conflict between the two spheres almost inevitable, and guaranteed that it would continue – and on the highest level: Did kings appoint popes, or popes appoint kings?

As the Merovingian line weakened, Pippin usurped the crown for himself, or rather was elected by the people if you accept his version of event, and began the line of the Carolingians (his son was Charlemagne)[153]. But, had he become King due to authority derived from his own supporters as he claimed, or by the authority of the Pope? Pope Stephen (752-7) had journeyed north from Rome to anoint Pippin and his sons. This can be understood as a conferred of power and authority. On the other hand, Stephen had appealed for Pippin's help against the Lombards, who were threatening his power. So, power given by the Pope, or a simple quid pro quo? Where exactly was the center of power, or the line between the two spheres of Gelasius?

The theocratic theory was also a justification of royal power. In that theory, the king was responsible to God for the direction of the church. So, kings intervened to solve problems in the church as they could, including summoning councils and presiding over them, founding churches, monasteries, bishoprics, and issuing orders regarding clerical administration and the filling of bishoprics and abbacies.[154]

Charlemagne's crowning in 800 in Rome provides an example of royal power in high politics and competition between the spheres. The Pope was in a precarious position, surrounded by enemies and accused of a creative assortment of crimes and vices. He had even been subjected to an assassination attempt. He swore a series of oaths, a normal practice in the law of the Middle Ages, and was considered to have cleared his name. The interesting thing is that he swore those oaths to Charlemagne, but not to the Emperor in Byzantium, (at that time an Empress, which was contrary to Frankish law).[155]

Germanic custom allowed the King who was most powerful to be Emperor over others, and clearly, Charlemagne was more powerful. He agreed to be Emperor. A Mass was held on Christmas Day, and the Pope carried out a ritual, and placed the crown on Charlemagne's head. Some sources say Charlemagne got the Pope to do so as part of a deal between them. Some report that Charlemagne said that if he had known what was going to happen at the Mass that day, he wouldn't have gone. We do know that in time, he advised his son to crown himself, and not let the Pope do it.[156]

Charlemagne's heirs were not able to keep his empire intact. As the initial division made for his heirs into three sections covering large parts of today's France and Germany crumbled, there was a transfer of power to the East, to the Germans under Otto, who reigned from 936 to his death in 973. Otto rescued Pope John XII from the resurgent power of the Lombards in Northern Italy, and was in return granted the title of Emperor in 962. "Then when John, who had finally awakened to the fact that Otto wanted more in Italy than just a title, began undermining Otto's position, Otto drove him from Rome, set up a new pope, and warned the Romans 'never again to elect or ordain any Pope without the consent and choice of the Emperor Otto and his son Otto II.'"[157]

Otto III appointed his tutor Gerbert (a famed scholar) as pope Sylvester II. A few years later Henry III began his reign, during which he appointed four popes. But then Henry III died early, leaving his successor, Henry IV the task of recovery. During that period of weakness various lords had taken back pieces of the empire. Henry IV waged a long struggle against the popes that in the long run probably weakened Germany.[158]

Competition for Leadership and Reform in the Church

Even as the struggle for primacy teetered back and forth between kings and popes, a struggle was developing within the church for purity and reform. The monastic ideal was respected by virtually all in society. Benedict had proclaimed his famous rule for monastic life in 529 at Monte Cassino, and the order of Benedictines, as well as several others, had proliferated throughout Europe. "Though the majority of monks seem to have held themselves aloof from direct participation in the work of reforming the Church and getting rid of the manifold abuses of the time, yet by accustoming people to think of the Day of Judgement they made clergy and nobility take up the work of reform with greater attention and energy."[159]

Simony and lay investiture began to be seen as violations of the freedom of the church, and in even more striking images. If bishops were bridegrooms of the church in their diocese (and were all collectively really one bridegroom), then simony was a violation of that symbolic marriage.[160] "The struggle against simony and the domination of the laity was never more full of hatred nor expressed in more unrestrained terms than when the leading thought was the fate of the Bride of Christ and the low and vulgar crimes that were being committed on her body."[161]

Celibacy was also a part of the struggle for reform within. It wasn't a new idea in religious circles, whether Christian or non-Christian. The Spanish church thought this a good idea very early on, and in the council held at Elvira in 304, decreed that bishops, priests, as well as lower functionaries like deacons weren't to have children, and were to remain celibate. This was rejected in 325 by the council in Nicea, although it did go as far as prohibiting marriage after ordination and not allowing women who were non-relatives to live in the house of a priest.[162]

It had value as an ascetic practice, it could symbolize total commitment to God, and free priests from the practical demands of home and family life, to devote their full energies to the church.[163] The idea of celibacy obviously wasn't going to go away, and would provide reason for conflict for the following centuries.

Marriage provided fertile ground (in many ways) for entanglement of the church with local rulers, and conflict between the two. Unmarried clergy, with no children, would not seek to leave inheritances from the Church for their families.

They might also be less likely to be tempted by marriage or family alliances with local rulers into a confusion of where their loyalties best lay. The easy remedy seemed to be celibacy, which could have advantages on several different levels.

Celibacy could also preserve the property and funds of the church. In a letter of Pope Gregory VII to William the Conqueror of England, Gregory wrote that William was to eject Bishop Juhel from the see of Dol in Brittany. Juhel was married, and had children, and "'he crowned a most frightful crime...by adding an abominable sacrilege. For by a monstrous outrage he married off the grown-up daughters of his illicit marriage, bestowing and alienating church lands and revenues by way of their dowries.'"[164]

The confusion and contention over all these issues began to rise to a high point in the mid-1000s. That highpoint is sometimes simplified as a movement of reform pushed by Gregory VII, a Pope of great energy and force, aimed at ending abusive practices in the Church, such as simony, investiture, and the marrying of priests, often termed Nicolaitism. On its face, that presentation of a desire for reform and reform process is quite accurate, but it includes all the other areas of conflict already existing between kings and popes. An examination of the time when tension began to escalate may help.

The Height of the Struggle

In 1046 a Synod was held at Sutri, just north of Rome. The King of the Germans, Henry III, deposed three rival claimants to the papacy, and installed another. Benedict IX, a Roman noble, Sylvester III, another Roman noble, and Gregory VI all claimed the papal throne. Gregory's claim was wonderfully simple – he testified to having purchased the title from Benedict. But, not having been paid, Benedict re-claimed the title of Pope. Sylvester's claim was that he had declared himself Pope after the departure of Benedict, since no other legitimate claimant was on the throne.

Henry's intentions were to be declared Emperor of the Holy Roman Empire, and to do this, a Pope of good title to the office held was necessary. Having been appealed to by parties within the Church, Henry came south over the Alps with a large number of clerical and royal supporters. Not coincidentally, he also brought a large army. The council sat, and the three claimants were all deposed, one after another. Henry then nominated a new Pope, who accepted the papacy as Pope Clement II. In return, he crowed Henry III as Holy Roman Emperor.

The actions at Sutri were praised by Henry's allies, the monks of the Cluniac order, as a very miracle of heaven, but others felt it as an insult. "Walloon and French writers venomously attacked this whole-hearted union between emperor and pope which gave the former a power of censorship over the pope."[165] Clement II died shortly, and after the short pontificate of Damasus II, Henry and a council of Romans meeting at Worms selected Leo IX.[166] He traveled throughout the Empire together with the Emperor, and discussed the problems of simony, and celibacy of the clergy, promoting reform within the Church.

The emperor and pope appeared even to agree on election to the papacy. Leo had demanded canonical election, which meant essentially approval by the people to ratify the choice made. Henry supported him, but then both died close in time to one another. The Romans then elected their own pope and questioned the position of the emperor in this whole contest. When that pope in turn died prematurely, and the Romans elected a new pope over the cardinals, the curia appealed to the emperor. Humbert, one of the curia, had in the meantime been busy asserting in his books that the emperor, as a layman, didn't belong in papal elections.[167]

Victor II succeeded him, having been selected by Henry and a Roman delegation headed by Hildebrand, soon to be Pope Gregory VII. Skipping a very short-living Pope or two, and the scheming for power involving the Normans in the south of Italy and their support for the Pope, we arrive at Pope Nicholas II.

As a result of his struggles with the "Antipope" Benedict X, Nicholas wanted to reform papal elections. In 1059, a synod he called in Rome adopted changes in the election procedure: "Encouraged by the success with which they had resisted the German court and the Roman nobility at the last two papal elections, the curia dared to issue an election decree, the aim of which was the abolition of all lay interference."[168]

That same synod, of 13 April 1059, passed a sixth canon, which stated that "In no circumstances shall any priest or cleric be invested with a church by a layman, whether gratis or for payment."[169] Gregory VII, involved or near the center of many of these issues for several decades, at last became Pope in 1073. Gregory held tight to the reforms made prior to his time, but then took this reforming spirit much further. If the histories are believed, the people elected him by acclamation, and the cardinals quickly voted his election. He didn't seek prior confirmation by Emperor Henry IV, but informed him of his election and delayed the consecration for enough time to receive Henry's consent. This was the last reported instance of imperial confirmation of a papal election.

Gregory was not a simple man – nor, given the greatly abbreviated recital of imperial and papal politics just given should that be expected. Gregory was credited by friend and foe alike with a great deal of cunning and guile. Cardinal Benno, in opposition to Gregory, accused him of sins including necromancy and torture, and of possibly even being the Antichrist. Of those who supported Gregory, "his admirer Peter Damian referred to him as 'my holy Satan.'"[170]

Gregory pursued his internal reforms with great energy. He held synods, and passed laws against Nicolaitism. He went so far as to label all carnal relations between priests and women, even if married, as sinful. He also attacked the problem of simony. He turned more obviously outward as well. At a synod in 1075 he forbade bishops, abbots, and other ecclesiastics from receiving appointments from any king or lord, threatening ecclesiastical punishment to both giver and receiver of investiture.[171] But when forced, he could compromise.

Gregory didn't only seek to insulate the Church from what he saw as attacks from the Emperor by internal reforms and reforms involving laymen like investiture, but went further, and higher. In 1076, Gregory excommunicated Henry IV himself, (after Henry had sought to depose him). Not only that, but Gregory then deposed him. This had never been done before. Henry's position with his own subjects was not strong enough to defy the Pope, and so some accommodation had to be sought. The Pope's position was stronger – if the Pope could crown an Emperor like Charlemagne, then wasn't there also an implied power in the papacy to take away the crown? The Pope strengthened his alliances with the Normans, and the friends he had in Northern Italy, his own soldiers in Rome, and waited.

Not finding any allies strong enough to help him keep his crown, Henry gave in, and his submission gives us the famous scene, on Jan. 21, 1077, of Henry standing barefoot and penitent in the snow at Canossa in northern Italy, waiting for the Pope's absolution, which came after it had been made clear enough who held the real power. Many later questioned Henry's real repentance, perhaps because they didn't want to follow an Emperor who had bowed before the Church. It has been said that "Canossa marks the deepest humiliation of the State and the highest exaltation of the Church,—we mean the political papal Church of Rome, not the spiritual Church of Christ, who wore a crown of thorns in this world and who prayed on the cross for his murderers."[172]

All was now not well between Gregory and Henry, and in 1080, problems broke out again, around the question of the real purposes and functions of kingship, and who should make or unmake kings. Henry was again excommunicated and deposed. That wasn't the last word. As Henry gained strength and allegiance in Germany and Northern Italy, he moved south, entering Rome in March 1084. The Pope's supporters dwindled away, and Gregory himself was deposed, and died in exile in Salerno.

This is only a brief sketch, omitting enough of the details to make a historian cry, or protest that a pivotal detail has been left out, such the ending at Worms in 1122. A more complete retelling, and touching on all of the contributing factors, would be far too long, but I hope I've emphasized the most important point: A strong papacy struggling with kings to define the border of those two spheres of Gelasius was a staple of Western European politics for centuries. The height reached in this struggle around the time of Gregory VII and Henry IV did lead to some black lines in the division of power between the spheres – sharper lines between sacred and secular than had existed before in Europe.[173]

Use of Law by the Contending Sides – Birth of Independent Universities - a New Role for Law in Europe

Naked power alone though, is not the full story, and one more element is necessary to explain the foundations of our Western European notions about Church and State: There is a thread of law weaving through this story which often gets lost in the scheming and maneuvering, and I must return to that for a moment. Beside passing laws, Gregory had tried hard to enforce those he and his predecessors had made, by sending letters and legates far and wide "He sought out industriously every conceivable legal claim from which an increase in the power of the Roman church could be expected…"[174] Both sides in the controversy had appealed to laws and precedents to provide authority for the actions taken.

Law often serves the function of legitimizing actions. Of course, that's a very weak legitimacy if an action is taken, and then a law is passed to confirm it. That violates our modern notions of the rule of law, and it violated notions of the rule of law then, although it may not have been expressed yet in those terms. "The law" was referred to in order to buttress arguments, and the strongest laws and legal principles that could be used were those of the long-prexisting Roman law.

There was a traditional view of the rights of the Emperor as a patrician of Rome. We can identify Roman law in the structure and working of the papal court. On a more theoretical level, the idea of the *translatio imperii*, or transfer of the imperial authority, was appealed to by the Emperors. Rome had, it was argued, transferred its power northward over the Alps as the Germanic tribes came South, residing at last in the Germanic Holy Roman Emperors.

Both sides appealed to law as this struggle reached its height, and as a result Roman law experienced what has been described as a rebirth, or rediscovery. Competition for legal authority, demands from imperial and papal partisans for law to use, that shared memory of Roman law as an authority, the growth of cities in Western Europe, all combined to raise interest in the study of Roman law and its dissemination, along with a new institution, the University.

Much education in the early Middle Ages took place within monastic orders or Cathedral schools. It was in other words, a matter primarily of the church, and the more public face of the church as the Cathedral schools became more dominant in the 10th century.[175] In the small Northern Italian states, though, not under domination of either a strong papacy or strong imperial power, universities began to grow. The revived interest in law, and growth of cities and commerce, spurred on the development.

Universities grew along two basic models, one driven by the students themselves, the other centered more around the professors. In a student-driven model, students themselves sought legal protection, since under prevailing legal notions a student from country x could be liable for debts of any student from country x, unless a form of legal entity gave them protection. Either emperor or pope could grant them a charter giving protection. Bologna was this type of university, with an imperial charter from 1155.[176] The students were either wealthy, or sponsored by someone, so they held financial power, and even graded and disciplined their own professors – censuring or fining those who began class late, or ended too early. By about 1200 cities were sponsoring the universities, so that professors (and all those students who needed to spend money for room and board) would stay around instead of moving on with their students.

In Paris, the university followed a master-driven model. It was made up of three schools, the collegiate church of Ste. Genevieve, the monastic school of St. Victor, and the cathedral school of Notre Dame, growing between 1050 and 1070. The Chancellor of the Notre Dame school was "empowered to confer the *licentia docendi* on all eligible applicants" and also claimed to be *judex ordinarius* of the scholars.[177] It asserted strong independence. "As an institution, it throve on conflict; perpetually at odds with officialdom (episcopal, papal and royal), for a long time obdurate in its resistance to the Mendicant Orders..."[178]

Conflict over the forces which wished to control it kept Paris independent. First the pope supported the university against the church in France, with which he was at odds. Forbidding a law faculty there kept the university from becoming too close to imperial power that had an appetite for trained lawyers to fill its bureaucracy. The French king likewise agreed, for the same reasons. The growth of a large number of resident scholars (Masters of Arts) meant that the cathedral school could be left behind, and both Chancellor's and bishop's power ignored, as the students fled with papal support. But all united to oppose the Mendicants (Dominicans and Franciscans), who wished to enter the university as teachers. At one point the university even dissolved itself to avoid their entry. In 1261 it re-opened under the stipulation that the Mendicants could not enter the faculty of arts, preserving its independence. By 1318 the Mendicants too were required to give oath of obedience.[179]

There was indeed substantial independence for the universities. Even where law wasn't taught, as at Paris, their very existence served to balance and keep in opposition the sacred and secular powers. Where law was taught, especially in the greatest of the law schools – Bologna - it was not the local law, it was the newly-rediscovered Justinian corpus of Roman Law, first referred to again by scholars in 1076, after a silence of nearly five hundred years.[180] But there were some important differences: Scholastics like Abelard contributed the idea of a dialectic, in terms of thesis/antithesis, and resulting synthesis of a subject as a complete and unified body, although it might need some gap filling by reasoning, or by making theoretical justifications.

It was possible then, to analyze the Roman law, to systematize it and make better theoretical categories for it than it had historically contained. For example, Gratian, in Bologna, in 1140, published his delightfully named "A Concordance of Discordant Canons." Scholars sometimes identify this as the first Western European legal treatise, where all of the laws of a society are seen to form a comprehensive, systematic whole. It is in that treatise that we read, "Princes are bound by and shall live according to their laws."[181] Spread by students who came and went from Bologna to their homes all over Europe, it was a universal European law.

The conjunction of the struggle to divide power into two spheres, the growing appeal (and need) for law by which Empire or Church might be ordered, and the new institution of the university yielded very important results for the West. It is difficult to say this better, or as entertainingly, as Umberto Eco summarized it in his fantasy of medieval times, *Baudolino*. In that book, Frederick I (Barbarossa) is discussing the question of his authority as Emperor, with his court and the protagonist Baudolino, sometime around 1157:

> "'We clearly saw what happened in Rome,' Frederick said. 'If I have myself anointed by the pope, I admit *ipso facto* that his power is superior to mine; if I grab the pope by the throat and fling him into the Tiber, I become a scourge of God worse even than poor Attila....Where the devil can I find someone who will define my rights without claiming to be above me? Such a person doesn't exist in the world.'
> 'Perhaps a power such as that doesn't exist,' Baudolino then said to him, 'but the knowledge exists.'
> 'What do you mean?'

'When Bishop Otto told me what a *studium* is, he said that these communities of masters and students operate independently: the students come from all over the world and it doesn't matter who their sovereign is, and they pay their teachers, who are therefore dependent entirely on their pupils. This is how things work with the masters of law in Bologna, and this is how it is also in Paris, where in earlier times the masters taught in the cathedral schools and hence were dependent on the bishop, until one fine day they went off to teach on the Mountain of Saint Geneviève, and they attempt to discover the truth without listening either to the bishop or to the king.'

'If I were their king I'd show them a thing or two. But even if this were the case?'

'It would be the case if you made a law by which you acknowledge that the masters of Bologna are truly independent of every other power, whether yours or the pope's or any other sovereign's, and they are in the service only of the Law. Once they are invested with this dignity, unique in the world, they will affirm that – in accord with true reason, natural enlightenment, and tradition – the only law is the Roman and the only person representing it is the holy Roman emperor – and that naturally, as Master Rainald has said so well – *quod principi plaquit legis habet vigorem.*'

'And why would they say that?'

'Because in exchange, you give them the right to say it, and that is no small thing. So you are content, they are content, and, as my father Gagliaudo used to say, you are both in an iron-clad barrel.'

'They wouldn't agree to anything like that,' Rainald grumbled.

'Yes, they would,' Frederick's face brightened. "I tell you they will agree. Only, first, they have to make that declaration, and then I'll give them independence.

Otherwise everyone will think that they did it to repay a gift from me.'

'If you ask me, even if you do turn the process around, if someone wants to say it was prearranged, they'll say so anyway,' Baudolino remarked skeptically. 'But I'd like to see anyone stand up and say the doctors of Bologna aren't worth a dried fig, when even the emperor has gone humbly to ask their opinion. At that point, what they have said is Gospel.'[182]

In a diet held at Roncaglia in 1158, three of the four doctors of law of Bologna said that the right of the Emperor was based on Roman law. Bulgarus, Jacopus and Hugo voted for the Emperor's position, and Martinus against. Shortly afterwards, Frederick Barbarossa promulgated his *Authentica habita* (a bit of a repeat of what he'd already passed in 1155) granting lay and clerical students privileges like immunity from taxes and tolls during travel to Bologna, freedom from the liability of debts incurred by fellow students, and the right to trial before one's own master or bishop. This was understood as the charter of the University of Bologna.[183]

For the first time in Western Europe there was a strong theoretical basis for a system of law, a law that could grow in independent institutions. It could be appealed to by both sacred and secular powers, to define powers and decide disputes. Laws were made and enforced by the Church, by Kings, cities, local lords, even groups of travelling merchants as history moves forward from the high Middle Ages in the West. As different jurisdictions competed in building their legal systems and taking or keeping power over certain types of cases, respect for and reception of the Roman law continued.

Although a revolutionary high point had come with Gregory VI, and been capped later in the universities by the revival and growth of respect for law as an independent force in the struggle to define the borders between the sacred and secular, strife in Western Europe was not finished. The Church in the 1300s tried to use the Donation of Constantine, a document probably fabricated in the 800s, to bolster Church claims of authority. Frederick II, the grandson of Barbarossa, fought with the Pope in the old-fashioned style, trying to confirm the *translatio* of imperial authority to himself in the face of opposition by the northern Italian cities that were supported by the Pope.

Frederick II argued in a letter to Pope Gregory IX in 1232, that "ecclesia and imperium are descriptive of two manifestations of the same society of men, one of these a healing balm, the other a cutting sword, but each having its origin in divine authority."[184] He pressed for a more explicit version of what Gelasius, and Augustine, had said years before, in a 1239 letter to the cardinals of the Church: "'God, at the creation of the world,' Frederick insisted, 'had placed two lights in the firmament, a large one and a smaller one, the large one to preside over the day, the smaller one, over the night. But these two are independent of each other, so that one never disturbs the other, although one communicates light to the other.'"[185]

Summary

By the high Middle Ages, following the close of the Papal Revolution, the foundations on which the struggle would continue had been laid. The weakness of disintegrating Rome, the necessity that compelled the Western Church to grow strong, its borrowing of Roman law and Roman nobility to organize and staff its hierarchy, the dispute between Kings and Emperors and this growing church over who was to rule, the recognition of law as a legitimating mechanism for authority, and the growing independence of the law in the new universities as a legal science independent both of the sacred and the secular, form that foundation.

Since the Middle Ages, this struggle in Western European societies has always been carried out in the context of an underlying supposition that *there is, and ought to be*, a substantial separation between the religious and the temporal, between the sacred and the secular. It has also gone forward under the assumption that knowledge, specifically law, is something not under the control of either sacred or secular power. Those powers may use it or manipulate it for their own ends, but it has an independent status, and does not depend upon either of those powers for its existence.

These are not suppositions widely held within Islam (even within global Christianity for that matter), and examining conflict between powers in Islamic societies, and the use and control of knowledge, is where we turn next.

Chapter 5 - The Mihna

The decline and failure of the Roman Empire in the West created the environment for the growth of competing powers and their competition that culminated in the Papal Revolution. To the South and East of the stable remnant of the Roman (Byzantine) Empire, it was the amazing success of the rising Islamic Empire that created the environment for its own formative crisis. That crisis and its underlying causes was every bit as convoluted as the struggle in the West.

The military success of the Arabic armies within the generation after Muhammad left the Islamic empire in possession of cities, buildings, sophisticated aquaducts, libraries, a large peasantry and educated citizens in the cities. The empire acquired great numbers of subject peoples of diverse ethnicities and religions, and it made the Umayyad caliphs in Damascus, and their successors the Abbasids, wealthy. The Abbasid period in Baghdad is called the golden age of Islam quite often, and caliph Harun al-Rashid's name, and the one thousand and one nights, are remembered to this day.

But that success brought both foreseen and unforeseen problems. The need to define identity as Islamic rather than Arabic and the tensions that caused shouldn't have been surprising. The need for an expanded state apparatus, as well as a stronger and more comprehensive organization of government, was also obvious. There was the issue of conversion or tolerance of the many non-Muslim subject peoples to Islam. Finally, there was one unexpected problem of greater importance than was likely realized at the time – the issue of foreign thought and knowledge. The Arab armies had conquered a good portion of the classical Greco-Roman world. Arab scholars could hardly ignore the intellectual products and resources of the territories the armies of Islam had taken.

Accumulating and Using Foreign Knowledge in the Golden Age of Islam

Those scholars had been laboring diligently to build a coherent system of law, of the methods of law, and of legal doctrine. Given the sources of law, it was natural that one strong strain within legal scholarship was to look back, to the traditions of Muhammad, to the Koran, to the customary practices of the *ummah*. At the same time, other scholars had begun to grapple with the philosophies and religious systems of the new subjects of the empire, and to study their thoughts and methods, the better to refute them. The origin of this group, the Mu'tazilites, is not clear to modern scholarship.

Some doctrines of the Mu'tazilites had common points with the Persian faiths around them. "Marked resemblances have long been noticed in several areas of theology: divine attributes, ethical principles, structure of treatises, methods of interpretation of scripture, and so on."[186] It is difficult for the modern scholars in this area to pinpoint clear adoptions of ideas. There were also many Arabic-speaking and writing Christians spread from Syria to Iran. There also, "[t]he total of resemblances and contacts makes it difficult to deny that there was an influence of Christian on Mu'tazilite theology, but the forms it took are elusive to the historian and will probably remain so."[187]

Greek philosophy also very likely contributed to formation of the Mu'tazilite arguments and methods of thought. Educated Muslims could study the old Greeks without it raising too many questions, since they weren't a threat like the larger contemporary groups of Christians and Zoroastrians. "Some of them did so intensely, in the small circles that cultivated the secular sciences and philosophy, from the days of Harun al-Rashid (reigned 786-809) and thereafter for several centuries; and these circles adopted Greek thought in form and content, with no attempt at concealment and with varying efforts to harmonize their theories with Islam."[188]

One quality common to the Mu'tazilites was a high regard for rational inquiry, and recognition that it was useful, if not necessary, in explaining Islam to non-Muslims. In missions work, "[b]eyond the particular sphere of ethics, rationalistic methods are normal in interreligious controversy, because if the adversaries are to be able to discuss religion at all they must find common ground and not presume the truth of their own faith. This is an idea that recurs constantly in the history of religion. Theodore Abu Qurra says he will argue with Muslims not on the basis of scripture but 'from common, agreed notions'"[189] But with all that new (old) knowledge available, how could it only be confined to missionary conversion efforts?

Many of the libraries and much of the knowledge of the Greco-Roman classical world was now contained within the Abbasid Empire. Modern scholars struggle to describe what happened, and sometimes make the error of reductionism, saying in effect that Islamic scholars only passed on what the Greeks and others had already produced. Others fall into the error of precursorism, arguing in effect that Islam took in former knowledge and improved it, forming the basis for a knowledge later exploited by the modern West. Both are partly true, but it is probably most accurate to characterize what started to happen under the Abbasids "as an act of appropriation performed by the so-called receiver."[190]

Not everything was appropriated, or taken in for consideration. Appropriation means taking in what appears to be useful, and using it. The libraries and knowledge of Greek and Christian scholars in Alexandria, Antioch, Edessa, and Nisibis were available, written in the Greek and Syriac languages. The knowledge of Persia and India, written in Pahlavi and Sanskrit was available through the school Shapur I had supported at Jundishapur. Even sources from as far away as China were taken in for translation.[191] Greek drama, history, and poetry, were by and large not translated. But Plato's *Laws*, or the *Republic*? Of course. Very often the materials translated were selected for their utility in answering a question of governance, or of the hard sciences.[192]

Not only knowledge was appropriated or attracted. "Jundi-Shapur, meaning 'Beautiful Garden', was a city in Khuzistan founded by the Sasanid Emperor Shapur I (241–272 AD)." He had settled it in part with Greek prisoners, and refugees from the conflict between the Byzantines and Persians, for example, the Syrians of Antioch after its capture. Nestorian Christians also took refuge there after Byzantine purges of the Edessa school in 457 and 489. When Justinian closed the Athenian school in 529 some of the traditional classic Greek scholars went there too. "Subsequently, a university, medical school and hospital was established by Khusraw (Chosroes) Anushirawan in about 555 AD."[193] The Umayyad and later Abbasid conquerors perpetuated and spread medical science and hospitals like this far and wide through the Islamic world.

Appropriation of knowledge was intentional, and directed from the top, by caliphs and other well-connected or wealthy people.[194] A mass translation movement of the knowledge of the ancient world into Arabic began, books that in some cases would be later passed on to a West which had forgotten them. A *bayt al-hikma*, or house of wisdom, was founded in Baghdad to house books, and assist with translation. Baghdad became a fabled city: "Ibn Battuta, cultured visitor that he was, introduces the city by calling it 'the City of Peace, the capital of Islam, of noble rank and conspicuous virtue, the resting place of the caliphs, and the home of scholars.'"[195]

The expanding Abbasid Empire was in an admirable position to take and assimilate what it wanted from both the East and West – and it did. There has never been an episode in history quite like this, a cultural explosion, especially under caliphs like al-Rashid and al-Ma'mun (786-809 and 813-833, respectively).[196] Scholars of this new material were prolific. For example, al-Kindi, who died around 850, reputedly had studied all of Greek science, and wrote 265 treatises. In his treatise on metaphysics he attempted to reconcile Aristotle with Islamic teaching on the creation of the world. In that work the quote for which he is most remembered today is found: "It should be no shame to us to honour truth and make it our own, no matter whence it may come, even though from far distant races and peoples who differ from us."[197]

In this golden age of Islam, there were Jewish, Christian, and Arab/Muslim scholars of note who synthesized, improved, and surpassed the knowledge of the ancient world. In math, Al-Khwarizmi took Greek thought and the earlier translated Indian works, and synthesized them in Arabic. In Latin translation, his work was very influential in the West. Many others could be mentioned, clustered in the great city of Baghdad, all within the context of a "secular tone that pervaded Iraqi society in these centuries, a society bustling, worldly-wise, business-minded and somewhat cynical, but full of ideas. All this is reflected in the literature of the period, as scholars and students from Arabia, Syria, Egypt, and Persia found a new freedom of circulation."[198]

The tone of that society, and the ideas, appeared to be spreading in the *ummah*. In houses, there were Roman baths, and Roman and Iranian decorations. Some had taken to building in the countryside, where life was more comfortable.[199] The Arab conquerors had gotten rich as the old trade barriers (the Byzantine and Persian borders) had disappeared creating an enormous Islamic zone for trade.[200] They could afford to sponsor translations, and poetry writing.

Foreign Knowledge – Should it be Adopted or Rejected?

But not everyone of the time thought as broadly as al-Kindi. Despite encouragement of translation and learning by the Abbasid caliphs, and their sponsorship of Mu'tazilites, traditional-minded scholars looked on the foreign knowledge with mistrust.[201] Their mistrust hinged on the effect that new knowledge, and new peoples, might have upon the Islamic *ummah* itself. So long as the Mu'tazilites kept their sometimes strange ideas to themselves, or used them against rival religions, they were not a serious threat to the rest of the scholarly establishment. But what if Islam could be examined using the same methods?

"They were applying to the ideas of the Koran the keen solvent of Greek dialectic, and the results which they obtained were of the most fantastically original character. Thrown into the wide sea and utter freedom of Greek thought, they had/lost touch with the ground of ordinary life, with its reasonable probabilities, and were swinging loose on a wild hunt after ultimate truth, wielding as their weapons definitions and syllogisms."[202]

This quote is delightful language, but may be misleading. The Mu'tazilites were not rationalists bent on discarding the Koran and God. They were Muslims, and Muslims they intended to remain. They saw themselves as bringing necessary reform and strengthening to the *ummah* in the face of the new challenges of success. "In the theological field, Mu'tazilism initially emerged as a school with its main focus on giving clarity to moral guidelines, introducing specific rules in Islamic religion and (only by the beginning of the eighth century) secondarily acting as a rationalist sect able to develop a dogmatic approach on *Tawḥīd* (the unity of God) and *ʿadl Allāh* (the justice of God, Theodicy)."[203]

Reasoning about the unity of God, and his justice, seemed necessary to the Mu'tazilites to preserve Islam. Justice was inextricably tied up with the ideas of free will, *qadar*, and predestination. The Qadariya, a school of theology preceding the Mu'tazilites, had reasoned that human beings had unlimited freedom to decide upon their own acts. The Mu'tazilite questions about God's justice "are linked directly to Qadarite doctrines whose implications the Mu'tazilites follow up and make explicit." To say that human beings were predestined to do certain things would be to call God unjust, if people were punished for acts they were pre-determined to do. Justice had to be united to God, who then must punish the bad and reward the good. The Mu'tazilite reasoning upon the Qadarite base was for the best of reasons – to uphold what they considered a high conception of a just God.[204]

The Mu'tazilites rejected anthropomorphic views, the idea that God sees or hears the way human beings do, an idea common to the traditionists. The Mu'tazilites argued that when the Koran or *hadiths* used such language, it was metaphorical and spiritual, and they developed their own method of Koranic exegesis following this. They attacked the authenticity of *hadiths* which were crudely anthropomorphic. They "called into doubt the inimitability of the literary style of the Qur'an. They questioned the authenticity of the hadith."[205] And well they might have, for it was beyond question that a significant number had been fabricated. The Mu'tazilite opposition showed this by their efforts to reform the science of *hadith* collection and to establish definitive reliable collections after the struggle between these contending parties had been resolved.

The Mu'tazilites didn't shy away from the big question of good and evil. The orthodox answer was that good is what God commands, and bad is what God forbids. The Mu'tazilites rejected this conception, and said there is absolute good and absolute evil. Reason can enable people to conclude what those are, and that "[a] thing is good not because God has commanded it, but God has commanded it because it is good."[206] In modern terms, God has made his laws and is bound by them. The Mu'tazilites at last went too far when they expressed the thought that the Koran itself was a creation of God, not the uncreated word of God. An uncreated Koran might almost be said to be a second god, something very offensive to the Mu'tazilite emphasis on the unity of God.[207] But on the other hand, a created Koran could be questioned with the new tools of the Mu'tazilites like an uncreated Koran could not.

Within the *ummah*, opposing points of view began to coalesce. One centered around the Mu'tazilites. They were not a school in the sense that they shared a unified theoretical outline of what Islam was. The term Mu'tazilite applies to those holding reason in a higher position than revelation (tradition), and for that reason they are sometimes called rationalists. Their positions could vary from those just as traditional as the staunchest collector of traditions to those that were decidedly less traditional. A speculative system of *kalam* (sometimes translated theology), was common to them all. It was based on the word *mutakallim* (speaker), and functioned by turning problems into discussion topics, offering logical and speculative proofs for answers.[208]

There was opposition to the Mu'tazilites. The opposition also went under several names, such as *ahl al-hadith*, people of the *hadith*, or *ahl al-sunna*, people of the tradition. The traditionists rejected the application of dialogue and reason to find solutions for problems, but insisted that the place to start was the Koran, and then the *sunna*. Within those parameters, and only within them, reason and logic could be exercised. The traditionists had studied the arguments and methods of the Mu'tazilites, and drawn an inference of outside influence, "which in their eyes amounted to an accusation of heresy."[209]

Was it possible that the Mu'tazilites had been poisoned by their contacts with other religions, even though those had originally been driven by a missionary intent? "Certain groups of theologians who contest dogma and interpret the Word of God under the influence of philosophy and reasoning are labelled as Zindiq by the Ahl al-hadith. The charge was levelled by some of the Ahl as-Sunna against the Mu'tazilites."[210] Zindiq didn't mean just a Manichee, but a Muslim who was really an unbeliever. It came to be an all-purpose form of abuse, hurled at Mu'tazilites, unbelievers, hypocrites, profligate or licentious people (such as poets), and even used as Ibn Hanbal did, for the kind of people who look for contradictions between verses in the Koran.[211]

The rationalists might have been a threat to the traditionalists for another reason. "If any intelligent person could weigh in on whether a law was right or wrong, based on whether it made rational sense, why would anyone need to consult scholars who had memorized every quotation ever ascribed to Prophet Mohammed?"[212] Fear of losing one's importance, place, and livelihood could be reason enough for the more conservative scholars to attack the Mu'tazilites. If that seems too cynical (and it may be), then reaction against those who found it necessary to depart from the plain text of the Koran and the *sunna* should be expected from sincere, devoted (and conservative) Muslim scholars.

Both rationalists and traditionists were spread through the different schools of Islamic law, which were beginning to develop at this time. The short summary is that schools of law were primarily personal – a master/disciple relationship, and there were literally hundreds, although their numbers began to fall as popular teachers attracted more students, and different types of schools became more or less popular in different locations.[213] "But the conduct of life in conformity to the law includes more than ritual. For in Islam, religious law encompasses all legal branches: civil, criminal, and constitutional. Not one chapter of the code could escape regulation according to the religious law. All aspects of private and public life fall within the province of the religious ethics by which the lawyer-theologians meant to assure that the lives of the believers were fully in harmony with the demands of their religion."[214]

A school of law meant not the institution, but rather a philosophical and methodological viewpoint regarding how law was to be understood. A crude comparison could be a lawyer in the United States who wishes to interpret the Constitution from a strictly textual viewpoint (the text doesn't say there is a right to homosexual marriage), compared to a lawyer who wishes to interpret by focusing on principles of law in the Constitution and reasoning about them (privacy is a protected liberty or equal protection interest which includes homosexual marriage). Both lawyers accept the Constitution, both seek to interpret it and the laws enacted upon its authority, and both understand the moral and religious implications accompanying their interpretations. They disagree about how the interpretation is to be done. Perhaps that is closer to what a school meant in Islamic law.

Questions of theology that might be labelled Mu'tazillite or Qadarite, then, had legal implications. Both traditionists and rationalists accepted that some interpretation had to be done, but how much? "The differences of opinion about the admissibility of such hermeneutic methods, and about the proper extent and manner of their application, comprise a large portion of the doctrines that set apart the legal rites into which the Muslim world is divided."[215]

Scholars steeped in the Koran and the traditions confronted those who were devoted to the idea of rational inquiry without the limits of the Koran and traditions. "In proportion as Mu'tazilism became more daring in its assaults on orthodoxy, the defenders of the citadel became more tenacious in their defiance. Rejecting everything that savoured of the hated heresy, refusing even to admit discussion, they fell back on the Koran and the Tradition and met all questions with *Bila kaif*, 'Don't ask "How?"' Their champion and the idol of the Baghdad mob, was Ahmad b. Hanbal (d.855), the foremost traditionist of his age."[216] The enmity between these different camps came to a head in Baghdad, the center of Islamic society, in the early 800s.

The Argument over Foreign Knowledge Comes to a Peak

The seventh Abbasid Caliph, al-Ma'mun, came to the throne in Baghdad in 813 after four years of civil war. His father Harun al-Rashid had likely intended his brother al-Amin to succeed on his death in 409, but factions gathered around each brother, and eventually al-Ma'mun won, after besieging and doing a great deal of damage to Baghdad itself to defeat his rival. Al-Ma'mun was from Persia, and had a Persian cultural background. He was a scholar in his own right, following the work of the eclectic school of Jundishapur. But he was Muslim first, and at the time of his father's death, had been campaigning in the East, where he had converted the Barmakids (an influential Central Asian clan) to Islam.[217]

Al-Ma'mun encouraged translation, and funded the translation of numbers of works of scholarship. "The interest of al-Ma'mun in theology is emphasized by all the historians. He had been thoroughly trained in the knowledge of Tradition, of the Koran sciences, and of the Koran itself from early childhood, and had had among his teachers Malik ibn Anas, Hushaim ibn Bashir and his own father [the great Caliph Harun]."[218] He was said to make thirty-three recitations of the Koran during the month of Ramadan. In addition he supported a great number of scholars, of all schools, even the most die-hard traditionists, with the exception of those like Ahmad Ibn Hanbal, who refused to accept the stipend offered.[219]

"Al-Ma'mūn was that paradigmatic enlightened ruler: theologically Mu'tazilite, Jahamite, Hanafite, and Zaydite; imbued of Islamic, Persian and Hellenistic principles and values."[220] Examining questions of the day was important, so "al-Ma'mun sought thinkers of various persuasions who could debate one another and address theological and cultural topics from different angles…It was expected of them to accept the assumption that human beings could and should discuss the essence and attributes of Allah, and to excel in these debates. Once this condition was met, it did not matter what specific position was espoused."[221]

The Mihna Begins

In 827 al-Ma'mun publicly agreed with the Mu'tazilites when he proclaimed that the Koran was to be regarded as created by God, not pre-existing with God. But after six years, something changed and he went farther. In 833 Al-Ma'mun sent out a letter (part of a series of four) insisting upon the "correct" answer, that the Koran was created. He directed that scholars be summoned to his court to interrogate them on their positions, and persuade or force them to accept his position, an event known as the *Mihna*.[222] The events themselves are fairly simple, but the conflicting and complementing reasons for the *Mihna* are not. What might look like a scholarly dispute or a caliph throwing around his power had great consequences for the future of Islamic societies.

A first group of seven scholars was called, and under examination in the caliph's court, including arguments and threats, all agreed that the Koran was created, and were sent on their way. Yet another letter was sent with additional reasons for accepting the "createdness" of the Koran, and more scholars were called, including Ahmad Ibn Hanbal.[223] He was one of the foremost traditionists of the day, if not the most important. His career as a collector and transmitter of *hadith* had begun early, and he insisted upon strict standards in the *isnad* (chain of transmission) of *hadith*, and the strong character and reliability of the transmitter. He regarded this as his major life work.[224]

In all, Ahmad Ibn Hanbal spent twenty-eight months in prison before a definite test and conclusion was reached in his case. During that time he sometimes led prayers, or studied in prison. From time to time, agents of the court came to him to talk and try to argue him into accepting the official position.[225] "Ibn Hanbal languished in prison at Baghdad until a well-meaning relative persuaded the authorities to let him defend himself. The ensuing disputation took place before the caliph al-Mu'tasim, who did not share al-Ma'mùn's penchant for theology. In partisan accounts, each side claims to have won the debate, or at least to have exposed the incoherence of the other position."[226]

The caliph and scholars from a variety of schools were present in the court when Ibn Hanbal was brought in, and an epic three-day trial began. The scholars asked questions. The caliph asked questions. Ibn Hanbal asked questions of his own. Each became more and more frustrated with the other. When presented with a claim made by the rationalists that relied on proofs and logic, Ibn Hanbal asked for a Koran passage or a *hadith* in support. In turn, when asked to answer, Ibn Hanbal either tried to answer as a rationalist and failed, according to some sources, or wouldn't answer at all, claiming ignorance of the theologians theories. It was clear that "…each of the sides perceived evidence and proof in a different manner."[227]

At last, when he didn't give in, he was flogged. A variety of stories surround this episode, some sources saying that he gave in under the lash, others insisting that he did not. Some say a golden hand came out from under his shirt when his pants or undergarment was in danger of falling off, and replaced the clothing properly. All agree that he was flogged and smuggled out of the palace under cover of darkness so that the Baghdad populace would not be so inflamed as to invade the caliph's palace. He was restored to his home, where he was attended by the prison physician until he was healed.[228]

The *Mihna* didn't end with al'Ma'mun's death shortly after it started in 833, but continued under the next two caliphs, through the episode with Ibn Hanbal, and just into the beginning of a fourth caliph. The actual events of the *Mihna* are fairly short, though there is some disagreement among the historical sources about what happened. There is an even greater dispute among scholars to this day on what it all meant for Islam and the *ummah*.

What was the Mihna - Really?

The *Mihna* may be characterized as a bid by the caliphs to assert their authority *over* that of the scholars, in a more purely political struggle:

> "It is of course true that religious authority was the
> prerogative of scholars rather than of caliphs in classical
> Islam, but we shall argue that this is not how things
> began. The early caliphate was conceived along lines
> very different from the classical institution, all religious
> and political authority being concentrated in it; it was the
> caliph who was charged with the definition of Islamic
> law, the very core of the religion, and without allegiance
> to a caliph no Muslim could achieve salvation. In short,
> we shall argue that the early caliphate was conceived
> along the lines familiar from Shiite Islam."[229]

The authors of this theory cite letters by several early caliphs claiming in effect that caliphs received authority directly from God. Caliphs were seen as the legitimate center of faith, under

God, to which all Muslims had to adhere, or face the peril of loss of salvation after death.

The fact that early caliphal decisions are incorporated in later *hadiths* is pointed to as an indicator of this strong authority. As the authors point out, other material contradicts this thesis (e.g., shows the caliph writing to religious scholars for opinions, but "[i]t is clear, however, that the classical point of view is the outcome of a reinterpretation."[230] Islamic law was God-given, and "there is no simple way of explaining how the Umayyad caliphs came ever to be invoked unless we accept that legal authority once resided in the caliphal office itself."[231] Reports by scholars of law cite *hadiths* from early caliphs, and new caliphs made new *sunna* for the community as they took office. That status, runs the argument, degenerated as a result of the growing emphasis on knowledge of *hadith* (and hence importance of specialists in this knowledge), until al-Ma'mun attempted to reclaim it.

If that theory cannot be accepted, then al-Ma'mun may have started the *Mihna* to restore a role in defining the substance of Islam alongside that of the scholars, a power which, again, had degraded as the different schools began to grow, and as the role of scholars became more important. After all, al-Ma'mun had put the scholars with the greatest social and scholastic standing to the test, ignoring those of minor rank. Also, enforcing one position, such as the created Koran, doesn't match well with his open-minded approach, and support of many schools of scholars up until this time, so the *Mihna* couldn't have been only about getting the right answer, goes the argument. His letters too, used phrases such as "God's deputy on earth", "inheritor of the prophethood" and "direct recipient of knowledge from God."[232] He was not so much looking for a correct answer, as asserting his right to a place in the intellectual dispute.

If what al-Ma'mun was after was to give himself a high place in determining the shape of thought within the *ummah*, "[t]he chief consequence of the Inquisition, or rather of its failure, was to discredit the caliph as arbiter of orthodoxy.

Henceforward, Islamic orthodoxy might be defined only by consensus of the community, or its spokesmen the men of religion; no longer, certainly, by the caliph."[233]

Once the *Mihna* started, it may also have been a chance for the two contending schools of thought within Islam to fight for dominance. Not all sources agree that al-Ma'mun started the *Mihna* to define his caliphal role (whatever that was), but state instead that the contest could have opened as a result of pressure from the traditionists.[234] The *Mihna* then, was an internal fight among the scholars, which would have consequences in the external world of Islamic society. "To put it in Ibn Hanbal's words, in one of his exchanges with Ibn Abï Du'âd, he replies: 'You have interpreted the Qur'an and you know best: [however] what you have interpreted [cannot be considered to have divine authority, and therefore] does not warrant jailing or shackling.'"[235]

It is certain that Ibn Hanbal himself was very reluctant in matters of *fiqh* (jurisprudence developed by human reason), giving strong opinions only where a tradition supported him.[236] Writing after events to tell their side of the story and win adherents, the traditionists emphasized this point. What mattered was certain knowledge on points of Islamic law and practice that were clear in the Koran and *sunna*. "One of the central points that the *muhaddithün* attempted to make in their narrative was that the *Mihna* was illegitimate. It was unacceptable to jail or punish individuals who disagreed over theological opinions. The *muhaddithün* critique was not based on liberal notions of the right of expression, but rather on total disrespect for the theological enterprise."[237] The role of the caliph here then, was at most to be the umpire of a doctrinal dispute, a role caliphs had already filled, even among disputing Christians.[238]

If not an exercise in (re)acquiring caliphal authority, or a fight between more or less evenly contending schools of scholars, the *Mihna* may have actually been a defensive action, where the caliph, a supporter of free expression and inquiry, came to the defense of the rationalists, who were on the ropes after sustained traditionist attacks. Records from the rationalists who clearly lost in the *Mihna*, "maintained that during the decades that preceded the Mihna, the mutakallimin [rationalists] and muhaddithun [traditionists] jockeyed for power. In the course of this struggle the muhaddithun succeeded in landing a sequence of hard blows on the mutakallimin. After al-Ma'mun came to power and extended his support to the mutakallimun, the pendulum of power swung in their favor and it was their chance to strike at the muhaddithin. Such a narrative implies that the mutakallimin were not the original aggressors but rather the victims of the muhaddith."[239]

Finally, several different scholars argue that the *Mihna* didn't really make much of a difference in the existing trends of power shared in society between *ulama* and caliph. After his release, Ahmad ibn Hanbul stuck to his traditionist beliefs, but more quietly. He affirmed that it was the duty of the scholars to revive and preserve the law. All Muslims had the duty to uphold law, whether or not the caliph was doing so. In general, he didn't oppose the authority of the caliph over the machinery of the state, and denied a right of rebellion,[240] but did uphold the authority of the people and scholars to disobey on specific matters, like the createdness of the Koran:

> "Whoever rebels against one of the Imams of the Muslims – once the people have agreed upon him, and acknowledged him as caliph, in any manner, whether out of pleasure [with him] or by force – that rebel has broken with the community, and deviated from the traditional practice handed down from the Prophet of God... Fighting against authority [*sultan*, here, the Imam-caliph's authority] is not permitted, nor is anyone permitted to rebel against it. Whoever does so is an unlawful innovator, outside the *sunna* and the way."[241]

Another scholar also argues that there was really no sharp break in the *Mihna* between caliph and *ulama*, nor a real competition for authority. There was rather, continued sharing of authority as evidenced by a number of Abbasid texts. Both caliph and *ulama* agreed on a great deal, but then "al-Ma'mun tried, through the *Mihna*, to bring their own 'orthodoxy' into question. The implication of imposing a criterion whereby to measure their 'orthodoxy' not only was that the authority of the caliph to institute such a procedure was being asserted, but also that the caliph would come across as more 'orthodox' than anyone else, and more worthy of being the guardian and defender of that 'orthodoxy'."[242] In other words, the struggle between caliph and *ulama* was for the power to shape the direction of thought, something they had already cooperated upon.

Al-Ma'mun may really have believed in the createdness of the Koran and wanted to impose his views. Perhaps his Persian (Shi'ite) tendencies pushed him that way, as the Shi'a schools and leaders in Persia were more receptive to the idea. He had declared the superiority of Ali over Umar and Abu Bakr at the same time as he declared the *Mihna*. Maybe his disgust at an ignorant populace, that after all had sided with his brother against him, drove him to impose a test on the heroes of the local populace. Or the chief *qadi*, who served through three of the four caliphs of the *Mihna*, may have substantially driven the *Mihna*. There is no lack of theories and combinations of reasons for the *Mihna*.

Caliph al-Mutawakkil, reputed to favor the traditionist position himself, ended the Mihna in 847. He suppressed the Sufi teacher al-Muhasibi, the Sufis being (after the Mu'tazilites) the next greatest enemy of the traditionists. He outlawed the Shi'a, and cracked down upon Christians and Jews with new laws. He "forbade men on 'pain of death' from asserting createdness."[243] Many of the scholars, as well as the Baghdad man in the streets, approved. Ahmad ibn Hanbal himself lived the balance of his life respected, in relative solitude, fending off offers of money and prestigious positions from succeeding caliphs.

Why the Mihna is still Important Today – its Consequences

Regardless of why the *Mihna* took place, and which one of the modern scholars is right about its short-term causes and consequences, it had enormous long-term consequences for Islamic society. Those effects appear in the areas of knowledge and in the formation of institutions of higher learning. Some appeared immediately, while others took a great deal longer to develop.

Al-Kindi, who had dedicated one of his books to Caliph al-Mu'tasim, successor of al-Ma'mun, who had wanted in that book to "honour truth and make it our own, no matter whence it may come," was flogged. His library was confiscated. Al-Mutawakkil ordered that he receive fifty lashes, in public, which was done before an approving crowd.[244] Al-Kindi's treatment couldn't have sent a clearer message: Reason could not, and would not, be used like the Mu'tazilites had wished; and the foreign sciences suggesting such things were even more questionable than ever.

Reason and foreign sciences weren't altogether discarded, but marginalized, by changing allowed uses and official attitudes toward that knowledge. One way was to narrow the use of the foreign science. Caliph al-Mutawakkil still employed mathematicians and astronomers. They were useful for large construction projects. Astronomers could be employed to calculate the exact time for prayers.[245] But calculating the time for prayer, while using the astronomer's knowledge and skill, is not the same as the contemplation of the heavens.

If knowledge couldn't be narrowed to the merely useful, then the scholars and possessors of the knowledge could be made less free to talk and teach. "Numbered among the greatest of Islamic natural philosophers are al-Kindi (801-873); Al-Razi (ca. 854-925 or 935); Ibn Sina (Avicenna) (980-1037); and Ibn Rushd (Averroes) (1126-1198). All were persecuted to some extent."[246]

Al-Ghazali, 1058-1111, warned against something as seemingly innocent as mathematics, stating in essence that people would observe the precision and exactness of that science, and impute that quality to their view of the other foreign sciences, concluding that religion as a result must be false, since it was not discussed by the foreign scientists in the same way.[247] A little later, "Averroes [1126-1198] seeks to determine 'whether the study of philosophy and logic is allowed by the [Islamic] Law, or prohibited, or commanded - either by way of recommendation or as obligatory.'"[248]

Ibn Salah, who lived from 1181-1245, gave a famous *fatwa* against teaching and learning logic and philosophy. "This *fatwa* by Ibn Salah is only the explicit formulation of an attitude that prevailed over a large part of the Muslim world during his lifetime; it was an attitude that certainly did not originate with this renowned religious scholar."[249] "The Hanbalite Ibn Taymiya [1263-1328] understood 'ilm [knowledge] as referring only to that knowledge which derives from the Prophet. Everything else he regarded either as useless or no science at all..." Ibrahim b. Musa in Spain [died 1388] thought that the "average orthodox theologian regarded only those sciences as worthwhile that were necessary to, or useful for, religious practice...."[250]

Other statements about the potential harm of these sciences could be cited, about how they were wisdom mixed with unbelief, and how they could only lead to less worthy thoughts about God. The last word is that of Ibn Khaldun, historian and theorist of history, 1332–1406, who "wrote that '[t]he problems of physics [he was referring to Aristotelian natural philosophy] are of no importance for us in our religious affairs or to our livelihoods. Therefore, we must leave them alone.'" Taken as a whole, such views have been summed up as "an instrumentalist and religiously oriented view of all secular and permitted knowledge."[251]

Despite this opposition, reason and the foreign sciences did not disappear in the Islamic Middle Ages, and great accomplishments must be recognized. The practitioners of the foreign sciences were not persecuted everywhere, and not evenly. In some times and places within the Islamic world they found favor. One Caliph might burn books, while the next promoted these sciences.[252] "Indeed, from around 1100 to 1500, sciences such as optics, astronomy, mechanics, mathematics, and medicine reached a higher state in Islam than in the medieval West."[253]

Narrowing the scope of use, and creating reluctance in scholars to use reason, was not the only way reason was challenged following the *Mihna*. Ibn Hanbal himself had "utilized analogical reasoning, though silently and not in a polished manner. He did not state explicitly that he was doing so, and this question was never completely clarified even among his disciples."[254] Hanbal though, would have preferred to find a *hadith* or legal opinion rather than to rely on reason. Even when traditionists gave a conservative answer in reply to a more Mu'tazilite position, Hanbal disapproved of both results! "By labeling both positions innovations, Ibn Hanbal took aim at the process that led to either position rather than at the positions themselves. His criticism was directed at the theological discussion and he chastised the mere act of raising the issue."[255]

But could there be some safe use of reason? A movement called the Asharites attempted to avoid a position like Hanbal's, and to make reason safe for use by defining the limits within which revelation from God allowed it to be used. Al-Ash'ari, who died in 935, was the founder of this school of thought in Baghdad. The argument of his school was that something like the value of good or bad didn't have an objective existence by itself, as the Mu'tazilites had held, but had to exist in reference to something – God – in order to exist at all.[256] This has been traced through a line of succeeding teachers down to al-Ghazali, 1059-1111, one of the greatest figures in Islamic thought. His book *The Incoherence of the Philosophers* didn't try to destroy philosophy, but "to bind it to the service of theology by combating the exclusive use of reason." [257] Reason, within the bounds of revelation only, was a good thing, and within the subsequent one hundred fifty years this became the dominant form of discourse within the Sunni Islamic world.

A theory of how to use reason in knowledge though, was not enough, since "any system of thought, in order to survive, had to be affiliated with one of the schools of law."[258] The traditionists had adherents in every one of the schools of law beside the Hanbali, and overall the most members. Mu'tazilism tried to survive in the Hanafite school, and Ash'arism by moving its adherents into the Shafi'ite school. "Ash'arism's object being legitimacy, any of the four schools could have served the purpose, at least at the start. The ideal situation was the eventual infiltration of all the schools of law."[259]

I hope by this time it is clear why law was so important within Islam, and why any significant system of thought would need to be accepted as legal thought. The schools of law determined what was orthodox within the Islamic *ummah*. Not to be present in a school of law meant that an intellectual position was not orthodox, and at worst might be non-Islamic.

One final reaction by the orthodox traditionists to the rationalist attack of the Mu'tazilites was in the area of hadith collection and transmission sciences. If a rationalist was able to easily exploit contradictory *hadiths*, or show by examination of the *isnad* that the *hadith* in question couldn't be authentic, then traditionist positions were in danger of falling. That critique spurred the definitive collection of the traditions and arrangement by subject area – something new – not just by the name of the transmitter. Al-Bukhari, who died around 870, and Muslim, who died around 875, were the most prominent, though four other authors and their collections of tradition also have great authority within Sunni Islam. For Sunni Islam, these collections are still today the normative sources of tradition.

Law is the Most Important Knowledge – Growth of Law Schools

The struggle over the content of knowledge, and the proper means to pursue knowledge – revelation or reason –

naturally had effects within the institutions of knowledge, the schools. As the schools were more greatly affected, they fed back in to the struggle over the content of knowledge, in a mutually reinforcing process. Schools within Islamic lands tended to organize both geographically and personally. A respected individual teacher would attract followers, who upon completing their education would attract their own followers, a process both highly personal, and one naturally influenced by geography.

There were as many schools of Islamic law as there were teachers. "Some five hundred schools of law are said to have disappeared at or about the beginning of the third/ninth century. [cite omitted] But even then the schools had not yet settled down to the number of four."[260] But as the struggle for knowledge in the Mihna reached its height, and subsided after its close by al-Mutawakkil, "The struggle between the two antagonistic forces becomes apparent when the schools of law change from the geographical designation to the personal one. For the change into personally designated schools of law is in itself indicative of a rallying call of the traditionalists to emulate the Prophet and his disciples (*ashab*). Just as the Prophet was the leader with followers, each school consisted of a leader (*imam*), with followers (*ashab*)...[and the number of schools decreased] because of a natural movement on the part of the traditionalists to close their ranks in order to present a solid front against the perennial enemy, rationalism."[261]

Another factor encouraging consolidation into fewer schools of law with greater numbers of adherents was a change in infrastructure of education. Education still took place primarily in the mosque, either the *masjid* (every-day mosque) or the *jami* (the "Friday" mosque). But mosques began to have *khans*, or inns, associated with them. Those money-making inns could assist with upkeep and maintenance costs of the mosque, and also provide places for students to live cheaply. The most sophisticated stage of educational institution, the *madrasa*, was soon reached, though the older *masjids*, *jamis*, and even shrines would still teach the law. The *madrasa* specialized in law, often only the law of a specific school. *Madrasas* were usually located in or attached to a mosque, providing teaching and housing in one building or complex of buildings. Some students still paid their professors, some professors taught for very little, some for high salaries, but the development of the *madrasa* evened out some of this chaos.[262]

The *madrasa* was quite typically endowed as a *waqf*, a charitable trust, by a founder, in order to teach the law. The founder could be quite specific in the founding deed about what school of law was to be taught, what the salary of the professor would be, the number and duties of the assistants, the stipends to be paid to students, etc. That encouraged students to declare an allegiance to a school of law – after all, following a specific school could mean housing, stipend, meals, and opportunities. Purists of course deplored this development as removing the pure joy of learning and dedication a student ought to have, at least to their minds.

The one basic stipulation of the law of *waqf* was that nothing contravening Islam could be taught in a school provided by the *waqf* – otherwise the *waqf* ran the risk of being declared invalid, and its lands and buildings seized by the caliph.[263] Since founders did want to do good deeds in founding an institution of learning according to Islam (or at least set up their progeny with livings as salaried trustees of the *waqf* after their own death, insulated from the caliphs acquisitive desires), the *waqf* by definition could not teach the ancients or the foreign sciences.

Those unwanted bodies of knowledge were squeezed out, and found their way into informal library settings, even into private homes, or might even be taught under the guise of teaching an accepted Islamic science. "This century saw the destruction of Baghdad's last *dar al'ilm*, [house of knowledge] in the year 451 A.H. [1073]."[264]

Legal Scholarship and State Power in Partnership

As the Abbasid power decayed and Seljuq Turks rose to power, they "came to realize that their power could be greatly increased by the ideological support of the Sunnite ulema, and an understanding, almost an alliance, grew up between the actual rulers and the religious institution.... The important step was due to the initiative of the great vizier, Nizam-al-Mulk, who about 1070 began to set up colleges – each called after him a *madrasa Nizamiyya* – in about a dozen of the chief cities of the empire, including Baghdad."[265] Al-Mulk knew just how to secure the support of the scholars, and "in his will and testament for the trust (waqf) of the Nizamiyyah school system, Khwajah Nizam al-Mulk ordered specifically that the teaching of falsafah [philosophy] be banned from the university system founded by him. This ban in fact continued in most of the Sunni world afterwards except for logic, which was always taught there."[266]

All knowledge was thus *not* created equal in these growing institutions of learning. Legal scholars were the top level. Below them were the scholars who used rationalism within the bounds set by revelation to support Islam. Finally, the philosophers (followers of the "foreign sciences") were ranked lowest.[267] Within the *madrasas*, the professors of law had professorial chairs. The other teaching positions did not. Those who still wished to use *kalam*, reason, had no teaching position at all.[268] And all knowledge had political and social implications.

A balance was maintained between the *ulama* and the caliph. "Both groups relied on each other, the ulama needing the financial support provided by the soldiers, the latter benefitting from the ideological legitimation which only the former could supply. Competition, both between the ulama and the military elite and also between members of each group, provided the system with its dynamic and at the same time placed limits on the authority which any individual, or group of individuals, could wield."[269]

Teaching was personal in character. There was as yet no fixed curriculum, and students went to the mosque or the *madrasa* to hear the teaching of a specific teacher. A student seeking education would find for himself the teacher that best fit his own developing beliefs about the law. If those beliefs changed as the student progressed, then the student could simply join the classes of a different teacher. It was not unknown for scholars themselves to change school affiliations during their careers, as their thought matured or changed.[270] After the *Mihna*, while the number of schools shrank and law consolidated to the familiar schools of Sunni Islam known today, up to the founding of the new Nizamiya institutions, teaching held its personal character.

A student aspiring to teach on his or her own could not teach a specific book without a certificate from his own teacher, indicating that he had the required degree of knowledge, and that he was in fact approved to teach the text to which the certificate was affixed. Teaching without the certificate was hence illegitimate, no matter the learning of the aspiring teacher in question.[271] Given this personal system, the pressure of the purse in the *madrasa/khan* combination, and ambitious young men who wished to move upward in the preeminent Islamic science, it is quite easy to see a very conservative body of scholars and scholarship as a result.

To become a doctor of the Islamic law was the highest goal a student could pursue. A *mudarris* was at once a doctor/teacher of the law, a *mufti* empowered to give legal decisions and a *faqih*, or master of law. This was a degree that had not existed in Islam prior to the *Mihna*, and developed in reaction to it. As the schools of law became more personal and diminished in number, "[t]hey were thus transformed from a loose and informal entity, to an autonomous, exclusivist unit, a professional guild, with rules and regulations to be adhered to by those who wished to become members. The purpose of these guilds was to place, in the hands of the jurisconsults *exclusively*, the machinery to determine orthodoxy in Islam."[272]

Summary

The *Mihna* had been a formative moment for Islam. The caliph lost his struggle to assert authority over a question in the body of knowledge possessed by the scholars. Declaring whether something was, or was not, properly Islamic was to remain their decision. Of necessity, the caliph had to have the support of the scholars to govern, or face accusation from them that he was not fulfilling his duty to command the good and forbid the bad, at which point his hold on power would be tenuous indeed as the scholars let it be known in every mosque that the caliph had failed. In return for that support, the caliph endowed *waqfs*, and appointed judges, positions that carried security, prestige, and salaries along with them for the scholars appointed.

Second, knowledge itself was firmly categorized and ranked in order of importance, as were the teaching institutions. There simply is no question that the study of law was the preeminent science within Islam after the time of the *Mihna*, and had no serious rivals. The foreign and ancient knowledge passed on in more unofficial forms and locations, and went without *waqf*-derived funding. Further, the institutions of learning themselves were under the firm patronage of caliphs and rulers.

After the struggle of the *Mihna*, Islam remained a unified whole. Power and knowledge were inextricably linked and supported one another. Neither could exist without the other. Neither was free to question the other except within fixed boundaries. Their relationship gave great cohesiveness and strength to society, yet at the same time inflexibility. The coming of modernity would present challenges.

Chapter 6 - The "Revolutions" Contrasted

Christianity and Islam began quite differently from each other. Those beginnings did not necessarily dictate the results of either the Papal Revolution or the *Mihna*, but helped frame the struggles, and encouraged different types of outcomes. The Papal revolution in Western Christendom in the high Middle Ages and the *Mihna* in Baghdad during the mid-800s were significant episodes which confirmed diverging paths of development. They have left results in Western and Islamic societies which are still felt and experienced every day, though rarely recognized.

There are a variety of results still with us, under the two broad headings of authority in society and the role of knowledge in society. In the West, authority was divided between the sacred and the secular – between church and State. In Islamic societies, authority existed in a unity within which the power of the state and that of religion were closely tied together. In the West, knowledge served competing authorities in society, and could even act as arbiter between them. In Islamic societies, knowledge served competing interests, but was required to serve a unified authority of society.

In both Western Christian and Islamic societies, these divisions or distributions of power were not always plain. Different authorities and interests did intrude upon each other's territory. The role of knowledge was similarly not consistent at all times and in all places. Often, the same events in the histories of Western Christianity, from the beginnings of Christianity through the Papal revolution, and in Islam from its beginnings through the *Mihna* can be part of the discussion of either, or both, authority in society and the role of knowledge in society. Let's try to examine some of the different results of these two great struggles, first in the area of authority, and then in the area of knowledge.

Christianity – Islam – Relationship of Doctrine to State Authority

Christianity from its beginning had no strong theory of the relationship between religious and civil authority within society. After existing as a tolerated, then persecuted, religion for roughly three hundred years, it was free to define for itself (or perhaps be forced into) the Byzantine understanding of a close relationship between religious and civil power. The Byzantine Emperor in his empire was a neo-platonic representation of a heavenly reality, or perhaps a successor in priestly authority to Melchizedek, to whom Abraham himself had given the tithe. The Emperor was in all events under God (while in Byzantine history we see Emperors removing Patriarchs of the Church, we never see this working the other way round).

The Byzantines show a long tradition of substantial unity between the authority of church and state. Starting with Constantine's adoption of the new religion as that of the state; proceeding through his laws favoring religion and establishing it; passing through the criminalization of heresy by Theodosius; touching the theories of the Byzantine Emperor as a priest himself in an order in which the forces of state and religion were happily unified under God; encompassing a central-government-approved monastic rule of Basil instead of independent rules such as monastics used in the West, a unity remained.

The weak social fabric of the West invited papal power to grow and compete with civil authority, while a strong central authority continued in the Byzantine Empire as it shrank in treasure and territory until Constantinople fell to the Ottomans in May of 1453. In other words, the Papal revolution could not have happened in Eastern Christendom. If Constantinople had not dwindled, a very different idea of relations between religious and civil authority would be current in the West today. But

Constantinople did fall, and even long before its fall, Western Christianity had opened the contest for authority within society.

The power struggle between Popes and Emperors was between competing hierarchies. Each can be imagined as a pyramid, with either Pope or Emperor at the apex (despite protestations of identity as servant of all); each had an intermediate level of cardinals, bishops, dukes, or counts, etc.; each had a machinery of administration filled with bright or aspiring lawyers, accountants, and other officials; each had a large body of foot soldiers (both in the literal and symbolic senses) to carry out its wishes. Reward and risk in the struggle came not from society as a whole, but came to the partisan of either side from those higher up within the structure to which he had given his primary allegiance. Both Church and state possessed sufficient structural and intellectual tools to exercise direct authority over its own hierarchy, as well as other people and lands.

An important triggering event of the Papal revolution was the argument over the appointment, or investiture, power for bishops. This simply illustrates the assertion that the Western issue was to be decided between competing hierarchies. While a common devotion to God could be claimed, there seemed an underlying agreement already between the parties that power gravitated either around the Church, or the State, and that it was these two as actors who must decide upon appointment of bishops, and other boundary lines between themselves in society.

After the Papal revolution, in the West the idea of two separate spheres governing the life of the individual was accepted. The ambiguities of the "render unto Caesar…" statement by Jesus meant that on a theoretical level the Christian religion *could* adapt quite easily to this idea of bifurcated authority in society. Pope Gelasius I's letter in the 400s; Saint Augustine's theory of two swords; the perennial conflict between Kings and Popes; Frederick II's lights in the heavens which didn't interfere with one another – this idea has a long history within Christianity in Western Europe.

Competition for and between authorities in the West undoubtedly drove the theorizing. But for the fact of real competition between popes and emperors, this model might simply have receded into history as an interesting but minor theological theme in the history of Christianity. But real competition and hostility did exist. The foundations of the familiar church and state idea Westerners accept today were built on through further strife to reach their modern forms. Separation of these two centers of power within society gave the opportunity for freedom of the individual to grow. If the religious and secular powers could be balanced in opposition against each other, there might be more freedom in both realms for the individual.

That of course is what Martin Luther did in subsequent centuries. His use of the power of the Elector of Saxony against that of the Pope was only possible because of the conclusion of the Papal Revolution. Scholars of the Reformation speak of the Magisterial Reformation of leaders like Luther who made use of the power of the state, in distinction to radical reformers like those who quickly led the city of Münster into a hell on earth, all too often without mentioning the struggle of the Popes that made this very reform possible.

Luther was free to develop his theories of what the Christian religion should be, simply because of the pre-existing separation between church and state. Had he lived in a society modeled on the Byzantine understanding of a unity between the forces of state and religion, he would likely have been stepped on speedily as just another troublesome heretic. The Papal revolution laid the foundation of that freedom by confirming the separation of authority in society. While that separation may be accepted as normative in the West today based on this long historical development, Christianity has retained the flexibility to also adopt a unitary social formation like that of the Byzantines, or none at all and become once again a social outsider.

Islam, on the other hand, began with a very distinct and strong theory of the relationship within the community of the religious and civil authority. They were one. That unified society was put to the test upon the death of Muhammad, but Abu Bakr and the other rightly guided caliphs insisted that the community remain unified around the Koran and the *sunna* of Muhammad. Tribes who wished to withdraw were compelled to remain within the community. The split between Sunni and Shi'a branches of Islam didn't significantly alter that unity, although the Sunni and Shi'a branches of Islam would weight community consensus, traditions, and charismatic leadership differently.

Within Islam, that struggle for authority was carried out not between competing hierarchies, but in an effort to gain the control of the sole existing hierarchy. While it is true that the caliph had officials to do his bidding who were not members of the body of scholars, and while the army could sharply influence events if it had the leadership to do so, there were not strong hierarchies capable of standing by themselves alone for a sustained period of time, either within the state or within the religious establishment. They were united in sustaining the constitutional balance within Islamic society, even while tensions and disputes flared.

The *Mihna* raised the question of authority in society in several ways. Some scholars today see the *Mihna* as a direct struggle between the caliph (to either take, or resume lost authority) and the *ulama* (to consolidate or hold on to theirs). Some scholars today don't see that direct struggle. After all, with a unified theory of religious and civil authority in society, it is difficult to see separate and distinct opposing parties, as in Western Europe. But whatever competing agendas were at work in the *Mihna*, there is no doubt that the question of authority was the center of the whirlwind.

Islam, in the scholars, had a hierarchy capable of exercising great indirect authority, through their power to define what was good, and what was bad, for society at all levels. Sometimes, they might even directly challenge a leader who failed to meet what the scholars said Islam required. Scholars did not hold offices in ranks as in the Christian Church, but there was nonetheless a hierarchy, which emphasized intellectual ability, influence on other scholars, and accumulation of followers more consistently and strongly than the Church.

In Islam, an important triggering event was the use of foreign or ancient sciences to help in understanding Islamic law and God himself. Neither scholars of any school or caliph questioned that Islam promoted unity – unity of God, unity of knowledge, and unity of the community itself. The only question was who was to be dominant in setting the method of explaining the unity. Which school of scholars, with or without caliphal assertions of his own power, could define the tools that helped Islam interpret itself?

The authority at issue, if not that of scholars and caliph in direct competition, was exercised indirectly in the body of knowledge that defines the Islamic *ummah* and sets its course. The group of scholars who wished to apply the tools of reason and Greek philosophy to the substance of Islam, supported by the caliph (or perhaps pushing him), or maybe being protected by him against other scholarly opposition, lost. The scholarly opposition insisted upon understanding and interpreting the substance of Islam through the traditions which had been given, and subordinated reason to the demands of those revelations. The traditionists won.

After the *Mihna*, it was clear that the scholars were the ones to decide which intellectual tools could be applied to knowledge to define how society was to work. It was clear that the scholars were the ones to select their own tools, and that the caliph could not do so. But at the same time it was clear that a caliph was necessary for order in society, for acts like appointing judges, and for the general policing of society. The caliph might even appoint professors to prestigious teaching positions. But all of his acts, his commanding the good and forbidding the bad, lay within the substantive boundaries defined by the scholars.

The unity of the Islamic *ummah* continued, with roles for caliph/sultan and scholars that were better defined and more distinct from one another than before that struggle. Unity of the community was preserved when religious scholars and leaders needed one another to maintain the balance of authority. Neither could stand alone in governing an Islamic society. There was agreement both on the mechanism of government, and the laws of Islam which governed all of society. In a unified society, there was no place for playing off forces against one another.

But was this result pre-determined by the nature of Islam? There might not be a *hadith* equivalent to "render unto Caesar..." which may be easily read to allow a separation between powers in society. There might be a great deal of substance in the Koran and *sunna* about how authority in a unified society was to work. But, law nearly always has room for interpretation. Could not that interpretation have been more favorable to strong caliphal power, or along the lines of the Mu'tazilite understanding of the use of reason as an interpretative aid, instead of the conservative insistence on revelation from God alone as the governing rule of interpretation?

Those understandings were of course possible, even if on a theoretical level there was less room for them than the room allowed by Christian theory for separated powers. But the Mu'tazilites lost, as did the caliph, in the *Mihna*. Perhaps that helps to explain the birth of the Sufi, or mystical, movement within Islam not too long after the conclusion of the *Mihna* and consolidation of the conservative official position within Islamic society. If one were to argue for more freedom of interpretation or theorizing within Islamic society today, then it seems that the Mu'tazilite controversy must reawaken.

In considering both the Papal revolution and *Mihna*, I'm not sure that trying to gauge the intentions of the actors would be helpful. It can be argued of any Emperor, Caliph, Scholar or Pope that he was either trying to purify religion of disgusting encrustations, or was trying to turn religion into his own tool of government. I think it fair to attribute at the same time both the best, and worst, intentions to any of the parties involved, unless the historical sources surviving agree that one or the other is more appropriate. In that way both events are similar to one another.

There is a different danger in identifying false similarities. The argument that standing in the snow at Canossa, or refusing to answer a question framed in terms familiar to Plato, shows the importance of religion to Henry IV or ibn Hanbal, may be sound, but it is so broad and basic as to be nearly useless. If both these men are assumed to have been equally pious, then the practical working out of their piety was done in very different ways, and yielded very different results.

Christianity is capable of filling different places in the constitutional order of society, depending upon its historical circumstances. The Papal revolution was a rejection of the Byzantine idea of a unified society, when the competition between parties didn't yield a universal victor, but different spheres of influence within which pope and king could each be preeminent. In Western Europe at that time there was no real possibility of Christianity taking back the outsider role in the constitutional order it had had prior to Constantine.

The Papal revolution shows a strong and enduring choice made within Western Christian society. It was a change from what Christianity had been originally. It was also a substantial change from the first position of accommodation reached between the forces of religion and state in the Byzantine Empire. It had become clear that Christianity could resist change, but when controlling social change was beyond its ability, it could also adapt to new conditions.

The *Mihna*, in contrast, does not show change from what the *ummah* originally was, but confirmation and amplification of qualities Islam already had. Islamic society from its beginning was a strong unity containing both religious and state authority within defined boundaries. The *Mihna* refined the methods by which those boundaries could be defined. The necessity of cooperation between scholars and caliph was brought home by their clash. Stability in society demanded their support of one another, since neither was strong enough, nor suited to be, sole ruler.

The *Mihna* also confirmed a conservative approach to understanding what the *ummah* itself was to be, and what it meant to be a Muslim within an Islamic society. Reason was used, but within the context provided by revelation. The words of the Koran, and of the *sunna*, contained in the biographies of the Prophet, and in his actions, sayings, and silences, were not to be overcome or controverted by reasoning, but were to be interpreted and understood with the use of reason. How this conservative conclusion would affect Islam when confronted with the need for future change is a subject for the remainder of this book.

Islam would move toward the modern world with its theory of authority, and its exercise in society, substantially unchanged from what had existed when Islam began. This in turn required that Islam look back when questions of the right structure and application of authority to society were asked. Christianity would move toward the modern world with a new theory of authority, not integral to the Christian faith, allowing Christianity more flexibility in the right structuring and application of authority in society. Christianity on the eve of modernity had the freedom not to look back to answer questions of authority in society, even if it did sometimes become confused and do so anyway.

Knowledge – Master or Servant?

The question of authority was linked to knowledge in both the Papal revolution and the *Mihna*. Whether the link was strong, weak, or even necessary was answered in very different ways in Western Christian and Islamic cultures during these two revolutionary events, leaving knowledge with different roles in each of these societies. The role of knowledge was defined in two ways: First, through the nature of the institutions in which it was taught and learnt; Second, through the types of knowledge considered most important, and the limits placed upon critical thought and inquiry. But before examining educational institutions and the content of thought, there are two threshold issues to be noted.

First, there are universal similarities in the educational cultures participated in by teachers and students. In both Western Christian and Islamic societies of the time there were lazy students, and perpetual students. Professors were sometimes diligent, and sometimes they placed the burden of lectures on their assistants. Both students and professors competed for positions with the most prestige and scholarships or pay. Some students were quite zealous in religious matters, and others were more interested in wine, women, or song. But there were differences in the status at law and the power of students between East and West.

Second, "[o]ne must guard against attributing to Muslim institutions of learning characteristics parallel to those which developed in Western Christendom. Therefore, from *jami'* and *masjid* to *madrasa*, we do not have a development similar to that of European institutions from theological to secular schools."[273] The reverse may be said with equal truth – one should not attribute to the law faculty at Bologna developments similar to that in a great *madrasa* in Baghdad. These institutions were different, so I shall use "*madrasa*" instead of "university" when discussing education in Baghdad in the years after the *Mihna* to try to avoid the unintentional confusion or attribution of qualities or defects which translating to "university" may bring.

One set of differences in institutions of learning centers around the organization of the body of students and teachers. Within the Islamic world, the *waqf* was the dominant mechanism for organizing that most important institution, the *madrasa*. As a private foundation, the *waqf* was endowed with buildings and land (often income producing) by its founder. In the legal paperwork (deed) creating the *waqf*, the founder often stipulated the particular school of law to teach in the *madrasa*, and who was to hold the post as the head professor. Salaries were laid down, as were different assistantship posts, even down to lowly positions like clerks or gatekeepers. The instrument establishing the *madrasa* could provide stipends for students (hence generating competition among the best students to gain a place where room and board were provided).[274]

In Western Europe, two different models were used. The first was centered around the professors themselves. They were in charge of organizing their lectures, courses of study, and setting the fees they would charge students, although they still had to contend with student attempts at taking power or fend off the embrace of the church. In the other model, the power was centered within the body of students. The students set salaries and paid their professors. They kept the time for lectures, and penalized professors who didn't start on time, or stopped too early. After all, if they were paying, they ought to get their money's worth![275]

The differences in the relationships between students, professors, and money, is striking. Within the Islamic *waqf* model, both students and professors were beneficiaries of the largesse of a founder. They had no substantial economic interests either in competition or cooperation with one another. Within the Western models, competing economic interests were at the center of the relationship between students and professors. Students financially penalizing a professor for finishing early? Professors making sure they'd been paid before admitting a student to a lecture?

Money may be a powerful motivator to either student or professor. Within the Islamic system money and prestige could follow as the natural fruit of effort in a good *madrasa* and recognition of a student's learning. So too in the Western world. Money (or lack) could also be a motivator, as students pursued the benefit of a place in the *madrasa*. But as part of the relationship between student and professor, the voice of money was more muted within the Islamic system than the Western. Of course, the relationship between the donor establishing a *waqf* and appointing a favored professor, especially if the donor was a public official acting in this private capacity, was another question altogether.

Another part of the difference between *waqf* and student or professor-driven models and the relationship to money is mobility. *Waqf* property was fixed, immovable property. In either the student or professor-driven models of the West though, the "property" was not in buildings or lands given by a benefactor, but in the economic give and take between students, professors, and their surrounding towns. Think of the demand for housing, scholarly supplies, food, and beer that a growing Western university might have generated. If the business community of the town failed to treat students or professors well, they could threaten to move away, taking their money with them. While *waqf* property could be seized by the caliph if sufficient pretext were found, there was no property in the early Western university for king or pope to seize.[276]

These differences between *waqf* and Western organization forms also were reflected in student consciousness. Within the Islamic system, competing for a place in the *madrasa* with its benefits of room and board was part of the student's concern, but the greater part was the question of which *madrasa* to join. Which of the emerging schools of law was taught at the *madrasa* was important, and even more so, the identity of the professor doing the teaching. The student in this system is more the disciple or follower of an important teacher, common in the ancient world, than we would assume a student to be today.[277] Within the Western system, the economic identity of the students, either in power over their professors, or as debtors who must pay for access to education, bred more of a class or group consciousness.

The idea of the faculty (or department) is also one of the differences in either a *waqf* or Western model. The *madrasa* was organized around a head professor, with varying numbers and grades of assistants, teaching a specific school of Islamic law, and was for this reason somewhat personal in nature. The Western university model was organized around the subject, not the professor himself and was therefore less personal in nature – another reason for the difference above in students as disciples versus students as a group. Since it was organized around a subject, the faculty idea – different professors teaching the same subject area, evolving a course of study for the student, was a natural growth. It was also possible to have different faculties within the same university, teaching different subject matter.

Within the Islamic world, a *madrasa* was by its nature quite limited in scope of study. It could not contain various faculties within it. An interested student could finish his study in the *madrasa*, be certified by the professor as fit to teach from a certain book, and could then go on to study different subject matter in a different *waqf*-funded school, or if his tastes ran to the ancient or foreign sciences, in one of the more informal library settings.

Studies of Western European universities during the Middle Ages show different faculties co-existing within one university. Those same studies show different mixes of faculties. Some universities tended to emphasize medical schools, others law, or theology. Regional variations in the number of faculties, and those emphasized, also existed. Within the Islamic educational world of the time, the differences were less. The strong *waqf* model was prevalent, and with the *madrasa* as preeminent school, the regional variation lies in the choice of school of law taught.

Authority to grant degrees was something granted by either the Emperor or Pope in founding or supporting a university, while it was the business of the faculty, not an individual professor, to decide if a student had met the required standard to earn the degree he wanted. The caliph had no voice in granting authority to confer degrees. That privilege in the Islamic world was the possession of the body of scholars themselves.

"It is well known that, from the Muslim point of view, knowledge (*'ilm*) has a sacred character. It is so regarded whether taught in a private home or public building, whether in a mosque where the canonical prayers are performed, or in another building not specifically for the performance of such prayers. Thus the founding of an institution of learning was an act of piety pleasing to God whether the institution was a *masjid* or a *madrasa*." I do not question that many *waqfs* were in fact founded for pious and charitable reasons.[278]

We know also though, that this was not always the case. A rich man could donate property to a *waqf*, appointing himself and his family line as trustees or administrators, naturally enough with salaries to continue for life. The theory was that in this way a rich man might avert the jealousy of a caliph, and preserve at least part of his property for his heirs.

There was an indirect state role in the institution and its maintenance. Questions of whether a *waqf* deed was being correctly interpreted and implemented could come before a judge appointed by the caliph. The caliph might even need to intervene and appoint a trustee or manager if one were lacking. And we do know that on occasion, a particularly greedy caliph might cast his eyes upon attractive *waqf* land or building, and if he were strong enough, confiscate it for state purposes. Sometimes there was a direct role for the caliph in *madrasas*. In the case of the Nizamiya *madrasas* of the 1100s, the caliph appointed the professors, and there was much political maneuvering surrounding that process.[279]

Founding of institutions in the West had a more public character. We do not see the existence of a strong body of trust or foundation law like the *waqf* theory in Western Europe. Instead, foundation of organizations was carried on by the Church, or by the Emperor, or was even a spontaneous development.[280] This immediately gave the founding of an institution of higher learning a public, rather than a private character. There simply was not the defining deed restrictions of which school of law to teach, and by whom, as there could be within the Islamic world.

Public founding under the conditions of the Middle Ages in the West also immediately raises the question of competition between Church and State for the control of education. The power to grant an institution the authority to confer degrees on its students was a power held by either Church or State in the West, but not by the founder of a *waqf* in the East. We also must not overlook the question of loyalty. To which party –

Church or State – would the graduates of any particular institution adhere? Faithful servants within the hierarchy of either Pope or Emperor could hardly be expected to come from an institution under the control of the other party.

High political maneuvers dictated that between 1309 and 1378 the seat of the Popes was in Avignon, France, and not in Rome. When Pope Gregory XI moved his court back to Rome, dying shortly thereafter, an election was held which resulted in the election of Pope Urban VI, who stayed in Rome, and also in the selection of Clement VII (sometimes called the anti-Pope), who presided over his own court in Avignon. Two rival Popes meant that secular rulers had to choose one or the other. France and Spain stayed loyal to the French Pope, while the German statelets of the Holy Roman Empire, and the Italian states chose Rome. So obviously, universities had to be founded in Germany, to avoid denial of entry to students or brainwashing by hostile faculties.

The Popes could play parties off against one another by granting charters to universities, allowing more universities to form, ultimately giving the chance to students of lesser nobility (or none), such as Martin Luther several hundred years later, to enter university and gain an education. There were even struggles within universities for control, as in Bologna periodically during the 1200s and 1300s, where the Church sought to slow the growth of the faculty of law which so helped its primary rival, the State, or as at the university in Paris, mentioned in the last chapter.

Economic competition between Church and State, and between States as the Middle Ages advanced, was also a powerful factor in the founding of new universities.[281] A free city, or a fledgling kingdom, needed educated men to staff its courts and state bureaucracies. What better place to find these educated people than a university existing in, and beholden to, the State which wanted the educated men in the first place?

The example of the Emperor Frederick I (Barbarossa) sums up some of the differences between Western Europe and the Islamic World in the nature and structure of institutions.

First, Barbarossa intervened in the university of Bologna and its law faculty not as founder, since it was already in existence, but in his office as Emperor. As Holy Roman Emperor he claimed certain rights in the Northern Italian city-states, which were, unfortunately, ill-defined. Frederick did in fact wonder, as Umberto Eco imagined it, "Where the devil can I find someone who will define my rights without claiming to be above me?"[282]

The answer was to appeal to the law faculty of Bologna to define those rights. The four famous masters of the faculty didn't act alone, but met in a committee composed of themselves, and two legal delegates (judges) from each of the fourteen towns involved, so that the full committee was thirty-two persons. An opinion for Frederick was given, with three of the doctors of law in agreement, and one disagreeing. Frederick in exchange had something he could give the university.[283]

In an 1155 decree, which was repeated again a few years later in the 1158 *Authentica Habita*, Frederick by law granted privileges (immunity from taxes and tolls) to lay students, just like those the students who were clerics already enjoyed. In addition, the students gained freedom from the system of reprisals. For example, under the reprisal system if a German student drank too much beer and couldn't pay his bar tab, any other German student with money could be seized and made to pay the bill. Right of trial before the masters of the university itself was also granted.[284]

This imperial law was soon understood as applying to any university student at any university. Its main importance lies in putting real force behind the independence the universities claimed for themselves. We are free to speculate as to whether the doctors of law in Bologna had a quid pro quo with Frederick, but whether they did or not, the result was still the same: The university stood on its own. There doesn't seem to be much, if any, piety in Frederick's law applying to the university. It seems rather a cunning exercise in power where Frederick got what he wanted, while elevating the status of the Roman law and the professors of that law.

The Papal revolution and the use of knowledge in it may have spurred the founding of more universities than the *Mihna*, since knowledge was already of great importance to the correct ordering of the Islamic world. The number of universities or *madrasas* in either society though, is not as important as what went on within those institutions. The shaping and qualities of the institutions themselves has already provided hints. Frederick I may or may not have made a corrupt bargain with the doctors of law of Bologna, but even if he did, law was recognized as a power in society independent of either emperor or pope with the power to decide political contests. On the other hand, the *waqf* was limited by its nature to subjects and content which did not offend the established political order.

In the West, competition between papal and imperial authority spurred on the digging for knowledge, specifically the nearly forgotten body of Roman law. In Islamic society, competition between the scholars and caliph (or scholars and scholars if the caliph's role is downplayed) also spurred on the search for knowledge, specifically the correct method of understanding what Islam was supposed to be. In both Western and Islamic societies, the reason for seeking the knowledge was in order to use it to win the struggles within those societies.

Knowledge then, had importance and limits directly linked to its use in affirming the proper shape of society. If in accord with society, it could be accepted and used, and if not, then it would be marginalized. Within Islam, law was clearly in the first position. "The collapse of the Inquisition [*Mihna*] and the consequent political defeat of the Mu'tazilites set in motion two developments of capital importance to the resurgence of conservative Islam. The first of these developments was the relatively rapid compilation of hadith collections; and the second, was the gradual monopolization of the masjid-mosque and its organization for the education of the jurisconsult."[285] Other knowledge faded away, although it might still be studied privately and great advances made. It is difficult to point to exactly when, and where, the ancient sciences died, and they dwindled inconsistently from place to place, but they did fade away.[286]

In Western Europe, despite the strong impetus to develop law supplied by the struggle between papal and secular powers, there was not a rank-ordering of knowledge placing law in a primary position and marginalizing other areas of knowledge. In fact, competition in the West denied Paris a faculty of law, since that seemed advantageous to both the French king and the pope, for different reasons.[287] Paris could continue to brag of its primacy in theology, the "queen of the sciences." Research shows differences between Northern and Southern Europe; the size and relative importance of different faculties - for example, Southern universities taught more law and medicine, while Northern taught more theology and liberal arts; the mix of graduate students to undergraduate differed; as did the student-driven or professor-driven models, and more.[288]

The reaction against unbridled reason which followed the *Mihna*, and victory of the traditionists and their method of interpreting law forced knowledge slowly but surely into narrow borders, and subordinated reason to tradition among the right-thinking in the Islamic world. "Orthodoxy in Islam is therefore legal, more a matter of God's law, rather than theological, which would concentrate on God Himself. When a conservative jurist and theologian of the thirteenth century was faced with the need to refute what he considered to be the rationalistic theology of a fellow Muslim of a previous century, one of the arguments he used goes to the heart of the matter that concerns us here:

> 'We have no need to know the meaning which God intended by His attributes; *no course of action* is intended by them, nor is there any obligation attached to them *except to believe in them*; and it is possible to believe in them without the knowledge of their intended sense. For indeed faith, with ignorance, is sound. God has enjoined belief in His angels, His scriptures, His prophets and that which He has revealed to them, though

we might not know of all this except the designation.'"[289]

With the marginalizing of the ancient sciences, suppression of the rationalists, and victory of the traditionists, a statement like that should be no surprise, nor should the primacy of the legal scholars within official Islam following the *Mihna*.
Western universities had faculties of theology, of course. But they were not automatically the most important faculty. That varied from place to place, and university to university. There was no rank ordering of knowledge from most important to least important in the Western university as there was within the Islamic world after the *Mihna*. "It is highly significant that the medieval universities gave their students no spiritual training or instruction."[290] And reason, far from being subordinated to tradition, began slowly to come into its own in the Western university.
"Persecutions and harassment of those who advocated the use of reason to explicate revelation are unknown in the medieval Latin West after the mid-twelfth century, when Bernard of Clairvaux and other traditional theologians opposed the application of reason to theology...After the 1240's, and for the rest of the Middle Ages, attacks on reason would have been regarded as bizarre and unacceptable."[291] As already noted, it was during these same years, and even later, when Islamic thinkers were still debating the extent to which they could use reason, and for what subjects.
Limiting and rank-ordering knowledge also helps define the possible roles it may fill in society. May knowledge act as a mediator, or independent source of authority, or will it act as only the servant of an established order? Within Islamic society, knowledge was a servant, even while a few scholars still fought to advance their marginalized areas of study, which in all events, must be subordinate to the law. Within the Western Christian tradition, knowledge had begun to be set free from servitude, and also set free to inquire.

In Western Europe, a rebirth of the Roman law drove the growth of the class of legal professionals - lawyers, notaries, and judges, displacing church-educated or clerical servants of the State, confirming the split between these two centers of authority, and appealing to the re-discovered Roman law as their basis for doing so. In Islamic society, the *ulama* remained an integral part of the state constitutional structure, and its reaffirmed and newly limited knowledge after the *Mihna* only confirmed and served the accepted ideas of governance.

From the limiting and rank ordering of knowledge, and definition of the social role of knowledge, it is quite easy to draw the conclusion that knowledge itself narrowed in scope. Of course not immediately, and not everywhere, but as a general proposition within Islamic society. The tools of free thought were discarded or severely limited by the conclusion of the *Mihna*. While the scholars of Bologna were still working within a cultural religious tradition, it was one that allowed Greek thinking tools inside. The idea of the dialectic, the respected knowledge of Artistotle, and Platonic ideals were applied to an older body of knowledge and law. In subsequent centuries the glossators, commentators, and humanists felt free to reinterpret, comment upon, and correct what had gone before. That did not happen within the mainstream of Islamic thought, because it no longer could.

In the area of authority, creation of competing spheres of sacred and secular power in the West during the Middle Ages spurred the growth of different bodies of law, and hierarchies of king and church that were independent of one another, even while they shared many of the notions of Western Christianity. "Out of the conflicts, especially between reason and faith, church and state, the sacred person and sacred authority, grew the ideals of freedom of thought and conscience."[292]

In the arena of knowledge, the division of sacred and secular in West allowed the university to diverge and grow, while the confirmed unification in the East narrowed the role of the institutions of higher learning. In return, the independent role of knowledge in the West helped uphold the separation of sacred and secular (and was to help widen that split further in subsequent centuries), while in official Islamic society controlled knowledge acted as the capstone holding the state and social order in one place.

The Papal revolution and the *Mihna* had very different results in the areas of governance and knowledge. Each one of them interwove issues of knowledge and authority in society in different ways, producing greatly differing results at the time of the events. Most importantly for the societies of Western Europe and the Middle East, they left a very different set of possibilities for the future development of these societies as the Middle Ages passed and modern times approached.

Chapter 7 - From the Middle Ages to Modern Times

If you've made it to this point, you've probably had as much history as you like, maybe even more. I can imagine the impatience. Why is all this ancient history so important? Why can't we just get to the real issues? After all, as I write this, a few days ago the Paris offices of the French satirical newspaper Charlie Hebdo were attacked, and several people were killed. So I'll try to quickly bridge the gulf between the end of the Papal revolution and modern times in Europe and the West. Then we must turn back to developments in Islamic culture after the *Mihna*, to show the differences growing between Western European and Islamic cultures as modern times drew near. Those differences gave fuel to the fires burning today.

From Papal Revolution to Modern Western Society

So in the West, we're skipping the Renaissance and Reformation, the birth of Protestant Christianity and the Wars of Religion and peace of Westphalia in 1648. We'll pass over the centuries-long withering away of the system of canon law and church courts, the rise of royal systems of law, and their morphing into national systems of law as royal power was forced to accept parliaments, and the slow rise of the European nationalist ideal and the modern participatory and democratic forms of government.

We're passing over the beginnings of European secularism in the intellectual ferment of the Enlightenment, English reaction, and proliferation of varieties of Protestants in Europe. The ability to choose between diverse and competing forms of the Christian religion, in a society tired of religious strife, also contributed to the secular impulse in society. This sort of secularism should be understood as a separation or privatization of religion in society, not the absence of religion, even though anti-clerical hostility and violence did break out sometimes, as early in the French Revolution.

Naturally urbanization accompanied these developments. They were also furthered by the growing modern banking system emerging from embryonic form in the states of Northern Italy as the Papal Revolution came to a close, and by the development of the business corporation, that structure allowing aggregation of unheard of amounts of capital, limitation of liability for the participants, centralization of management and continuity of existence across generations. And to cap it off of course, the great Industrial Revolution.

All of these developments up to the beginning of modern times in Western Europe were not possible without the long competition for power of the Middle Ages. There, separation of church from state and establishment of independent spheres each occupied and in which each busied itself with its own concerns had been confirmed. Also, we saw the rise of knowledge substantially free from tutelage of the church or the state and free to apply itself in new directions. That knowledge produced the great scientific and industrial revolutions of Western Europe.

These are the foundations of modern Western culture, rarely questioned or even recognized. Summarizing some of them, even though it may seem tedious or too obvious, is important simply because Westerners too often don't even realize that their lives rest on these assumptions – assumptions not shared by the rest of the world.

Unquestioned Foundations of Modern Western Societies

For our purposes, that means assumptions like: There are two different spheres of competency and authority between the State and Religion; and, education and knowledge have a degree of independence, and carry independent authority, within society. The power of the State is expressed through law, and law gives norms defining legal and illegal behaviors, but the power of religion expresses itself through aspirations and calling to a better or higher good. Education and reason are not the servants of religion, but may in fact be an enemy either of religion or of the state.

Older possibilities of the power of religion in the state don't exist any longer in the West. Does anybody really think that the Catholic Church, or the Protestant denominations, plan to take over and govern Western nations? The Christian Church lost the ability and machinery for that sort of administration as its power in society dwindled following the Papal Revolution. Priests inspecting your cupboards for illicit booze, or requiring a tithe before you receive that unexpected inheritance? Church leaders understand that that won't happen, no matter how much they dislike alcohol, or how interested they might be in funding their churches through inheritances. Nor do they expect or want it.

On the other hand, does anybody seriously think that Western governments want to run vibrant and dynamic communities of faith, and get involved in matters of theology or doctrine? Western States seem quite content to modestly fund established national churches serving essentially ceremonial functions for the remnants of royal families, or inspiring a law-abiding (docile) congregation toward good works and private acts of religious devotion. Government and political leaders are quite content to leave religion alone, so long as it stays on its own side of the dividing line. Even in the U.S., where separation of these two structures in society arguably reached its high point, there is little worry that the State will establish any time soon a Church of the United States.

Certainly there are tensions between the Church and the State in the West. Bigotry and ignorance have not been eradicated in either State or religion. These tensions can and should be argued about within civil society - the accepted social, political and legal institutions that exist. Those tensions are relatively minor when the historical conflict in Western Europe between the forces of law (State) and religion is considered. It is clear that by now there are established spaces for both the Church and the State in the constitutional order of Western society. Sure, there are going to be border skirmishes, and maybe they're increasing in our time, but neither sacred nor secular is claiming it should control most or all of the territory of the other.

Think of the modern Western freedom to have no religious faith at all, or the freedom to loudly criticize religion on both popular and academic levels – a Western tradition possible precisely because of the separation between the spheres of law and religion. Rodney Stark and Roger Finke, in their *Acts of Faith: Explaining the Human Side of Religion*, provide a quick historical survey of the background to modern sociological assumptions that when studying religion, what sociologists are studying is something false, that ought to be explained by the tools and substance of either sociology or psychology. Religion is definitely something which is not true in and of itself.

They skim quickly through scholars or writers like Jean Bodin, whose underground book of 1593 made the argument that since religions were in essence similar, they couldn't all be true, therefore refuting each other. Boyle in 1697 emphasized the sexual (mis)conduct within pagan religions. Fontenelle in 1687 showed widespread "trickery" by pagan priests. Shaftesbury in 1711 spoke of "minds" predisposed to fear and anxiety, which create religion. Hume asserted the irrationality of religion. Frazer in 1890 in *The Golden Bough* argued that since so many gods traditionally die next to a sacred tree, all refute all, and all religions are false. And one could speak of the greatest Enlightment personality, Volataire, or of Freud, and many others.[293]

To a separation between the spheres of authority for state and religion, the substantial freedom of each from the other, the freedom of choice among religions, and the freedom to doubt or reject all religion, we must add the shaping of society brought on by industrialization. Industrial societies, born first in the

West, brought increasing complexity to life. Growth and specialization in knowledge encouraged a corresponding growth and complexity in social structures, and the authority they provided in different spheres of life, including the life of the mind. As Patricia Crone has stated:

> "Members of (non-Marxist) industrial societies do however tend to invoke different value systems in different contexts where their pre-industrial forebears would invoke one and the same. Thus a modern Englishman will legitimate his actions with reference to democracy in connection with politics, to animal rights in connection with vegetarianism, to the growth of knowledge in the context of science and scholarship, and so on, reserving his religious values (if any) for questions to do with the transcendent. By contrast, a pre-industrial Englishman would have marshalled his religious values in all of these connections and a host of others too. Modern religion typically limits itself to a special aspect of life, but pre-industrial religion was for multiple use."[294]

She concludes that "Science and scholarship have indeed caused religion to decline in the West, not so much because their conclusions run counter to the Bible or Christian dogma, but rather because they have made God severely under-employed..."[295]

These developments caused some Western intellectuals to predict that religion would wither and die. A few hundred years later on it has not, and religion may even be making a comeback in modern life in the West.[296] But at any rate the role and importance of religion has diminished among some intellectuals, and in some segments of the modern Western population. Even so, a protected role for privatized religion, a religion separate from and neutral toward the state, safely existing in its own sphere, is so basic as to be written into the laws of Western nations.

The U.S. Constitution is the oldest and in some respects the most radical constitutional document in the Western legal tradition, when it states in Amendment I (ratified 1791) that: "Congress shall make no law respecting an establishment of religion, or prohibiting the free exercise thereof..." There have been many court cases since that time, trying to define when an action by the state might have the effect of establishing religion; and equally as many cases and arguments where a religious group complains that the state is violating its free exercise of its religious beliefs.

Many Western nations are more active in supporting a national church than the U.S., but even so, they accept the same basic premises as the U.S., and face similar arguments on freedom of or from religion. Acceptance of different social roles for church and state, and independence and non-interference with one another is why a mostly independent church structure with no need for state oversight can exist in Western states without causing serious conflict with government or the state.

That's also why switching churches, or even religions, isn't taken as a very serious matter by many Westerners. After all, maybe it is all a bunch of mostly harmless nonsense anyway. And really, it has nothing to do with whether one is a loyal citizen, a good neighbor, or productive member of society, and presents no challenge to the rule and order of the State.

In December of 1952, a month before his inauguration, President-elect Dwight Eisenhower, speaking off-the-cuff, explained that "[o]ur form of government has no sense unless it is founded in a deeply felt religious faith, and I don't care what it is." That's a great line, and almost always gets a chuckle or a few grins from students in the lecture room. He went on to say that in the case of the U.S. that felt religious faith forming the roots of the U.S. democracy was the Judaeo-Christian tradition.[297]

But Eisenhower's statement assumes Western Christianity, as sixteen hundred years of development had shaped it and its idea of proper relations with the State. His statement assumes the most privatized, generic, mainstream version of Christianity, a religion that could provide hopes and aspirations for society, without interfering in government provision and enforcement of legal norms of order. It assumes a partnering, if you will, of partners providing different good qualities to a stable society. This distinctive social partnership arrangement is not possible under either the Eastern Christian or classical Islamic theories of the relationship of religious and state or legal authority. So even if he didn't articulate it, Eisenhower *did* care what "it" was.

For people interested in religion, there is freedom in the West today to wander the aisles of the supermarket of religion, selecting desired items, or leaving them all on the shelves. The religious equivalents of spam, roast beef, and organic free range chicken are all there – and that's only the meat section. This shopping is done without any substantial negative repercussions for a person's constitutional, legal, or social standing in the community, and reaches a frenzied peak in the U.S. where there is a free and competitive market in religion. Look at the wide variety of religious bodies and practices present in any large Western city for confirmation.

Different spheres for law and aspirations, freedom of choice, a certain lightness and ease in shifting between, or out, of religious faith, a live and let live mentality, even a disdain for the religious, free rein for thought, multiple sources of authority to whom an individual may turn in making his or her life choices, those are all assumptions of modern Western society.

So long as the West stayed at home, or made trading voyages sporadically, the peculiar assumptions of Western life weren't very important to the world as a whole. But that importance grew when the West began to expand into the Middle East and North Africa in the late 1700s and through the 1800s. There the West ran headlong into a sophisticated and organized Islamic culture (with regional variations to be sure), with a long history of underlying assumptions very different from those of the West.

it; or, finally, law comes from positive power, where a legitimate ruler, be that king or parliament, has the power to declare what the law is.

These three basic sources all blend within legal systems, and sometimes one is more dominant than the other two. There is no question that Islamic law emphasizes the theory that law comes from God, specifically by direct revelation, not the method by which God's law may be discerned using reason. The reason approach had been rejected in the *Mihna*. Revelation from God included the Koran, and also the *sunna* of the Prophet, so it had a strong historical element as well. The theory of Islamic law then, demanded that positive acts by the Sultan must fit within the outer limits of what God had laid down either by direct revelation or as in the approved *sunna* of the Prophet. If not, then acts by Sultan Suleyman might have lacked legitimacy, especially the new changes or reforms to fiscal and tax policy.

Ebu's-su'ud looked back in time to concepts and terms that were without question accepted as coming from God, and lying in the *shari'a*. For example, he conceptualized the Ottoman fiscal institution of land law as being within or related to the Islamic concept of *waqf*, something dependent upon allowable custom. He borrowed older terms of Hanafi jurisprudence, and applied them to new *kanuns*. "Seen therefore from a secular viewpoint, Ebu's-su'ud's pious work of harmonisation served to legitimise and uphold the existing Ottoman order and, above all, to enhance the authority of the Sultan."[305] Seen from a more skeptical point of view, "Ebussuut was notoriously willing to perform legal acrobatics in questions dealing with the state and sought thereby to ingratiate himself with men in power."[306]

The Sultan got what he wanted, but what of Ebu's-su'ud and his brothers in the *ulama*? The Ottoman legal system and practice were unified by the Sultan's authority, and he made appointment of governors, local and district judges, and other officials. The top of the Ottoman legal system was a Kadiasker for Europe, one for Asia, and over them both, the Mufti in

Istanbul. That office, known thereafter as that of the Sheikhu'l-islam, was organized and given much of its continuing prestige and power, by Ebu's-su'ud.

The scholar holding the Mufti's position issued *fatwas*, written opinions in response to questions from the Sultan or his officials, or from lower judges. The judges quite often followed the opinions. The opinions regarding administrative or government matters themselves did not have executive authority. The Mufti needed to petition Sultan to enact his recommendation as a decree. The Sultan in his turn would seek a *fatwa* from the Mufti before any risky action which might be seen as lacking in legitimacy.[307]

Ebu's-su'ud ordered and trained permanent clerks of his ministry better than had been done before, so that the quality of the work produced by the office didn't fluctuate so much with the strength or weakness of the officeholder, as it had in the past. Ebu's-su'ud demanded a procedure where the manner in which a question was presented in the *fatwa* presented an opportunity for a simple yes or no answer. That way, a great number of cases could be gotten through in a systematic way. The bureaucracy he helped form continued even when office of Mufti or Sheik turned over more quickly, as it did after his tenure, but without a loss of prestige due to the continuing high quality of its work.[308]

Determining whether or not an act of the Sultan or his government was acceptable within the *shari'a* sounds a bit like setting the jurisdictional boundaries of a constitutional court. As Chief Mufti, "…it was a sign of his freedom of judgement and his power to curb and rebuke the holders of power that he was not a member of the sultan's *divan* of high officials."[309] But while it sounds like the scholars kept their power and relevance in the constitutional order, they did so at a cost. "Between 1542 and 1559, only three seyhulislams were dismissed. From 1599 to 1703, no less than thirty of the forty-two chief muftis were removed from office, a staggering 75% rate of dismissal."[310]

Absorbing the *ulama* into the structure of the state, under the caliph or sultan, had been attempted before. One of the reasons for the Mihna may have been such an attempt by al-Ma'mun. Nizam al-Mulk may have generously opened so many *madrassas* to get the kind of law and legal scholars he favored, all knowing clearly who their benefactor had been. Through a long gradual process, this may at last have happened in the Ottoman period.[311]

Ebu's-su'ud himself got a higher salary, and wider powers in the appointment of judges than the Mufti's office had had before. "Whatever the obscure nature of details, it is immediately evident that the şeyhülislam had assumed a more political and temporal role than had been typical before this last period."[312] It was the State which created and filled offices, and if the State ever wanted to limit the authority of those offices, it just might be able to do so.

The knowledge and orthodoxy of legal views were still established by their own schools of thought, but even here, the *ulama* may have been challenged by the growing Ottoman state. A scholar didn't have to receive a choice *madrassa* appointment in the formation of a *waqf* by an official in the government hierarchy, but even if disfavored by the government he was still a member of the *ulama*. It has been argued that:

> "The only man who could ordinarily discredit a scholar within the educational system was the Shaikh al-Islam in each community. So it is for this reason that the Shaikh al-Islam of Istanbul was proclaimed Shaikh al-Islam of the entire empire. The independence of the scholarly community was being continually sapped from the time of Nizam al-Mulk onwards by the steady expansion of official patronage, yet it remained at least theoretically independent until the creation of the Ottoman Shaikh al-Islam. After that the Ottoman government possessed for the first time the authority to control the entire religious hierarchy since every religious appointee had first to pass through the educational system. The independent scholarly tradition had finally succumbed."[313]

That may overstate the loss of power by the *ulama*, as we'll see in the late Ottoman Empire. But I think it is fair to say that the machinery of the state had grown more powerful than that of the *ulama*, even if the scholars remained custodians of the knowledge and law necessary for the state to function. Both the state and the *ulama* were now guardians of a very strong and coherent theory of law, but a theory with a weakness in its ability to assimilate change.

How, or why, is one to lightly change what God has ordered, especially when it has been around so long without any apparent necessity for change? "This rigidity showed its serious character in the nineteenth century when Islam felt the impact of the West and extensive adjustments became necessary. These could only be made with great difficulty."[314]

Unchanging Law on the Eve of Great Change

Bernard Lewis, in his *Jews of Islam*, relates events illustrating the difficulty of confronting change within the Islamic tradition.[315] The difficulty grew with trade and commercial relations carried on across the narrow strait between British Gibraltar and North Africa. Some of the population of Gibraltar was Jewish, and from time to time a British subject of Jewish background would show up in Morocco. To the Moroccan authorities, these were Jews, not British subjects. To the British, they were British subjects.

The British authorities in Gibraltar thought that jurisdiction – the right to say what the law was and to apply it to an individual, was based on notions like national boundaries, or national territory, or citizenship, ideas bound up in geography, or place of birth. Therefore, a Jew living in Gibraltar was a subject of the Crown, even if he went to Morocco on business. The Moroccans used the traditional Islamic rule to define jurisdiction. That centered on confessionalism – of what religion was one a member? Confessionalism was closely linked (if not sometimes confused) with ethnicity or race. Thus a Jew from Gibraltar was a Jew, and subject to the Islamic laws regulating non-Muslim *dhimmi*. He was not British.

It hadn't always been that way in the West. Remember when the students of Bologna had been excited to get the same kind of legal protection at university that the clerics had? And what of the times when Jews were the money lenders for petty European lords, since Christians were forbidden to engage in lending and taking interest? Recall that the Jews were expelled from Spain in 1492, and accepted by the Sultan in Istanbul, so that the Islamic world gained a rich heritage from Sephardic Jews and their Ladino-language literature. Law in the West had focused on religion and status to decide which body of law applied to an individual, but on the eve of modern times, Western society had substantially rejected the confessional system of jurisdiction in favor of a territorial jurisdiction.[316]

Islamic law, on the other hand, hadn't changed its basis of jurisdiction over an individual during this time. Some Muslim states, such as Morocco, regarded treaties they had made with Christian governments as applying only to Christians, and since Jews were by definition not Christian, then they were not *musta'min,* but instead were classified as *dhimmi*. It couldn't *be* any clearer than that. Let's pull this confusing statement apart.

A *dhimmi* within Islam, since almost the very beginning, was a non-Muslim protected person subject to certain restrictions, (like special taxes, and in some places and times, especially as Islamic states grew weaker, to sumptuary laws – laws requiring different *dhimmi* communities to wear distinctive clothing and colors). *Musta'min,* on the other hand, were foreigners of allowable types temporarily present in Muslim lands, like merchants, messengers, or students.

The shocking claim to the authorities in Morocco that a Jew wasn't a Jew first, but a British subject first, flew in the face of a thousand-year-old classification by religion, a confessional classification substantially abandoned by the West as legal systems diverged following the Papal Revolution, and as the Church legal system withered away. How could a Muslim accept this foreign (British) view of jurisdiction and the Jew? That would mean that Islam no longer meant what it had.

A Growing Gap between Islamic and Western Ideas on the Eve of Modern Times

So why was modernity less shocking in the West than in the Islamic world? One answer given too easily and quickly, as if it actually explains anything, is that the West is at fault for the shock to Islamic society, since the West came as a colonizer and oppressor. Yes, there is truth in that answer, but not enough. Since the Middle Ages, a gap had developed between the Islamic lands of the Middle East and the West. After the *Mihna*, and its residual effects in the area of thought and knowledge, growth had slowed in the East, while the West had grown progressively more free to modernize.

Modernity, first of all, is Western. The economic, political, and military strength, the technology of the new industrial world, and relatively free and creative growth of knowledge, and organizational structures and abilities (and desire) necessary to effectively apply those strengths on a global basis converged in the West. Don't mistake what I am saying as an argument for some sort of Western superiority. It is simply that the West assembled all of these potentials and tools into a single coherent culture first, even if others had some or all of these ideas before the West. It is relatively easy to scan through history and find superior technologies, organizations, political and military forces, etc., in other parts of the world, but other parts of the world did not use them in a united fashion before the West did, or to the extent the West has in modern times.

Political, technological and economic strength, and the rest, were only the tools which enabled the West to shape a world which it calls modern. The tools themselves, and the abilities and desires to use them, were shaped by the ideas and assumptions shown in the history of the West. Modernity then, at its simplest form is the most recent stage of growth out of what has gone before, and that means those Western ideas and assumptions, whether spread intentionally or without their Western proponents even realizing what they were spreading throughout the world.

We in the West regard the shape of modern life as normative. It's the way things are, or at least the way things ought to be. We rarely question, or even think about the historical process and choices which resulted in modern Western society. That is a great mistake. After all, as the global majority culture (in influence, not in population) that has shaped a comfortable set of social rules, what need is there to examine them again? Do we realize that those assumptions may be recognized by others as a challenge or an attack on the way they live?

It seems natural that a dominant, or majority, culture (colonial, economic, or military authority) would impose the assumptions of that dominant culture on the minority, or weaker culture. Sometimes this is done because it is thought that changing the ideas of society will be best for the weak or minority culture. Sometimes it is done without any conscious thought at all. However it happens, it did happen as the ideas of the dominant Western culture were spread over the globe as modern times began.

That is why a Jew as *dhimmi* versus a Jew as British subject in Morocco seemed so outmoded or backward. The West had forgotten by that time that it used to think the same way and have similar legal rules. Evolution and growth in religious, legal, and social institutions, and divergence away from one another, had become the norm in the West through the great struggle of the Papal Revolution and after.

From the Middle Ages on, the West had been accustomed to thinking of Church and State as if they had always been two. The West had forgotten the more unitary expression of Church and State power in society in Byzantium, and the struggle in Western Europe for that same united society, culminating in the separation of roles in the Papal Revolution and after. It was difficult for the West to comprehend that "in classical Arabic and in the other classical languages of Islam, there are no pairs of terms corresponding to 'lay' and 'ecclesiastical,' 'spiritual' and 'temporal,' 'secular' and 'religious,' because these pairs of words express a Christian dichotomy that has no equivalent in the world of Islam."[317]

As modern times came, how would the Islamic world of the Middle East and North Africa react to these new ideas and powers? Was a Jew to be a Jew or a British citizen? Could law be something separate from religion? Was knowledge a servant of the established order, or a challenge to that order? What of all the new technology? The varying reactions within the Islamic world to alien Western cultures and ideas is the underlying structure of today's problems, and what the West must seek to understand. It is what the balance of this work discusses.

Chapter 8 - Challenges and Defensive Reactions

When was the last time your homeland was invaded? When was the last time territory and population of your country was stripped away by a stronger neighbor? How often do you even think about this subject? For someone from the U.S., Japanese presence on a few remote islands far West of Alaska in World War II, or the British landing and attempt to torch the White House in 1814, are curiosities of history. But in majority Islamic cultures, invasions and losses were a constant threat and reality as modern times approached.

The Invasion by the West

After the wars between the Ottomans and Safavid Persians had subsided in the mid-1600s, a period of relative peace set in, but:

> "This period, too, ends with yet another invasion, this time from Europe. The kingdoms of Islam had tried several times to conquer Europe—the Arabs in Spain and Sicily, the Islamized Tatars of the Golden Horde in Russia, the Ottoman Turks in southeastern Europe, twice reaching as far as the walls of Vienna. All three attempts to dominate Europe failed, and as the Europeans expelled the invaders and conquerors, they themselves, in turn, began to follow their former masters into their own homelands. The Spaniards and the Portuguese, and later the other maritime peoples of Western Europe, pursued the Moors to Morocco and then, sailing around Africa, carried their war against the Muslims to south Asia and the southern approaches to the Middle East. The Austrians and Hungarians, recovering from their defeats, began to push the Ottomans back through the

Balkans toward Constantinople. The Russians, having freed Moscow from the "Tatar yoke," embarked on a vast series of conquests that took them southward to the Black Sea, the Caucasus, and the Caspian and thus to the northern approaches of the Middle Eastern heartlands of Islam."[318]

Are you feeling surrounded yet? A little defensive at the relentless advance of the West? If not, go back and read that passage again. Try hard to put yourself in that frame of mind.

Eugene Rogan, in his recent *The Arabs – A History*, starts one chapter with a retelling of the appearance of the French fleet off Egypt's shore in 1798, and the invasion by Napoleon's army. The rapid advance on Cairo, the battle South of the city, and the near total destruction of the Mamluk cavalry by an infantry force with modern rifles, firing, moving, and killing with precision and efficiency, was something alien and frightening – to say nothing of the modern French culture of the people who arrived after the army.[319]

Tamim Ansaray picks up this theme as well, in his book *Destiny Disrupted: A History of the World Through Islamic Eyes*. Invasions like the Crusades, and the even greater disaster for the Islamic heartlands of the Mongols and their sack of Baghdad in 1258, had caused struggle and reaction within Islamic society. In early modern times defeat appeared again, and "...the question arose now, as it had in the wake of the Mongol holocaust: if the triumphant expansion of the Muslim project proved the truth of the revelation, what did the impotence of Muslims in the face of these new foreigners signify about the faith?"[320]

Abdel Rahman Munif's novel *Cities of Salt,* set in a fictional Middle Eastern country which sounds a lot like Saudi Arabia (but of course is not, though the book is banned there), is painful to read as it recounts Arabic and Western cultures misunderstanding one another completely. It describes the dislocation and bewilderment of a traditional society invaded by modern technology and organization in the search for oil in the early 1900s. There is no escape, no going back to the old ways, only the struggle to adapt, or fail.

It is no accident that all of these authors, and many more, touch on the same themes of military defeat, loss of territory, dislocation of peoples, the shock of an alien Western culture, and the question of what it all means for the community of Islam in modern times. How to respond to the modern challenge of the West is still the object of social debate and strife throughout the Islamic world today. The way that Islam began and grew, how the *ummah* responded to the challenges of governing and interpreting Islamic society in the *Mihna*, and the resolution of those questions in the aftermath of the *Mihna*, all shaped the ability of Islamic society to respond to these new challenges from the West.

Defeat in battle, and victory as well, were nothing new in the history of Islamic armies. There had been battles between Islamic armies in several early civil wars, losses to the Byzantines as far back as the unsuccessful siege of Constantinople in 674-678, crushing victories over the Byzantines like Manzikert in 1071, victories and losses as greedy Europeans and crusader armies were driven out of their little kingdoms at the Eastern end of the Mediterranean, devastating invasions by Genghis Khan, and later Tamerlane, final victory over the Byzantines in 1453, steady expansion Westward and Northward for two centuries through the Balkans, and Ottoman attempts on Vienna culminating in a catastrophic loss in the 1683 siege.

But all of these battles had been between equals. There was grudging respect, even admiration, for great generalship by the enemy. The weapons and technology used were more or less equal. Sometimes the technology on the Muslim side was even better, as the Sultan was quicker to adopt artillery than his Byzantine foes, and used it with great effect to batter down the walls of Constantinople. But if the West were to develop technology and adopt advanced arms faster than Islamic society, then the Ottomans as foremost power in the Islamic world could only expect more, and sharper, defeats.

That is exactly what happened as the West grew more powerful with the approach of modern times. After the failure of the 1683 siege of Vienna, the West almost immediately went on the offense, with Buda and Pest lost to the Ottomans by 1686, along with Hungary itself. Only a few years later, the Venetians took the Southern portion of Greece – the Peloponnese. A series of disastrous wars with Russia was fought through the 1700s.

The pace of industrial and technical development in the West, and competition in warfare, raised Western standards more quickly than those in Islamic societies. Lacking modern technology and training, the Mamluk cavalary was destroyed outside Cairo in Napoleon's 1798 invasion. The Greeks gained their own independence in 1832 (with Western help). The Serbians in a series of uprisings finally gained their own independence in 1867. Wars in Bosnia, Montenegro, Albania, and Bulgaria, and finally Romania throughout the 1800s only resulted in more loss.

It was becoming obvious to the Ottomans that something had to be done. The French invasion and its aftermath incited one initial reaction in that part of the empire. Napoleon had better things to do in Europe, and the British navy made supporting his soldiers in Egypt all but impossible, so in a few years the French were forced to withdraw. That triggered a local power struggle as the Mamluk notables tried to regain their positions. Muhammad Ali, the young leader of the Ottoman Albanian regiment, schemed for power, eventually slaughtering the Mamluk leaders. Muhammad Ali understood that to win, he had to use European technology, organization, and ideas. Naturally, those things must first be applied to the military.[321]

What Muhammad Ali created as a result was the first peasant army (Nizami army) in the Islamic world. The Sultan in Constantinople had tried a tentative experiment with this earlier, but the Janissaries, privileged traditional warriors, were too powerful for him, so that experiment had failed. In Egypt, where the power of the traditional warrior class had been broken, the experiment worked. Muhammad Ali began to win, and win again, and moved East and North around the end of the Mediterranean.

In Istanbul, the government watched Muhammad Ali's progress with alarm. Beside the threat to the throne itself, though, there was something else: The growing realization that the Ottoman empire as a whole had to develop technology and learn, or face continuing defeat by the West and Western technology. If the career of Muhammad Ali is traced through his victories in Greece, and up through Syria, into Western-central Turkey, uncomfortably close to Istanbul, it isn't hard to imagine that but for the intervention of the Western powers and the 1840 London Convention for Pacification of the Levant, Muhammad Ali might have been a very successful modernizer and settled himself on the throne in Constantinople.[322]

But the realization that change was necessary was not yet fully accepted in most of the Ottoman empire, or the Islamic world of the time. The dominant force in that world was still the Ottoman Empire. It was creaky – and growing more so - and wildly inefficient at times, with power distributed among a wide variety of local rulers. But slow and poorly directed as it might have seemed to onlookers, it was in a fashion stable. So long as society was stable, the opportunity for change which Muhammad Ali had seized in Egypt couldn't come to society at large, or at least couldn't come as fast as would-be reformers hoped.

Initial Reaction of the Ottoman Empire – Adoption of Technology and Learning

With each new defeat, displaced people moved South and East out of the Balkans. Rich estates and well-watered agricultural lands were lost, and the borders of hostile powers moved a little closer. In Istanbul, pressure began building to implement reforms to save the state. In addition to coveting the latest and best in military technology and training, the Ottoman government tried hard to save the state through a variety of other reforms. Modern history survey courses in the West that label the empire the "sick man of Europe" obscure just how hard the Ottoman government tried to reform and preserve the established social order. Reform to preserve was the first, and most natural, reaction to the challenge of the West in most of the Islamic world.

Muhammad Ali had been impressed by French technology, but not particularly by French people or their culture. The Ottomans in the capital felt the same way. There was widespread acceptance of the idea that while the barbarians had good weapons and technology, their culture itself wasn't necessary, as the rooted and local Islamic culture was clearly superior. For those paying close attention, Muhammad Ali proved that adoption of Western methods, technology, and arms was possible without taking on the culture of their providers. Even more, those successes proved that Islamic rulers could adapt and succeed under the right conditions. Change though, required more than just purchasing weapons.

But change was hard, even in an area like printing, which might be thought neutral. In 1727 during the "Tulip Era" of tentative reform, the printer İbrāhīm Müteferriḳa had persuaded the Grand Vizier, who in turn persuaded the Sheik al-Islam, to issue a *fatwa* allowing Müteferriḳa's printing press in Istanbul to produce works in Arabic. Sultan Ahmet III confirmed the ruling with his own order on July 5, 1727. Permission was conditioned on no Koran, or other religious work, being printed.[323] With that condition, "all opposition ceased. Apparently those who opposed printing saw that they had little to lose if religious books – including, of course, legal works – were exempted, since material on subjects other than religion was not considered worth serious attention."[324]

The press was open until 1743, when it closed for almost forty years, due to resurgent opposition. It had managed to produce eleven histories, three works on language, and three on useful sciences: A work on modernization, one on magnetism, and one on geography.[325] A work by Müteferriḳa himself dated 1732 justified the existence and work of the press, arguing that "the Ottomans could survive only if they borrowed not only the military sciences but also the geographic knowledge and governmental techniques developed in the modern world."[326]

Some within the Ottoman government agreed that more knowledge was necessary, so in 1826 the Ottomans sent a mission to the West to study languages and sciences and to bring some learning home. This wasn't anything new, since as far back as Suleyman Kanuni in the late 1500s Ottomans had from time to time studied the West. There isn't much doubt though, that due to European technological and military successes, the need to learn was felt more sharply than at the time of the great Suleyman. A young Egyptian scholar, Al-Tahtawi, from Al-Azhar was one of the members of the mission.[327]

He wrote on many points of French culture. He analyzed the Constitution, and thought that if adopted it could make the Ottoman society successful. Admittedly though, he said that most of it was not from the Koran or *Sunna*. Ideas such as freedom of expression, separation of powers, an opportunity for the poor to advance, limits on the power of nobles and ruler himself – these were all very challenging ideas. On his return to Egypt, Al-Tahtawi was placed in charge of a translation bureau, and eventually published his observations as a book.

Printing in Muhammad Ali's Egypt was promoted vigorously. One study notes publication of four hundred and seventy-two different works in five hundred and seventy editions in Egypt between 1822 and 1851.[328] Presses that quickly rivaled that in Istanbul were established and run by the school of medicine, the school of artillery, the ministry of military affairs and the school of engineering, among others.[329] Muhammad Ali saw education as the key to success and the future, and pushed his own children hard to acquire it. He "had an enthusiasm for education that verged on being a fetish."[330]

Traditional and traditionally-educated scholars were resistant to some of the new ideas. Al-Jabarti and others at the time of Al-Tahtawi had attacked and disproven the idea of equality of men that Napoleon had announced when he led his armies into Egypt. Willingness to accept such a patently absurd notion hadn't grown in wider society since that time.[331] The *ulama* in Istanbul had grudgingly accepted the use of the press, even breaking their own limitation by publishing a work with an Islamic subject in 1801, and a steady trickle of similar works thereafter.[332] But just how far could one go with these strange new European ideas?

Printing even traditional Islamic texts instead of foreign matter could be a problem. "The problem was that printing attacked the very heart of Islamic systems for the transmission of knowledge; it attacked what was understood to make knowledge trustworthy, what gave it value, what gave it authority."[333] The *ijaza*, the permission to teach a work given by a scholar personally to a student has already been mentioned. The required oral recitation and approval by the *ijaza* enabled scholars to ensure that knowledge had been transmitted correctly and would be taught correctly in the future. The availability of a plentiful supply of printed books that a student could read in private upset the traditional method of checking understanding and compliance with accepted doctrines. It disrupted the geneology of knowledge[334] and made illegitimacy possible. That worried the *ulama*.[335]

The *ulama* tried hard to hold on to their monopoly on the flow and content of knowledge. Even after the advent of printing, they still controlled libraries and storage of books, the guild of booksellers, and the scribes or copyists. They could choose to release for printing what they thought most appropriate, such as commentaries, works on logic and rhetoric, and of course on law. In places like Egypt where printing had a higher degree of acceptance, even works on mysticism within Islam were published.[336] "Muslims came to adopt printing only when they felt Islam itself was at stake and print was a necessary weapon in the defence of the faith."[337]

Western knowledge was to be held at arms-length, while the Ottoman Empire selectively incorporated the learning that could help it strengthen and save itself. Military organization and equipment were obvious choices as well as their adjuncts

laborers. Ottoman and loosely or former Ottoman territories sank deeper into debt.[343]

The loans went on. So did the spending, and so did the mounting interest. The Ottoman government desperately tried to reform itself. The budget process was overhauled, but sharp-eyed Western auditors still saw the budget truthfully as nothing more than a guess about revenues, and then another guess about expenditures. A bank (after several failures) was launched in 1863 under Western governance to act essentially as agent for the government, both for dealings in the West, and to fulfill collection and payment (treasury) functions within the Ottoman Empire. None of it worked.

Finally, and in desperation, the government caved in to the pressure. Sultan Abdülhamid II gave the Decree of *Muharrem* in 1881, establishing the Ottoman Public Debt Administration (OPDA). The OPDA was run by a committee of Western representatives, and until the debts to the Western powers were paid, was entitled to receive and disburse "the revenues from the salt and tobacco monopolies, the stamps and spirits tax, the fish tax, the silk tithe of certain districts, the Bulgaria tribute, the revenue of Eastern Rumelia and the surplus of the Cyprus revenue" all together about one-third of state revenues.[344] This lasted even during the first World War, up until the Republic was founded. The OPDA provided stability and continuing access to credit markets, while at the same time protecting the creditors – at the price of a substantial blow to Ottoman sovereignty.

What may be most important in this area of economics is a failure of intellectual vision. Throughout the 1700s and 1800s, Islamic intellectuals tended to blame economic decline on a failure of technology and weapons – holding fast to the idea that adopting Western technology alone could save the state, while overlooking, or ignoring if they saw it, the new economic ideas and institutions which the West was using to fuel its success.[345] Think again of the resistance by the *ulama* to foreign learning, and the painfully slow process of adopting modern printing. A conservative outlook only willing to look for cures in the past glories of Islamic civilization couldn't remedy ills that demanded vision for the future.

Western Expansion Continues and Unrest Rises

Meanwhile, European expansion into Ottoman territory had continued.[346] It was relatively easy for the European powers to colonize North Africa. These lands were a short voyage South from Europe, and a much longer voyage from Istanbul to the South and West, and with the increase in the length of that voyage, the Sultan's power diminished. By 1870, France had planted nearly 250,000 European settlers in Algeria. It then annexed Algeria and gave it parliamentary representation, (except for the "subjects" living there, who were not citizens). England was never able to successfully disentangle itself from Egypt after the time of Muhammad Ali, even if it wanted to do so. As plans for and eventual construction of the Suez canal got under way in mid-century, England realized just how important Egypt could be as a link to India. In 1882 England occupied Egypt, and didn't leave until after World War II.

These French and British actions sparked the race to acquire the rest of North Africa, as each European power feared losing out to its rivals. There were long negotiations over just what to do with Morocco, since citizens of France and Spain were both doing business there, and German firms were increasingly involved. The Fez Convention of 1912 eventually awarded a protectorate to France. The French had taken Tunisia the year before, spurred on by competition with Italy, which imagined repossessing ancient imperial lands. The Italians took Libya in 1911. Their navy shelled Beirut, and assisted with occupying the Dodacanese islands, off the Southwestern coast of mainland Turkey. In sum, the whole coast of North Africa was under European control, either directly or through protectorates and local rulers. Those parts of the Ottoman Empire in the Western and Central Mediterranean were lost.

The Ottoman territories in Europe were also in turmoil, as mentioned. The great idea of the 1800s – nationalism – was gripping Europe. Balkan independence movements were often stirred by imperial Austrian and Russian to meet their own strategic desires. England had historically wanted to keep the Ottoman Empire together, but the Gladstone government turned against this, and with the other powers began to think about breaking up the Ottoman Empire. Toward the close of a long century of defeat, the Berlin treaty of 1878 approved independence for several substantial states, and the Ottomans lost two-fifths of their imperial territory and one-fifth of the Empire's population.

Even in territories not lost to the foreign powers, the Ottoman population was stirred up, as long-established ways of treating non-Muslim minorities were challenged or overturned. As Islam had spread, large native populations of Christians fell within its boundaries. Although forced conversions did occur, there was at least an attempt to acknowledge the Koranic injunction about not using force in matters of religion. Christians and Jews could keep their religions, provided they paid special taxes. There was continuous pressure to convert, given these taxes and other disabilities (e.g., occasional mob attacks if times were hard, or a ruler needed a distraction from his own shortcomings), but on the whole, these minorities were probably better treated within Islamic society than were non-Christians in Medieval Europe.[347] These protected non-Muslims were known as *dhimmi*, "a development of the Arab practice whereby a strong tribe 'protected' weaker tribes and groups."[348]

The Ottomans usually termed groups of these protected people a *millet*, (sometimes translated as "nation") a religious affiliation that usually corresponded to an ethnic grouping. *Millets* included people like the Jews, Armenians, Greek Orthodox and Syrian Orthodox. The *millets* did have some privileges in matters of marriage, inheritance, and other legal issues that were governed by the religious law of the group in question, and not the Islamic law of the majority Ottoman population.

But what is very clear is that these people were not Muslims. They were something other, and were defined that way by law. I think it is fair to say that for a nation, it is easy to be tolerant when strong, but harder when weak or threatened. As the Ottomans (hence Islam) grew weaker in comparison to the West, more repression took place. Any history of these years recounts riots and killings of different Christian or Jewish groups in the lands around the Mediterranean.

As Western nations moved into the Middle East and North Africa for trade and colonization, they naturally took what they viewed as oppressed and threatened co-religionists under protection of their own laws. That only made things worse. The Westerners themselves were business and economic winners under the system of capitulations, which gave them a lighter tax regime than the Muslim Ottoman population at large, and hit traders and commerce particularly hard. If convinced that an Armenian or Greek, who already had a religious affinity with the West, was also entitled to a consul's status, or citizenship, then former Ottoman subjects were converted into privileged Westerners overnight.

This happened to significant enough numbers of Ottoman minority populations that Muslim Ottomans could not help but notice it. As *millet*-member businesses performed better, "the millet system became a mechanism for exacerbating existing fault lines in Ottoman society."[349] Ottoman Muslims thought that the balance of how things ought to be had been distorted. While protected as *dhimmi*, there had been a Muslim feeling of superiority and a more full set of legal rights enjoyed than those given to the *millets* – and now that had changed.

There was naturally resentment about the capitulations and unfair tax treatment, but to have that tax regime actually discriminate against the dominant culture within the empire – unheard of! Resentment easily turned to outright hostility. That hostility was even further fueled by the Western supply of evil inventions like the "blood libel", (in which Jews were said to mix the blood of Christian infants into matzoh for the Passover Holiday), quickly seized upon by some within Islamic society.[350] Taken together, foreign interventions to protect minorities, granting of citizenship, tax-favored status, a claim of equality to Ottoman Muslims (if not even superiority), and the growing national aspirations of the *millets* were yet another hard blow to the established imperial order.

Military reforms hadn't reversed a steady trend of defeats. Economic reforms hadn't worked, and temporary borrowing hadn't helped - taking loans to buy guns or steamships only dug the pit of debt deeper. Restive minority populations complaining of inequality to the Western nations only invited interventions. At last, reforms across a much broader span of social life, through change in law and governance were also tried.

Reform in the Legal System and Constitutional Structure of the Ottoman Empire

The Tanzimat is usually treated as having begun with the 1839 Gülhane Rescript, ending in 1876, although at least two proceeding Sultans had made substantial reform attempts.[351] Maybe it is most accurate to say that a fruit of those reform efforts finally ripened in 1839 at Gülhane, part of the Sultan's grand palace complex in Istanbul. That proclamation stated that good administration and the fortunes of the empire could be restored by reforms in three major areas.

First, there was a guarantee "insuring to our subjects perfect security for life, honor, and fortune," and text explaining that if a man were secure in his life and honor, there would be no reason for rebellions or disturbances. Similarly, if property were secure, then men would be free to work for the interests of their ruler and country, instead of worrying about loss of their possessions. A related point was the "regular and fixed assessment of the taxes," and abolishment of the system of tax farming (shortly thereafter reversed, as we've seen). This would remove the "violent and avaricious passions" from single persons in the process of collection of taxes and would be fair for all.

Reducing the terms of military service to four or five years, and fixing the uptake of new troop levies more fairly from district to district was the next subject. This would ensure that the needs of agriculture and industry from province to province were not disastrously affected. The councils and assemblies of the Sultan, including those of the military hierarchy, were to meet to frame the laws and procedures to carry out these aims. "In short, without the several laws, the necessity for which has just been described, there can be neither strength, nor riches, nor happiness, nor tranquility for the empire; it must, on the contrary, look for them in the existence of these new laws."[352]

Interestingly, this was all followed by promises of criminal conviction and punishment for any official failing to carry out these reforms. Bribery and favoritism were condemned, and in their place, a declaration of a sufficient salary for public servants.

In 1847 a new system of Commercial Courts was established, due to continuing pressures from the Western powers. But was it really possible or acceptable to establish secular, civil courts outside the jurisdiction of the Sheikhu'l-islam? And there was a related problem: What sort of law would these courts apply? If the traditional Islamic legal framework and substance weren't good enough, could they both be borrowed from the West?[353] Cevdet Paşa summed up the problem when he commented on the proposed adoption of the French Civil Code in 1855:

> "With the increase in the number of Europeans coming to Turkey, and with the increase of contacts with them because of the Crimean War, the scope of trade widened. The commercial courts became unable to deal with the commercial lawsuits arising every day. The foreigners did not like to go to the şeriat courts. The inacceptability of the testimony of non-Muslims against Muslims and of Musta'man (non-Muslim foreigners) against dhimmi (non-Muslim Ottoman subjects) in the şeriat courts became very annoying to the Europeans and they

objected to the trial of the Christians in the şeriat courts. Thus, certain persons took up the idea of translating French civil codes into Turkish for judgment in the nizami courts. This idea was not acceptable because changing the basic laws of a nation would entail its destruction. The ulema believed that those who had gone astray to hold such Frankish ideas were unbelievers. The Franks, on the other hand, used to say 'bring forth your code; let us see it and make it known to our subjects.'"[354]

The establishment of the Divan-i Ahkam-i Adliye (Ministry of Justice) in 1868 served as a legitimate reason for considering civil, secular courts, and Cevdet Paşa seemed the perfect person to deal with this difficult task. He had been a member of the *ulama*, but left to become a secular government minister. He turned to the authority of the Diwan-i Daf'i Mazalim (a special purpose court – one could almost say a limited constitutional court – that existed to give opinions on the acts of the government toward its people). It found and stated that secular courts were compatible and necessary to Islam. The next step was to codify civil law, but according to what precepts, what models?

Cevdet Paşa did not support a wholesale borrowing of the French Code, nor a rejection either, but a middle road. The government asked him to begin the codification of the *shari'a*. The partial codification of the *shari'a* which resulted was called the *Mecelle*. It cannot be properly called a civil code, because a civil code within the Western legal tradition is thought of as a comprehensive whole, containing important basic subject areas of the law like marriage and family law. It was precisely the parts of the *shari'a* setting out family, marriage, and inheritance law that were left out of the *Mecelle*. It did cover the areas of obligations, civil procedure, and contracts, and for the content of these areas drew from Hanafite *fiqh* – the legal jurisprudence of the Hanfi school within Sunni Islam, the predominate school within the Ottoman Empire.

This was legal reform treading carefully. On one hand, the sensitive matters of family life were left where they had customarily resided – the *shari'a* tradition defined and made by the scholars. That tradition was augmented by the framers of the *Mecelle*, who followed the work of earlier Ottoman legal scholars, and compiled what was more a summary of the existing customary law than a code in the Western sense. On the other hand, the areas of commercial life where new challenges were presented by the West were (following the *shari'a*) cast in the mold of a new code, the type of presentation of law expected by the Western merchants and government officials.

Since the law was now rationalized and summarized in a set of books, anybody with at least a minimal level of literacy could go read it. Monopoly of knowledge in the scholars was lost. Probably most importantly, it was the executive power of government issuing this code, reversing the role of lawgiver. The scholars were of mixed opinion. Some didn't like the *Mecelle*, (the Sheikhu'l-islam's opposition brought work on it to an end in 1870) and some assisted with it, but it isn't clear whether as a class they recognized the gravity of this new legal development.

While the substance of the law might not have changed in any earth-shattering ways, such that merchants, judges, and monied classes weren't unduly disturbed, the larger constitutional structure of boundaries between things sacred and things secular, arguably did move. The scholars, as guardians of a legal tradition formed of long custom, set forth in many hundreds of treatises and commentaries requiring expert knowledge to plumb their depths, ended up with a weakened door-keeping responsibility.

The code *did* leave some areas within the traditional *shari'a* framework, and choosing Hanafi interpretations would have been thought appropriate by the scholars. Perhaps that was enough to placate the most upset. The real damage, though, was hidden more deeply: "Once ultimate law-making power came to be located within the state, the scholars lost the theoretical basis for their position as the ultimate source of legitimation for the entire constitutional order. Once legal decision making shifted away from scholar-judges, their practical basis for providing legitimacy to the entire system was eroded as well."[355]

A variety of other reform measures were implemented in these years as well, all copying Western institutions with the aim of unifying the empire: Post offices, a census, national identity cards, establishment of Ministries of Health, and Education, and the first modern (Western-style) Universities, an Academy of Sciences, even modern steamboat ferry service in the Istanbul area, and many others.

The stubborn and perennial problem of *millets* was addressed in several ways: A national anthem was adopted, as well as a national flag. A common citizenship was decreed by law for all, regardless of religion or ethnicity (usually only two ways of saying the same thing). In 1856 the promises of equality in the Gülhane Rescript were addressed again, in the "Hatt-i Hümayun" (which means simply a command of the Sultan, of which there were thousands). This one of 1856 is famous though, since it specifically promised again, equality in education, government appointments, and the administration of justice to all, regardless of faith.[356]

The 1876 Constitution was another step toward the ideas of Modernity.[357] It had a form of parliamentary system, but one working essentially on borrowed powers of the Sultan, not from powers derived from the nation. It provided for elected Members, and a higher house appointed by the Sultan. The first several articles state very strongly the sovereignty of the Sultan: Article 3 "Ottoman sovereignty, which includes in the person of the Sovereign the Supreme Caliphat of Islam, belongs to the eldest Prince of the House of Osman…" or in Article 4, "He is the sovereign and padişah (emperor) of all the Ottomans." The Sultan, among many other substantial powers in Article 7, had the power to call or dissolve the Parliament.

Some provisions sound very progressive to the modern ear: Article 8 said in essence that being Ottoman wasn't a matter of faith, and Article 11 promised the free exercise of faith, even while stating that Islam was the State religion. Article 17 stated that all Ottomans were equal before the law, and anyone could hold public office, so long as they spoke Turkish (Article 18). Security of real and personal property was guaranteed (Article 21), and confiscation of property was prohibited (Article 24).

Other articles seemed more an affirmation of the status quo: Art. 27. "His Majesty may appoint as Grand Vizier and Şeyhü'l-İslam whomsoever he confides in, and thinks right to nominate to those posts." Note that this article allowed appointment of a Şeyhü'l-İslam, but had no description of that office nor its powers. Traditional legal functions and offices of the scholars were to continue, in Article 87, which stated that "Affairs touching the Şeriat are tried by the tribunals of the Şeriat. The judgment of civil affairs appertains to the civil tribunals."

While this may, with wishful thinking, look like the start of a constitutional monarchy, it was not. The Constitution itself stated that the Sultan-Caliph was supreme, and not under law. And make no mistake, the Sultan was still in control. As Article 54 provided, a bill could be made in either higher or lower house, but "[t]hough passing both Chambers, no Bill will become law until it has been sanctioned by the Imperial İrade [order]." The Sultan, Abdul Hamid II, confirmed that he was still in control by closing the Parliament shortly after its second term began in 1878, using social unrest in the Balkans as his excuse. The Parliament next met thirty years later, in 1908.

By 1908 the Ottoman Empire was in enough trouble that Enver and other energetic young Ottoman officers could force Parliament to open again, and force changes in the Constitution in 1909. For example, Article 3 now read "The Imperial Ottoman sovereignty, which carries with it the Supreme Caliphate of Islam, falls to the eldest Prince of the House of Osman, according to the rule established *ab antiquo*. On his accession the Sultan shall swear before Parliament, or if Parliament is not sitting, at its first meeting, to respect the visions of the Şeriat and the Constitution, and to be loyal to the country and the nation."

In Article 7, the "consent of Parliament is required for the conclusion of Treaties which concern peace, commerce, the abandonment or annexation of territory, or the fundamental or personal rights of Ottoman subjects, or which involve expenditure on the part of the State..." If it were felt that any decision of the Council of Ministers, on the other hand, needed Imperial assent, Article 28 stated that that assent "shall" be given.

Parliament now met without being summoned by the Sultan (Article 41), and the role of Ministers was strengthened, and made necessary, in approving decisions within their areas of responsibility. (Article 30) Bills could become law even if rejected by the Sultan, so long as a two-thirds majority approved them after his initial rejection.

The Failure of Conservative Reform Measures

But even as the Ottoman Constitution moved toward a more modern form, we must remember that the Ottoman reforms were at the end of the day conservative in nature. They aimed at keeping Islamic society in its accustomed shape, while borrowing technology, arms and arms training, constitutional and legal forms, and other expertise from the West. Reform and centralization would make the government stronger. A policy of Ottomanism, the treatment of different *millets* equally in areas like education and government service, would bind all subjects together peacefully under the Sultan.

The Ottomans sought to preserve their existing political, social and religious ideas from the challenges and changes of the West by protective reforms. They tried new law codes, even a Constitution like Western powers were drawing up for themselves. They tried declaring equality among subjects to remove the cause of Western interventions. Decreeing equality only seemed to provoke more Western intervention, though.

Of course the conservative elements in the majority Muslim Ottoman population didn't like these reforms. Central government actions provoked them, and sometimes local authorities themselves whipped up the crowds. The Ottomans even tried, especially under Abdul Hamid II (sometimes called "The Red Sultan" by the West) more old-fashioned measures of brutal repression to unify the empire, for example, sponsoring quasi-military operations by Kurds against the Armenians. None of it worked.[358]

All of the reforms had one thing in common: Every time the Ottomans either lost a war, or were faced with overwhelming pressure and threats from the West (economic or military) they tried reform as a way to placate the powers, and remove any excuses for intervention in Ottoman lands and affairs the greedy West might seize upon as a reason to invade and partition. A liberal-secular Turkish professor friend told me some years ago that I must always remember that in Turkey, reform only came as a result of outside pressure. Given the history of this time period, that's a fair assessment.

A book published in 1903, *The Turk and His Lost Provinces*, by a correspondent for The Chicago Record-Herald, set out the accepted wisdom of the West for American readers: The European powers would "compel the Turks to respect their moral, political, and financial obligations." It recognized the competing interests of the great powers in the Balkans and resistance of the Sultan. It predicted that a universal war forecast by Germany's great general Von Moltke might well be fought under the walls of Constantinople, and that his prophecy "is soon to be fulfilled."[359] It was fulfilled, as the Balkans spun out of control and Enver led the Ottoman Turks to seek an alliance with Germany and the Central Powers. I'm not sure that World War I did much to compel the Ottomans to respect their moral, political, and financial obligations, but it did end the Ottoman Empire.

Islamic cultures had three basic reactions to the competition, and outright aggression, of Western imperial powers. The impact of the West on traditional Islamic societies drove them to choose from among these alternatives. The first reaction, chosen by the Ottomans, was to take the technology and a limited amount of learning of the West, and apply them within the legal and constitutional framework of a traditional Islamic society. As we've seen, that didn't work. Could it have? Possibly. This is fertile territory for the writers and dreamers of alternate histories.

The other two reactions are the subject of the next chapters: Some in the Muslim world want only a modern, secular state, with religion restricted to very narrow, private, areas of life, arguing for a society structured like the West, but one that would still be Islamic in culture. The second group is made up of those Muslims who have reacted to the rapid changes of the last century by calling for a wholesale return to the old ways and old days, and rejection of new innovations altogether.

All nations either identifying themselves as Islamic, or where a majority of the population identifies as Muslim, have groups more or less fitting the descriptions of the three different groups above. They vary in size and power from place to place. For example, Turkey has a very strong competition between secular/modern and religious/traditional groups, while Saudi Arabia has a much stronger religious/traditional grouping, and the secular liberal types must remain quiet or face serious state interference, suppression, and penalties. How would these groups meet the challenge of the West?

Chapter 9 - The Reaction Continues: Adoption of Western Ideas

I read John Buchan's *Greenmantle*, an adventure/spy thriller set against the backdrop of World War I, as a 7th or 8th grader, and was gripped by its exotic locations and people. In the book, the Germans planned to exploit an Islamic prophet to raise the East in holy war against the British, and sweep down upon that most cherished of colonial possession – India. The British sent a small team of secret agents to investigate and counter the plot, with action ranging through Eastern Europe into Istanbul, and then East through Turkey toward Erzerum, to an unexpected climax in the face of the advancing imperial Russian army.

David Fromkin's book, *A Peace to End All Peace*, spans the years of World War I and roughly three years afterward. It focuses on the deal making, and political and bureaucratic backgrounds to the peacemaking by the victorious allies after the war had fizzled to an unexpected end. It emphasizes the European impact upon the heartlands of the Islamic world in the Middle East, and the consequences that followed. The future of the Islamic Middle East was determined with finality after the war, but as early as 1914 "largely unnoticed and undiscussed, another major step had been taken. In the 100 days between the outbreak of the German war and the outbreak of the Ottoman war, Britain had overturned the foreign policy of more than a century by abandoning any commitment to the preservation of the territorial integrity of the Ottoman Empire."[360]

That foreign policy, of keeping the Ottoman Empire afloat, had aimed at averting a rush to either colonize the Middle East or exact one-sided trade concessions, either of which might have led to armed conflict between jealous European powers. The Ottoman Empire could serve as a convenient buffer between the conflicting desires of the powers. That policy also anchored the Western end of the "great game" line, along which the British sought to keep the Russian Empire comfortably North of British India and its approaches in Afghanistan and off into Central Asia and Iran.

With the Ottomans now an enemy, the old worries resurfaced with a new face: What if the Ottoman Turks or their German allies moved East aggressively through the relatively undefended territories leading to India? They couldn't be allowed to win there. That of course, led to thoughts of victory and who ought to control those territories after the War. The great game moved from circling and watching to darting in and grabbing whatever a player thought he could take. The secret deal-making got off to a blazing start before the war was even half won, with the treaty negotiated between Britain and France by Sykes and Picot in 1915-16, signed by May 1916.

Back to John Buchan for a moment: He based *Greenmantle* on facts he knew, as I hope this short summary of Fromkin's work has made clear. The British *were* worried about a jihad. The Kaiser's generals *wanted* a *jihad* declared by the Ottomans, and a small band of German agents spent almost a year trekking East through Turkey, Iran, and much of Afghanistan to Kabul, where they intrigued for an uprising against British India. They failed, and no grand *jihad* was declared as part of World War I, but Buchan was right in a way, for a feared result did come from the war's upheaval: Peoples throughout the Islamic world awoke.

There had already been colonization across North Africa. Oppressive trade policies had been forced upon Islamic nations. And now, after the War, the Ottoman Empire, home of the Caliph, and of the Sultan, a mighty empire to which Muslim minorities as far away as India could look, was beaten. The Western powers sat down to formally divide up the Ottoman territories they had already for the most part occupied. French opposition to British interests, and vice versa, and Soviet opposition to British interests, all helped to stir the populations of Arabic, Turkic, and Persian peoples as the Western powers fought diplomatically for territory and advantage.

Britain had made its own position more difficult by wartime politics. In the Arabian Peninsula and elsewhere in the Middle East, Britain had backed Arab uprisings against the Ottomans during the war, sending gold to buy allies and armed opposition to the Ottomans. More important than gold, Britain had made promises to induce action by its wartime Arab allies, and now had to make good on them, in the form of grants of States and Kingships.[361]

The Egyptians had been told by the British that they were now free from the Ottoman yoke, and had been vaguely promised some sort of freedom and independence. When the Egyptians didn't get what they expected to receive after the victory in late 1918 and early 1919, widespread strikes and protests resulted. The British had fully realized during the War how important control over the Suez Canal was to their interests. They tried to negotiate with Egyptian political leaders, but at last grew impatient and asserted control and a formal military occupation over the wishes of the political classes in Egypt.[362]

The British had backed both Hussein and Ibn Saud in the Arabian Peninsula itself. After the war they fought each other, at least initially while still subsidized by Britain. Ibn Saud of course won, and by 1924 expelled his rival from the West coast of the peninsula. Hussein had to have something for his service, and got the newly-created Transjordan (Jordan). Iran had a weak government, and British gold for the reigning dynasty wasn't enough to preserve it when caught between Soviet and British interests. Demands for concessions and control by Great Britain didn't sound as generous as what the Soviets had to offer, and eventually the British wound up helping Reza Khan carry out a coup to keep their position in Iran.

In Syria, Feisal was in charge.[363] An Arab from Mecca, he had led Arab forces in support of the British advance Northward after the retreating Ottomans, and been left in control at the end of the war. No fool, he realized that presence at the peace negotiations was imperative, and angled to elect a Syrian assembly that would legitimize his position. He didn't get the assembly he wanted, but instead one that included members with strong national leanings, who rejected the deal he had struck with the French for a very loose oversight over a Kingdom he would rule.

In fact, they went farther, demanding a greater Syria including most of what is now Lebanon, Israel, and Jordan, rejecting Jewish settlement in Palestine, yet another promise of the British now coming home to roost. In the East, their partisans proposed independence in Mesopotamia, with Feisal's brother on the throne. Britain and France united in their opposition to these plans, and Britain withdrew its support for Feisal, allowing France a free hand in Syria. France easily won against ineptly led forces, and took control of Syria, dividing off Lebanon.

Iraq was in no better condition than Iran or Syria, with competing Arabic and Kurdish tribal groups, to say nothing of the Sunni-Shi'a rift running right through Iraq, as it does to this day. There was widespread though uncoordinated opposition to English rule, and after his ouster from Syria, Britain was compelled to award a kingship to Feisal in Iraq.

The new Afghan government carried on a short military campaign and in 1919 succeeded in winning independence from Great Britain. Their goal had actually been an invasion of India to touch off an uprising among the people, but quick reaction by the British military (including something new – bombing towns from the air) forced back the Afghan forces to their own frontiers. While they might not have succeeded in India, the Afghans had thrown off British claims to control the foreign policy of Afghanistan and taken their own full independence.[364]

The uprisings, diplomatic and military maneuverings by great powers and by a variety of local groups in these areas form a complex and confusing puzzle. The common element is resistance to foreign control, control that lasted until after World War II in most of these lands. The Ottomans had tried hard in the face of internal opposition to borrow selected ideas and technologies of the West to preserve the State, and had failed. The question wasn't any longer the preservation of the State – it had already gone. The question became: On what basis could a new State be founded, strong enough to resist and endure the competing interests, mandates, and controls of the great powers? One answer was given quickly and forcefully in Turkey.

If you Can't Beat Them, Join Them – Republican and Nationalist Turkey

Mustafa Kemal didn't wait for a European decision about the Ottoman Empire or its lost provinces, but as the war ended during a slow retreat from Syria, began to hide away weapons and ammunition in the far corners of Anatolia.[365] He was the only undefeated general officer of note in the Ottoman army, and the hero of the Gallipoli defeat of the British forces. Turkey itself had not been an occupied or colonized land, nor had its armies been conclusively defeated by the West. That left Mustafa Kemal the personal status and opportunity to organize and to declare a national pact to unify a new nation against the plans of the Europeans. "The Middle East was overwhelmed by Europe; self-affirmation in nationalistic terms was part of its defense."[366]

By 1923, Mustafa Kemal had driven the French, the British, and the Greeks out of Turkey, and established a new national capital in Ankara, comfortably out of range of battleship guns, and not inextricably tangled in the Ottoman and Islamic past like Istanbul. Old forms were initially observed – the Sultan was said to be captive in an Istanbul occupied by foreign powers, and the first republican parliament debated separation of Sultanate and Caliphate in traditional Islamic terms.[367]

On November 1, 1922, the Sultanate was abolished; on April 23, 1923, the Republic was proclaimed; on March 3, 1924 the Caliphate was abolished, leaving Mustafa Kemal Atatürk, (the family name he took later) the dominant figure in Turkish politics. "What was his vision? To break the authority of the *ulama* in Turkey, unseat Islam as the arbiter of social life, and authorize a secular approach to the management of society. In the Western context, this makes him a 'moderate.' In the Islamic context, it made him a breathtakingly radical extremist."[368]

The Western ideas of secularization and secularism had both taken steps forward within Ottoman society during the 1800s. Secularization must be understood as a process taking place beyond the control of the individual. The change in individual ideas, attitudes, beliefs, and interests of a person are secularism.[369] An individual may be very pious and religiously observant, yet live in a secularized culture. Reform in the Tanzimat era had found both enthusiastic supporters and determined resistance. "This bifurcation in the response to the Tanzimat served to clarify the problem of the adaptation of Islam to modern civilization – the principal element in the problem of secularization."[370] That adaptation was now forced with vigor and speed.

Turkey's form of secularism, sometimes called Kemalism, is usually described as having six basic qualities: nationalism, laicism, republicanism, populism, statism and reformism.[371] Those meant enormous and jarring changes to many people with traditional Muslim attitudes, even those not considering themselves particulary observant. The acceleration of adoption (or imposition) of these ideas in Turkish society created unrest. Independence Tribunals were created to help settle by a very summary judicial process and execution some of the conservative backlash. In fairness, those Tribunals were abolished as soon as reasonably possible, though strong efforts to change society continued.[372]

A great amount of fundamental legal work was needed to implement the new secular view of State, society, and the individual: A new Constitution, new legal codes, and specific laws crafted to meet immediate needs, "which aim to raise Turkish society above the level of contemporary civilization and to safeguard the secular character of the Republic." They included laws unifying the educational system (1924); mandating the wearing of hats (1925); closing Dervish monasteries and tombs and abolishing associated offices (1925); mandating civil marriage before a government official (1926); adoption of international numerals, and a new alphabet based on a Latin, not Arabic, script (1928); abolition of titles like *Efendi*, *Bey* or *Pasha* (1934); and prohibition of traditional and religious clothing (1934).[373]

Radical Legal and Constitutional Reform

Atatürk understood the need for a new Constitutional and legal structure for society in addition to these specific laws, as shown in his speech before the Faculty of Law on October 5, 1925:

> "The Turkish Revolution signifies a transformation far broader than the word revolution suggests... It means replacing an age-old political unity based on religion with one based on another tie, that of nationality. This nation has now accepted the principle that the only means of survival for nations in the international struggle for existence lies in the acceptance of the contemporary Western civilization. This nation has also accepted the principle that all of its laws should be based on secular grounds only, on a secular mentality that accepts the rule of continuous change in accordance with the change and development of life's conditions as its law... The time has come to lay the legal foundations and educate new men of law satisfying the mentality and needs of our Revolution."[374]

The 1924 Constitution[375] concentrated political power in a single legislative Assembly, headed by Mustafa Kemal, who served as President and exercised executive authority until his death in 1938. There was no judicial review of the Constitution, and no effective guarantees for fundamental rights and liberties, although it had a set of rights which in brevity read much like those in the US Constitution. The judiciary did not have full independence. It was adopted after the victory over the Greeks at Izmir, and also after the Lausanne treaty negotiation victory, so this was not something imposed by the West, or adopted only to placate the powers. It was a Turkish product, incorporating secularizing and secular ideas borrowed from the modern West. It was amended in 1928 and 1937 to further secularize government. For example, religious references in the Constitution were deleted and secularism promoted as a basic characteristic of Republic.

Codes of law to support the new Constitution and Republican form of government soon followed the revolution. The Civil Code was adopted in 1926, from a Swiss model, and the new Penal Code was heavily influenced by that of Italy.[376] There were others as well. During the post-World War I negotiations for a final peace at Lausanne, there had been pressure for Turkey to adopt appropriate laws, (driven in part by desire to see the Bosphorus open for international shipping of goods). That pressure and the actual adoption of a code later have caused some to misunderstand and believe that the Civil Code of a Western nation was simply translated and its alien forms of law imposed on an Islamic society. But if so, then why did it take a committee of twenty-six scholars roughly a year and a half to do a simple translation?

Ruth Miller noted precisely that point and explained the articles of the Swiss code that were either missing, or different, in the Turkish version, and claimed that this was no mere translation, but "...it is...precisely the fact that the code was altered which indicates that its institution was a genuine attempt to change the society, and not just a bit of decoration to throw off the international community." There was a re-introduction of previous Ottoman and Islamic legal ideas. All of this was a true effort to join the stream of Western civilization, while at the same time trying not to create major stress or discontinuity from Islamic civilization.[377]

Despite efforts to cushion the blow, a new secularized constitution supported by codes and laws, with new content for the people of Turkey, was still a blow to traditional Islamic society. Seeing that partial adoption of Western ideas and techniques hadn't worked, Mustafa Kemal had led the republication revolution to a more wholesale adoption, and adaptation, of those ideas. Let me draw your attention to these points, which have possibly slipped by the reader too easily in the last few paragraphs:

The source of law had abruptly changed. Islamic law comes of course, from God, as revealed to the Prophet in the Koran, and as further amplified by the biographies of the Prophet's life, the mass of traditions around his deeds, statements, and silences, and the long tradition of scholarly commentary and decision. In this new secular state, law came from the State itself. This was part of the dominant Western jurisprudential trend that either rejected or de-emphasized historical (customary) or natural (from God) theories of law, in favor of positive law – the law made by the legitimate ruler in the appropriate way.

This results in the problem of legitimacy. Which law is most legitimate when there is a disagreement between the two? The law of the State, or the law of God? What is a well-meaning but religiously observant person in a newly secular culture to do when faced with such a choice? The further one lives from the centralizing authority, or weaker that authority is, the easier it is for that regime to be ignored or disobeyed, especially when its law isn't "right" anyway.

The substance of the law itself also changed. Doing away with the fez in favor of the hat? Prohibiting the garments indicating the status of a scholar? And what of marriage? Something which had been done before a local Imam now required a visit to a government building, official government papers and stamps, even proof that a young woman was now of the right age to marry, at least according to the government. The substance of something as fundamental as marriage law (even where not changed) no longer came from Islamic tradition, but from the State. Adding insult to injury, if you did marry in the old way, that wouldn't be recognized as valid, and a wife might find herself not entitled to the husband's pension after his early death, and their children might be labelled bastards. Even if this law was voluntarily adopted, how was the indigenous Islamic culture to react to it?

The institutions of law changed. There was no more Sheikhu'l-islam. This had been the highest legal and judicial office within the Ottoman Empire, but one that preserved an important degree of freedom and status from the State – the Sheik did not sit within the Divan of the Sultan, but kept his own offices. Instead, there was now a Diyanet, a State Presidency of Religious Affairs, for the administration of religious life. This was not a cabinet position, nor a department, but an administrative division of the State itself. It was clearly not a legal or judicial administration – those functions were all placed within a separate judicial branch of government.[378]

This is an enormous shift within the institutions and power relationships of society, the State and of the Law. "Atatürk's policy on secularism was to remove religion from the public realm and reduce it to a matter of the faith and practice of the individual, so that the principle of freedom of religion was to protect 'individualised religion' only."[379] Though hard-core secularists could protest against a State apparatus and support of religion, the more moderate argument was that since most people were Muslim, having an administration of religion to help supply imams and regulate mosques and prayers was simply a public service.

No longer did the law have an independent income from its wide array of pious and charitable foundations. Those foundations were now administered by the State. The State granted a budget and supplied it to the Diyanet. No longer was the law something independent of the State, with insitutions of its own that while closely related, weren't really part of the State. Now religion was administered by the State, and law was something else – separate – also administered by the State.

Even while the State still supported Islam (and ignored the similar needs of its Christian, Jewish, and non-mainstream Muslim citizens), this is a separation of Church and State that looks much like the modern Western understanding of what the relationship between law, religion, the state and the public should be. And don't forget that these institutions didn't gradually diverge and struggle over hundreds of years to define their roles as happened in the West, but were abruptly separated in 1923 and 1924.

The people of the law also changed. No more was there a class of scholars, passing judgment upon the qualifications of new aspirants to join their ranks, based on their knowledge of the Koran and traditions. No more *Mufti*, which a *Qadi* might turn to for an opinion when deciding a tough court case. Legal scholars were now educated in State universities, to an approved curicuulum, and passed a test to be appointed as Judge. They served according to civil service tables and procedures of the State. These new judges "generally understood their position in much the same way that modern European judges applying their own legal codes did: they saw themselves as faithful servants of the state."[380]

In sum, this change in the Constitutional order abruptly removed Islam from its place as part of the public and constitutional order and diminished its role to that of a private matter, as the West had come to treat religion within its own Constitutional structures. The scope and impact of such a rapid change is not to be underestimated. It had taken many hundreds of years for role differentiation of state and religion within society to evolve in Western Europe, starting from a more flexible basis of original teaching and content in this regard than Islam possessed. Within Turkey, that change was compressed into a decade or two.

The weakened or absent role of traditional scholars in maintaining the constitutional balance created a dangerous vacuum of power. No longer did the scholars have the power to pronounce the State legitimate or illegitimate in its exercise of power. That legal structure was gone, along with the check that it provided on the wrong exercise of state power: "With the executive as the source of law, and the judges charged with applying the law conceived as servants of the executive, the state became a totalizing sovereign entity such as never existed before in Islamic history."[381]

While many in Turkey accepted the new ideas and structures of society, many others did not, and sometimes the military was even called on to deal with outright rebellions, as in the province of Tunceli (Dersim) in 1937 and 1938. Discussing such events is beyond the scope of this study, as they involve questions like Kurdish identity and national feeling, and efforts to impose Turkish names and identities on Kurds and other minorities, efforts of social engineering and demographic relocation and purification. The point to be grasped is that this could happen precisely because Turkey was engaged in "replacing an age-old political unity based on religion with one based on another tie, that of nationality."[382]

Continuing Reforms Struggling for Legitimacy

Tracing out even this quickly some of the constitutional changes in Turkey may be too tedious for many, but it should illustrate the point of secularization for a Western reader by the very familiarity of terminology, ideas, and institutions which follow.

After the great changes of the republican revolution, the pace of change slowed, but change remained a constant in Turkish life as the single-party period ended after World War II, and free elections brought new leadership and enough chaos that the military felt obliged to intervene in 1960. The army promised to bring reform, and then get out of politics. It was accepted that the 1924 Constitution had weaknesses and needed updating. The new Constitution was drafted by law professors, and (later) a constituent assembly including members from the Chambers of Commerce and Industry, from Unions, Bar Associations, Universities, Teachers organizations, etc. There is no question of dominance of the elite, secular establishment in the process. In referendum (a first) it received 63% of vote.

The 1961 Constitution had a more detailed set of rights, including more effective judicial guarantees, partly through a stronger separation of powers, and partly through the principle of judicial review in a Constitutional Court (following German and Italian models), established in this Constitution. The aspiration was replacement of a majoritarian democracy with a liberal democracy. More modern Western concepts like the social (welfare) state; social and economic rights; and a new definition of sovereignty designed to work through institutions under a constitution – limiting the too expansive powers of the Parliament.

As the 1960s and 70s went on, Turkey experienced increasing separation between right and left, and violence between these sides; culminating in economic reform that, while needed, in the short term made life for painful. The Constitution was amended in 1971 and 1973, (under military influence) to strengthen executive power and to restrict the scope of some rights and liberties, and weaken the role of the judiciary. The idea was to strengthen the authority of the state, eroded by right-left terror and violence. It didn't work.

In 1980, the military intervened in politics again. The aim was to restructure the constitutional and legal order of the country and restore democracy. A National Security Council stayed in power until the end of 1983, when general elections were held. During this period they not only prepared a new Constitution but also adopted several hundred laws, which entirely restructured the constitutional and legal order of Turkey. But make no mistake, this was still a secular Republic.

The Preamble of the Turkish Constitution of 1982 (as amended in 2001) is quite clear on this: The Constitution is still "...in line with the concept of nationalism introduced by the founder of the Republic of Turkey, Atatürk..." It includes "...the nationalism, principles, reforms and civilizationism of Atatürk and that sacred religious feelings shall absolutely not be involved in state affairs and politics as required by the principle of secularism..." The Constitution is also clear that this Preamble is not just a statement of high-sounding ideals, since Article 176 states that "The preamble, which states the basic views and principles the Constitution is based on, shall form an integral part of the Constitution." There isn't much room there for judicial interpretation contrary to the grand secularizing vision of Mustafa Kemal.

The 1982 Constitution, currently in force, has been amended substantially between 1982 and the present. Initial amendments were part of a trend of liberalizing democracy within Turkey, but following roughly 2011, the trend reversed, and at the present time we are to stay tuned as former Prime Minister (now President) Erdoğan has said. We'll come back to those developments in a further chapter.

When the basis of law, in the eyes of some Turks, has changed from the commands of God to the commands of the State, what ought to be done? There is no question that some conclude that God ought to be obeyed rather than the State. Turkish courts have struggled to decide cases where a religious marriage has been entered into, but there has never been a civil marriage in the way recognized by the state. Are the surviving spouse and children entitled to the pension of the deceased?[383] A great variety of other cases raise similar questions of *which* law ought to be obeyed.

Turkey's answer to the challenge of the West and necessity to form a new strong state was to discard the old ideas that had not proven strong enough, and to adopt Western principles of secularization, and nationalism, and separation of religion and the state, and to mold them into a particularly Turkish form. It may have made the strongest and most comprehensive efforts to impose those new ideas and new ways of all the Middle Eastern Islamic nations, but Turkey was not alone. Nationalist and other new ideas were also stirring through the newly-created nations and protectorates of the Middle East, strongly in some places like Egypt, and more weakly in others.

Adoption of Nationalism Outside Turkey

As the authority and even nominal unity of the Ottoman Empire disappeared in the Middle East, European power politics created multiple new countries. National feeling became the rallying point for leaders trying to help their people coalesce. But first nationalists had to define just what it was that they meant by nationalism. The first part – opposition to European powers occupying and directing national life – was easy. Nationalism often includes a focus on an outside enemy, or an oppressive occupier, and Western nations gave plenty of opportunities to place that focus squarely on themselves. Egypt, as already mentioned, had been occupied in 1882, and was still subject to occupation by the British army after the end of the War. Arab nationalism also involved a second and more difficult question, that we'll come to a little later.

Saad Zaghlul and other nationalist leaders in Egypt had had enough of British rule during the War, and asked that the British government end the protectorate that had begun in 1882, and allow them to send a delegation to the peace-making conferences in Paris to make their requests.[384] These positions enjoyed strong support throughout Egypt. The Wafd (Delegation) Party had grown during the War, and was a focus of national sentiment and resistance to the British after the War. As protests spread, Zaghlul and other leaders were arrested and exiled to Malta, and in the Spring of 1919, the revolution began, with wide and united popular support. "It was the first real nationalist movement in Arab history, in which nationalist leaders enjoyed the full support of the masses, from the countryside to the cities."[385]

The British partly backed down, declaring unilaterally that Egypt was independent in February of 1922 - though not fully independent. There was no question of British military forces leaving the zone around the Suez Canal, vital for contact with India. The Wafd Party, King, and British struggled within and among themselves in an uneasy balance for the next thirty years.[386] Fuad, the 9th Sultan in the line which had started with Muhammad Ali in the mid-1800s, took the title of King when independence was recognized. Zaghlul became the first elected Prime Minister in 1924, in a legislature easily dominated by the Wafd Party.

Fuad was a Constitutional monarch, in that the Wafd Party had drafted a Constitution, adopted by royal decree in 1923. It stated that the source of power was the nation itself, and provided for a parliament of two chambers to share legislative power with the King. One chamber, the House of Representatives, was elected by popular vote, and the higher chamber, the Senate, had 2/5 of its members appointed by the King, and 3/5 elected to their positions.[387]

The King had the power to dissolve the House of Representatives. He didn't hesitate to exercise it. He even went so far as to throw out the Constitution, replacing it with one he liked until compelled in the mid '30s to take back the 1923 Constitution. The King of course was the executive power, and judicial power resided in the court system, which included both courts run on traditional *shari'a* lines with traditionally educated *ulama* as *qadis*, and also courts modeled on Western lines, with judges educated in the Western tradition. This was an attempt at compromise rather than going so far as Mustafa Kemal had in Turkey. Egypt had made some of the first modernizing experiments prior to the end of the Ottoman era, and doesn't seem to have provoked such a sharp revolution against the old ways as in Turkey.

Muhammad Ali had been open to Western ideas and learning, and that influence found its way into law, in his time and afterward. "In 1875, a system of 'mixed courts' was established, to administer the so-called 'mixed codes', being different civil, commercial, penal and procedural codes governing relations between foreigners or between foreigners and Egyptians. These codes, notably the Civil Code of 1875, were modelled on the corresponding codes in force in France. In fact, the Egyptian government would only adopt them after their approval by those foreign countries (principally Britain and France) which enjoyed a privileged status in Egypt."[388] A similar system was adopted in 1883 to apply to Egyptian citizens. In parallel, courts and judicial officials for Muslims and Coptic Christians also still operated.

Lacking the strong ideological basis of Mustafa Kemal's Turkey, Egyptian nationalism sought to blend new ideas with old. "Not surprisingly, considerable confusion and jurisdictional conflict arose out of this complex legal and judicial structure, leading to demands for simplification and rationalisation."[389] After World War II, reform work went on in earnest, and the court system was consolidated, but "family law, although now administered in a unified judiciary, continued to be subject to the 'personal law' of each of the principal religious groupings within the population, in accordance with the "Personal Status Law" of 1929."[390]

All of these nation-building attempts were balanced with the demands of the British presence. If nothing else they provided a continuing focus for nationalist animosity, especially after a young King Faruk signed a treaty with Great Britain in the run-up to World War II, strengthening the British military presence.[391] Nationalist agitation gained momentum after the end of the War, even as Faruk weakened. Guerilla attacks against the British army in the Canal zone in 1951-52 brought over-reaction, and produced rioting in Cairo, where confidence in the government was gone.

On July 23, 1952 the Free Officers struck, and General Naguib ushered Faruk out.[392] Gamal Abdel Nasser, the real driving force behind this group of young officers, took power soon after. It was Nasser who brought Arabic nationalism to its height. He insisted on an independent course without providing assurances and accomodations (peace with Israel, military bases), which the Western powers desired, and when they predictably refused aid and arms sales, Nasser didn't hesitate to strike deals with the Soviets and their satellites. He asserted a strong independence when he nationalized the Suez Canal.

Probably the most interesting aspect of his nationalism was in tackling the harder question of Arab Nationalism. Did it mean national feeling and identity of Arabs country-by-country (within the boundaries created by the West) or within one large Arab country including all of the Arabs?

National borders are usually considered a necessary part of nationalism, although some Arab nationalists had early on insisted on comprehensive borders in which all the Arabs could live, and disparaged those they called "regionalists". The British and French were enthusiastic cartographers during and after World War I, creating lines on the map that had never before existed, or had existed in a very ill-defined state, and "regionalists" weren't slow to take the opportunities this provided.

This wasn't a new tension within the Islamic world. There had been no unified political or state structure containing all Muslims since around 750. The reasons sometimes appeared as disagreement over doctrine (e.g., Sunni vs. Shia), or cultural opposition (e.g., Persian vs. Arabic), but today would likely be summed up as nationalistic. That wasn't necessarily a problem. The *ulama* "have at all times been passionately concerned with the integrity of the Muslim territory as a whole but not too much interested in its momentary distribution among the competing princes of the day."[393]

The old tension had now found a new vocabulary for ethnic solidarity, and the universal ties of Islam could help extend the nationalist idea beyond borders, and against regionalists.

Nasser, through Voice of the Arabs radio, spread a message of pan-Arabic nationalism, and found believers.[394] Believers, not converts, since they had arrived at some of the same conclusions as Nasser, but along their own path. A group of young military officers is Syria, encouraged by members of the Ba'ath Party, liked what they heard and saw in Egypt, and took a plane to Cairo to throw in their lot with Nasser in the United Arab Republic (UAR) of 1958 to 1961. When they joined Nasser militarily, the rest of the Syrian establishment had no choice but to follow, into the unified scheme of party and government that Nasser demanded.

The Ba'ath Party was founded sometime in 1943, by Michel Aflaq, a Sorbonne-educated Syrian, and Salah al-Din al-Bitar, likewise French-educated. While in France, both were exposed to communism, Aflaq probably remaining a party member until 1943, although some sources indicate he broke away earlier. They were also exposed to socialist ideas, but did struggle with those, since they were regarded as tainted by the West. While they both may have changed their ideologies as needed, the Ba'ath Party from the beginning was fiercely nationalistic, and dedicated to building a state strong enough to stand up to the West. This desire for a strong state against the West attracted support, especially as Nasser began to declare a similar message from Cairo.[395]

Syrian nationalism too was willing to look outward, and to use both Islam and Arab ethnicity as common ground. The Preamble to the Constitution of September 5, 1950 stated that the Syrian Constitution was formed "by the will of God and the free wish of the people." It declared its "attachment to Islam, and its ideals" and the desire of the Syrian people to "build their modern state on those sound ethical bases advocated by Islam and the other Theistic Religions and to combat atheism and moral decadence" but all as "part of the whole Arab nation" to be united at some time in the future.[396] With the rise of Nasser, it looked like that time had come.

The United Arab Republic was under tremendous strain from the very beginning, for the most elementary of reasons: Someone would have to lose power when two systems of governance coalesced into one. Differences between the Syrian and Egyptian systems, and the clear dominance of Nasser and his ideas, began to push the UAR apart. If that weren't bad enough, the momentum of this pan-Arabic advance was broken when the Iraqi branch of the Ba'ath Party refused to bring Iraq into the UAR after the 1958 revolution when the Iraqi sovereign was deposed and the Ba'ath took power there. The UAR ended, and Nasser himself began his decline, aided by the disastrous defeat in the 1967 Six-Day war with Israel. "Once Arab nationalism began to suffer reverses and setbacks, and Abdel Nasser's ability to work his magic came into question, all the particularistic, anti-national tendencies reemerged and even surged to the forefront."[397]

The Ba'ath Party persisted through a confused period of several years, both in Syria and Iraq. Party organizations brought strong rulers to power, through yet another round of plots, coups, and counter-coups, rulers from military backgrounds who diluted the pan-Arabic message of the old Ba'ath party. By 1970 Hafez al-Assad was in power in Syria, and by 1979 Saddam Hussein was firmly in charge in Iraq, although he had been wielding the real power for several years before that time.[398]

The Preamble to the latest Syrian Constitution of the al-Assad regime opens with the pan-Arabic recitation that:

> "The Arab nation managed to perform a great role in building human civilization when it was a unified nation. When the ties of its national cohesion weakened, its civilizing role receded and the waves of colonial conquest shattered the Arab nation's unity, occupied its territory, and plundered its resources. Our Arab nation has withstood these challenges and rejected the reality of division, exploitation, and backwardness. . . In the Syrian Arab region, the masses of our people continued their struggle after independence. . . [which is] the joint Arab struggle against imperialism and Zionism, regionalist disputes, and separatist movements, and which was confirmed by the contemporary Arab revolution against domination and exploitation..."[399]

There's much more in that vein, but I think that's enough. The struggle against the outside forces continues, mostly as many commentators point out, because it *must*. To declare the struggle over would mean that questions could now be asked about what the actual program of the government was, and when all the grand promises were going to come true.

The Syrian Constitution of al-Assad provides a very strong executive in the President of the Republic, who may assume legislative powers for a variety of reasons, can take measures necessary in an emergency situation, and can form special organizations, councils, and committees, defining their powers even as they are created. In Article 3, subparagraph 2, it states that "Islamic jurisprudence is a main source of legislation[,]" and further on defines a judicial system, presided over by a Higher Council of the Judiciary, chaired by – you guessed it – the President.

Stating that Islam still provides a main source of legislation is not as radical a shift as the Republican revolution in Turkey fifty years prior to that time. However, coupling that notion about the main source of law with the idea of the nation or state as the source of power as in Egypt, Syria, or Turkey is still a body blow to the traditional Islamic order.

Of course these are not the only Western ideas adopted in the Middle East, but they are the dominant ideas. Parties have flirted with socialism, or with communism, but these ideas have either been co-opted into a nationalist agenda, or have never gained enough followers to leave the margins of political and social life. "It is obvious that at different times and places European ideas have been enthusiastically accepted by particular groups. It is not so obvious that, despite the enthusiasm, this acceptance has been only partial and limited."[400]

Nationalism, whether pan-Arabic or country specific as in Turkey, socialism, secularism, communism, ethnicity, and other Western notions were enthusiastically taken in by some leaders and nations of the Middle East. While all of these involved some element of reaction against the Western or colonizing forces, they aren't to be confused with the initial defensive reaction to the West, which aimed to make reforms within the existing order to save it. Adoption of these "isms" was about building a new state and a new society.

But what if it didn't work? What if getting beyond mere technical borrowing, to appropriation of the ideas of the West for a Turkish, Egyptian, or Arabic nation didn't work? How could the effectiveness of the new ideas even be measured? Some within Islamic societies had rejected this attempt from the very beginning. Others began to reject the ideas as implementation proved painful, even oppressive. They only other option which seemed possible was to revive Islam altogether, to look back to its roots for a pure society.

Chapter 10 - The Reaction Continues: Rejection

The Ottomans had tried a middle path of selective incorporation of Western ideas and institutions to preserve the state, and that hadn't worked. The new Turkish Republic adopted ideas like secularism and dramatically reshaped traditional Islamic ideas and institutions where it didn't do away with them. Others like Egypt and Syria didn't go quite as far with the adoption of Western ideas, but still chose nationalism as a center for society. While some in the Middle East tried to preserve the old order, and some tried full or partial acceptance of Western ideas, another group was just as whole-hearted in its rejection. That group thought the answer to the challenge of the West was to revive the ideas and practices they believed had made Islam great in the past.

Traditional Islamic Society Continues into Modern Times

Not so far away from Turkey, Abd al-Aziz ibn Saud had "had a good war", as they say. English gold during World War I was enough to buy his raiding bands' help in defeating the Ottoman allies of Germany and Austria-Hungary. After early victories against the English at Gallipoli and at Kut, in Iraq, the Ottomans had been slowly driven back from their Arabian possessions, up to Northern Syria. The map drawn by the victors confirmed the ejection of the Ottomans from the Arabian Peninsula, Syria and Jordan, and along ibn Saud's other former frontier with Ottoman power, the Mesopotamian strip running along the Tigris and Euphrates down to Basra in Iraq.

The Al-Saud family was thus left in possession of the interior of the Arabian Peninsula. They had some coastline, excluding eastern enclaves like Kuwait which the British had created, and Yemen. But to their dismay, they did not have the Hijaz strip of coastland in the West, the location of both Mecca and Medina. Ibn Saud concentrated his energies and forces there, and by 1924/25 drove out Huseyn, another wartime ally of Great Britain, who was then awarded Jordan as a consolation prize. Continuing with a mix of "patience, diplomacy, and opportunistic moments of aggression"[401] Ibn Saud united a land he would name after his own family - Saudi Arabia – when he declared the Kingdom in 1932.

For the family of Al-Saud, this was the culmination of almost two hundred years of expansion from their small town of al-Dir'iyyi in the arid Najd plateau of central Arabia. They hadn't done it alone. In 1744 a young reformer, driven out from a nearby town when his zeal to purify the message of God led him to personally destroy the tomb of a companion of the Prophet Muhammad, and to sentence a woman to death for adultery, arrived in Al-Dir'iyyi. His name was Muhammad ibn Abd al-Wahhab.

The "Wahhabi" strain of Islam was born with Muhammad ibn Abd al-Wahhab. Depending upon who is talking, Wahhabi is either a pejorative term, or one standing for a laudable stripping away of unnecessary and harmful accretions to the faith that distract people from God. After studies in Mecca and Medina, al-Wahhab had made his way to Basra for more study.[402] In Basra he wrote "The Book of God's Unity" and after a fitting silence on returning home as his father was declining and dying, started to proclaim that message in his home town. The key was part of a *hadith* text stating that a true believer believes in "no god but God and denies all other objects of worship." That explains his destruction of the tomb – it was a distraction and wrong focus of worship.

The Wahhabi argument was that pilgrimages to tombs of companions of the Prophet, or praying for intercession from saints, angels, Jesus, or holy men, led people to confusion and misplacement of their worship. Worship should be concentrated on God alone. These weren't just confused people – it was worse than that. Since the *hadith* insisted on God *and* denial of other objects of worship, it was clear that people who used other objects of worship, made sacrifices, or swore vows, weren't even Muslims. They needed to be converted to Islam.[403]

This was the stark and uncompromising message disturbing local society which led to al-Wahhab's expulsion until he could find someone powerful like the Al-Saud family to support him. Al-Saud and al-Wahhab reached an understanding of mutual support in 1744, and that pact has continued to our day.

By the early 1800s, the Saudi-Wahabbi emirate had expanded to the borders of Ottoman territory. The Ottoman *ulama* recognized a threat to Ottoman order in the uncompromising message of the Wahhabis, and sent anti-Wahhabi tracts to their local *ulama*. When the Al-Saud took Mecca and Medina in 1803 and 1805, the blow to the Ottoman Sultan's prestige as protector of these holy cities was too much, and the Sultan sent Muhammad Ali and his armies into the desert.[404] By 1819 Dir-iyya was razed to the ground, leading the Al-Saud family to build up the nearby town of Riyadh when they grew stronger again in the mid-1800s.

Through the late 1800s (and a disastrous split over succession which ended the second attempt of the Al-Saud family to rule the Peninsula in the 1890s), Wahabbi doctrines had been developing and solidifying. They included the proper constitutional structure of the state. One group of Wahabbi *ulama* had opined that in this environment of strife over the succession, the proper Wahabbi stance would be to support the winner, so long as that emir supported the Wahabbis themselves. Another group thought that rebels were not to be approved unless the ruler had commanded something clearly unlawful. The Ottoman rulers clearly couldn't be supported, since their corrupt Islamic faith had made infidels of them.[405]

If this sounds familiar, it should, since this is the traditional Islamic constitutional balance between a ruler who commands the good and forbids the bad and the *ulama* who support that ruler so long as he rules within those acceptable bounds of Islam. Tracing some episodes in Saudi Arabian history allows a view of this updated and newly purified constitutional balance in action, as the 1900s opened.

The cities of Mecca and Medina were an early area of difficulty. Muslims following the four dominant law schools of Sunni Islam lived there, as well as a few Shi'a, even followers of some Sufi orders. In addition, in the Hijaz a tolerant attitude toward the judicious use of tobacco and alcohol prevailed, extending even to the new phonograph machines. The Saudi family had to somehow satisfy Wahhabi doctrines that didn't approve of those beliefs or actions, and yet keep open the pilgrimage routes for all the different kinds of Muslims of the world.

The solution was publication and enforcement of a stricter legal regime, especially when it came to alcohol and tobacco, but a legal regime which was quietly relaxed unless the King and his Wahhabi *ulama* were in town. Everybody could give a little in their positions, so long as they didn't lose too much. Maybe granting the King something he wanted would lead to gains elsewhere. For example, the late 1920s saw the emergence of Wahhabi-led local Committees for Commanding Right and Forbidding Wrong (today popularly known as the religious police).[406]

During the 1920s, the Bedouin tribesmen, stricter Wahhabis, kept up with their practice of raiding into Jordan and Iraq. These Ikhwan ("Brothers" – but not to be confused with the Muslim Brothers of Egypt), couldn't understand why ibn Saud wanted them to give up what Wahhabi doctrine so clearly allowed. Weren't these people infidels, after all, and fair game for the taking? The King didn't want to anger the British over raids into their territory – after all, he couldn't claim international borders himself if the protections of borders only worked in one direction – and he needed support to crush the obstinate Ikhwan.

The Wahhabi leadership agreed to support the King in resolving this problem and stopping the raids, in return for bringing back some of the stricter laws the King had relaxed.

When some of the Ikhwan refused this compromise and wouldn't surrender, the King used his new British machine guns mounted on cars in the 1929 battle at Sibila, and that was the end of that.

This is the traditional Islamic constitutional balance at work – a continual conversation at the highest levels of government between competing desires and agendas, varying in pace according to the relative power of either the King or the *ulama* at the time. The balance is usually struck in a peaceful way, but it may even involve force. I know some might object that a constitutional order is about law and principles, and that constitutional change can't be, or at least shouldn't be, worked out in a rough way, but it sometimes is.

Keeping a constitutional balance requires balancing two competing tensions within law. For law to be respected and followed, it must be predictable, and steady enough that the population may make business and personal plans in reliance on what the law is. At the same time, law must allow for change, so that it doesn't become so fossilized and irrelevant to social needs that people would disrespect and disregard it. Whether it is the *ulama*-royalty partnership in Saudi Arabia or the Supreme Court in the United States, both countries have within their legal systems a mechanism which is designed to manage social change at an acceptable pace.

It worked in a rough way at Sibila after failed negotiations. There the power of the Ikhwan was broken, the order that ibn Saud desired was restored, and the Wahhabi *ulama* took a step closer to the desires of the ruling family. More new things not violating the essentials of Wahhabism were pushed upon them by ibn Saud, who understood the need to open up to international commerce. Motor cars were greeted with suspicion by the *ulama*, and it took ibn Saud to point out their pious advantages for them to be granted acceptance. Women's voices on the radio were another problem, but then again, eventually acceptance came. In the 1960s the introduction of television caused riots by the more conservative, and it took restricting broadcasting content to what was acceptable under Wahhabi norms for this new invention to be accepted. But slowly, very slowly, change came.[407]

This really isn't so different from the pace at which the constitutional balance changes and is maintained within the U.S., using the much different mechanism of the United States Supreme Court. After the civil war had nearly ripped the U.S. apart, partly driven by the issue of slavery, the 14th Amendment to the Constitution was adopted in 1868. It made the newly freed slaves into citizens, and promised them that "[n]o state shall make or enforce any law which shall abridge the privileges or immunities of citizens of the United States; nor shall any state deprive any person of life, liberty, or property, without due process of law; nor deny to any person within its jurisdiction the equal protection of the laws."

Yet only a few years later in 1892, the Supreme Court in *Plessy v. Ferguson* upheld the proposition of "separate but equal" and black people were forced to use different train cars, bathrooms, drinking fountains, etc., that were usually anything but equal.[408] In 1954 the Court declared in *Brown v. Board of Education* that "separate but equal" was out.[409] The text of the 14th Amendment hadn't changed during that time, but society's needs had changed, as the court's opinion made clear, and the court moved in interpreting the law to keep in balance with demands from legislators, presidents, and society at large. It moved slowly, and painfully, but it moved.

Saudi Arabia today doesn't have a Constitution, for how could man make such a thing where God has already given law? But the King did move under social pressure, "having taken into consideration the public interest" to preserve the constitutional balance in society when he promulgated The Basic Law of Governance in 1992. Article I of that Law states that "The Kingdom of Saudi Arabia is a sovereign Arab Islamic State. Its religion is Islam. Its constitution is Almighty God's Book, The Holy Qur'an, and the Sunna (Traditions) of the Prophet (PBUH). [Peace be Upon Him] Arabic is the language of the Kingdom. The City of Riyadh is the capital."[410]

This couldn't be more different than the Turkish Constitution of 1982 with the secular nationalism of Atatürk forming its Preamble. In Saudi Arabia, unlike Turkey, the source of law has not changed. God is not dead, as many in the West, and some in the Islamic world, think. And even though change slowly comes to Saudi Arabia, the long traditions of memorization of the Koran, of the science of *hadith* collection, of study of the life of the Prophet, and his *sunna*, the scholarly comments – it all remains. There is no choice of legitimacy between the law of the State and the law of God. Sometimes the *ulama* disagrees with the royal decision, or vice versa, but this all happens within a system respected and recognized as legitimate by both parties.

The substance of the law itself has not changed. Nobody in Saudi Arabia took away the traditional headgear or robes indicating the status of a scholar. Marriages and divorces are still solemnized in courts applying the *shari'a*. Granted there are special purpose, or administrative courts, created by the king to rule on new areas of law not contemplated within the *shari'a*, such as royalties on oil and other minerals produced within the Kingdom. But creation by the caliph or sultan of bodies of law supplementing – but never replacing – the *shari'a* is almost as old as Islam itself.

The institutions of law did not change in any major way. There is still a most respected and highest member of the Saudi *ulama*, and groups and councils of senior *ulama*, all of whom are appointed to positions by the king, after they prove themselves to the members of the *ulama* as knowledgeable enough to be accepted. The people of the law haven't really changed either, although a set of Western-educated lawyers and judges exist to staff non-*shari'a* specialty courts.

Legal reforms have been made, but must be made carefully to preserve the constitutional order and balance. They may be phrased in *shari'a* terminology, such as has been the case with mineral interests. *Shari'a* ideas themselves, such as the *zakat*, intended for relief and help of the poor, have been redefined as a sort of income and property tax. Reforms may refer to the *shari'a* itself as their reason for being made, or may state that they don't conflict with the provisions of the *shari'a*. Reform moves slowly as the balance between *ulama* and royalty is preserved – large parts of the 2007 court reorganization have yet to move ahead. But when in doubt about a position, a Saudi ruler may do what Caliphs and Sultans over centuries have done: Ask for a *fatwa* from a *mufti*, legitimizing the decision he wishes to make.[411]

Saudi Arabia preserves to this day what is likely the purest expression of the classic Sunni Islamic constitutional balance still existing. But Saudi Arabia, in that post-World War I period where we took up the story, was nearly alone in the Islamic world in not being occupied by Western militaries or colonizers. Most other countries with majority, or at least substantial, Muslim populations were colonial possessions, or under Western occupation or governance.

If opinion of the Muslim majorities in those countries rejected the ideas of the West, how was a correct system of legal and state relationships with the Muslim community to come in to being? Should there be armed resistance, either open or guerilla war? Should the ideas of the majority find their expression through the ballot box, if that even existed? Should a non-violent but strong resistance be waged? Let me try to answer this question by focusing first on the ideas and actions of two very influential Muslim thinkers, and then placing them in their wider context of Islamic reformer or revivalist thought.

A New Kind of Islamic Scholar

The Mawlana (respected scholar of Islam) Sayyid Abu'l-A'la Mawdudi (Mawdudi), was born in 1903 in British India, and lived his life there or in the new country of Pakistan after the post-World War II division of British India, dying in 1979. I realize Pakistan is geographically not a country of the Middle East, but intellectually it may be. Mawdudi must be discussed here since his ideas, and the way he formulated them for his age, were so influential throughout the Islamic world.

Why Mawdudi even had his ideas in the first place, and put them in writing, is also important. British India was obviously British India. Muslims no longer ruled, the last of the Mughuls who ruled their empire in the North having gone in 1857, in the wake of what the Western history books usually call the Sepoy Mutiny. Mawdudi faced the same problem as the newly independent States built from the ruins of the Ottoman Empire – how to rule; and a sharper challenge yet, how to rule where Muslims were a minority.

Mawdudi realized that there was no hope for rebuilding the machinery and institutions of the Mughul Empire. He watched the failure of the Khilafat movement, a pan-Islamic dream of reviving Islamic institutions which came to a bitter end when Republican Turkey abolished the Caliph's office in 1924. The British governed India, but Hindu nationalism was growing fast. This was the era in which Gandhi was building his movement, and challenging the ruling British Empire for control of India. Democracy in an India with a large Hindu majority would be no answer, since Muslim desires could easily be submerged under the Hindu movement.

It seemed that the only course of action left for Muslims was to band together for protection. All of these factors combined to create in Mawdudi the need to put before (especially educated) Muslims "a systematic political reading of Islam and a plan for social action to realize his vision."[412] Mawdudi wrote seventy-three books explaining what needed to be done, along with an extensive Koran commentary, many more pamphlets and magazine articles, and gave many speeches.

Community cohesion was a necessary part of this vision, and a major theme of Mawdudi's work is strengthening of bonds between Muslims – no matter the area, from worship to economics. In all areas of life, there was a proper way for Muslims to take part, and all must be educated to take part in that way of life. Mawdudi himself practiced what he preached, coming gradually to cast off his Western clothing in favor of traditional dress, and at last growing the beard he'd been chided for not wearing as a younger man.

Education was at first the main tactic, and the books and journal articles proliferated. As the 1930s went on, the dangers of Hindu nationalism only seemed stronger. On a 1937 trip back to Delhi, Mawdudi was displeased to see Hindu dominance, and a secularized group of educated Muslims. Secularization and a pluralist society could only take Muslims away from the community, ultimately weakening those who remained. The presence of a Muslim majority in the surrounding population from which to build the correct type of society became increasingly important.

Politics began to seem more attractive, and Mawdudi moved to Lahore, a majority Muslim city where he lived the rest of his life. Around him, the Ahmadis, Hindus, and Sikhs all had their political parties, and it now seemed necessary that Muslims should have a party too. In 1941 the Jam'at-I Islami (Islamic Party) was established. In 1947 Pakistan became an independent State, and the lure for the Islamic Party to stay within the political arena to fight for its desires at the ballot box was too strong for Mawdudi to resist any longer. Some party members in both India and Pakistan quit since they desired to stay true to the original aim of bringing change by education and building community cohesion.

The nature of the movement changed. The ideal was the same, but politics could be pursued, and Western ideas and institutions could be borrowed, as vehicles to reach the goal. Building cohesion in the Islamic community was always important, but could no longer focus on right practice of the individual alone. "In traditional Islam there had been a balance between religion as individual piety and religion as social order. It was the piety of men that created and sustained a religious order. In Mawdudi's formula, although individual piety featured prominently, in the final analysis, it was the society and the political order that guaranteed the piety of the individual."[413]

Action was to be carried out in the political realm where appropriate, and within the organs of the State itself. Mawdudi didn't favor violent resistance, but rather the displacement and destruction of what existed by a gradual taking over and reshaping of the institutions of the State. The modern Western ideas of secularism, nationalism, and democracy would go, in favor of the new Islamic polity.[414] Gradual and lasting change, rather than sudden change that would only produce reaction, was best for the community. Mawdudi stated he would not use the methods of the Muslim Brothers, though the temptation to violence was too strong for some of his followers.

It was clear to Mawdudi that "[i]n Islam, the religious, the political, the economic, and the social are not separate systems, they are different departments and parts of the same system."[415] Once a man had made the choice to submit himself to Islam, he had no continuing choice in life except to obey. As the party of God's soldiers, the Islamic Party similarly had no choice but to take control of the political power of the state to preserve this system. Once the proper Islamic State was formed, even coercion could be used to keep the Muslims of that state on course.

The only possibility for dissent was from a ruler who performed a wrongful act, or had wrongful intentions, and then the consent of the whole community itself was required in order to show that wrongful act, not the complaint of one individual. "The basic human right was the right to demand an Islamic order and to live in it, not the right to differ with the rulers of the Islamic state or defy its authority."[416]

A judiciary and legislature could exist, but their function would be to advise the executive power. This sounds a lot like what I've called the traditional Islamic constitutional balance, just modernizing by replacing "caliph" and "*ulama*" with "president" and "legislature/judiciary". An Islamic constitution could be fashioned to set out this basic structure, though this would require a great deal of work in struggling to make the unwritten constitution present in the *shari'a* into a condensed modern written form.

Within the state, there was to be an attempt to balance the needs of the individual against the needs of society. Capitalism and socialism both erred, and proper Islamic economic thought could strike the proper balance. *Zakat* would be collected for the poor, *riba'* would be prohibited, and besides helping to establish a proper Islamic economy, one avoiding both egalitarianism and enrichment of economic exploiters, these devices would strengthen the community by a refusal to use the economic devices of others.

Mawdudi claimed that this was all democratic somehow, and trying to prove that resulted in "complex, muddled, and often contradictory arguments."[417] The democratic idea requires some sort of accountability of the state to its citizens, and how could a citizen ever hold the state accountable when as a citizen he had no real choice except to submit to the Islamic vision which the state enforced? Non-Muslims and *dhimmi* could exist within the state, though they certainly wouldn't be citizens, and could be excluded from office and voting. To hold otherwise would be absurd, and undemocratic. What, in Mawdudi's definition of democratic, could be less democratic than forcing the majority to abide by what a minority wanted?

Within Mawdudi's body of work, there were many familiar ideas taken from traditional Islam, yet there were important differences. The greatest point of difference is that traditional Islam called for advice, petition, even admonishment of state leaders by the scholars and the Islamic community. The scholars and community were not to actually *be* the leaders themselves by inciting and directing political action, as Mawdudi did.

There was no love lost: Mawdudi might call traditionalists "*cahil*" (ignorant – hearkening back to that "time of ignorance" prior to Muhammad), and they might label his thought "*bid'at*" (innovation outside the bounds of proper Islam).

The New Scholarship and Activism in Egypt

Meanwhile in Egypt, a similar revivalist movement had been growing. A young teacher named Hasan al-Banna lived in a Suez Canal Zone city and saw the higher standard of living of the foreign technicians, directors, and military men every day.

In 1928 he reacted to foreign superiority and the subservience of Egyptians in their own land by founding the Muslim Brotherhood. He went back to basics – the ideas of the Koran and the rightly-guided Caliphs. He talked about this a lot, but not in the language of the *ulama*, who never accepted him as one of themselves, but in plain language, in coffee houses and cafes where ordinary Egyptians gathered.

As the Muslim Brotherhood started to spread out from its first center, al-Banna was plain about what this group was:

> "You are not a benevolent society, nor a political party, nor a local organization having limited purposes. Rather, you are a new soul in the heart of this nation to give it life by means of the Qur'an...When asked what it is for which you call, reply that it is Islam, the message of Muhammad, the religion that contains within it government, and has as one of its obligations freedom. If you are told that you are political, answer that Islam admits no such distinction. If you are accused of being revolutionaries, say, 'We are voices for right and for peace in which we dearly believe, and of which we are proud. If you rise against us or stand in the path of our message, then we are permitted by God to defend ourselves against your injustice.'"[418]

It just doesn't get any more plain than that. If you skipped that quote, or read it too quickly, go back and read it again. Each sentence deserves thought.

In Egypt in the late 20s and 30s, up until World War II, there was plenty standing in the path of the Muslim Brotherhood's message. Defending against injustice seemed in that period to be a matter of education and missionary work, especially among young men, who flocked to the youth sections of the Brotherhood. Young men were also flocking to nationalist youth organizations, others, including older men, gravitated to the Wafd – the party of nationalism. It won several elections in the post-World War I period overwhelmingly, but

Islamic and illegal'." That is because "Islam knows only two kinds of society, the Islamic and the jahili'."[426] An illegal society may be fought against. Jihad as aggressive fighting was the norm. The "greater jihad" of inner spiritual struggle was a modernist and apologetic definition that Qutb rejected. He began to teach the necessity of a vanguard, or elite group committed to these principles who could lead the rest of society. Struggle with arms would only sharpen and develop the inner man of these followers – much further than any of them could progress spiritually without taking up weapons.

While these doctrines were being written in prison, the Muslim Brotherhood began to form again, carefully representing to the government that they were interested in teaching and missionary work. But again, a Secret Organization was formed, and Qutb while still in prison agreed to lead it. He was released in 1964 in a move designed to gain political favor for the Egyptian government, and by 1965 had met with the heads of the Secret Organization.

Qutb knew that the 200 men undergoing training, and the weapons they had were not enough. The first goal of the movement must be education and recruitment, since the state was simply too strong. The Muslim Brothers must wait. But in the late Summer and Fall of 1965 the arrests began – the government knew something was brewing. Perhaps it had learned of the shipment of arms into the country. Qutb was arrested, tried, and in the middle of the night of August 28, 1966, he was hanged.

His ideas lived on, and his writings continued to inspire. Some ran with the idea of the Kingship of God and the ignorance of surrounding Muslim societies, and through the 70s, 80s, and 90s, from time to time armed rebellions broke out. Others tried to pull back, and emphasize the teaching and missional aspects of Qutb's thought. Yet others left Egypt which was too harsh an environment for them, and moved to other Arab countries, including Saudi Arabia.[427] There they contributed to the "awakening" movement of the 1980s, showing increased hostility when U.S. military forces were stationed there during the first Gulf War. The apparent failure of the Egyptian experiment with Western-style nationalism and economic deprivation only drove more young men to join the Muslim Brothers.[428]

Common Threads Uniting these Modern Scholars and Activists

The Wahhabis, Hasan al-Banna, Qutb, Mawdudi, and the Muslim Brothers all have in common a rejection of the Western model of society (even if some of them borrowed Western tools to promote their own programs). All of them look back to find the answer, through a time-honored chain of scholars, to a time or times when everything in Islam was done perfectly. With that comes the insistence that later encrustations of culture or tradition must be scraped off to get back to a pure Islam, free from regional and cultural variations, an Islam to be accepted by all.

Sometimes boundaries between different groups overlap. A Wahhabi may be included within the general class of *salafi*, but not all *salafis* are Wahhabis. The term *salafi* can be understood as an umbrella big enough to shelter disparate groups like the Wahhabis and the Muslim Brotherhood, because of their common wish to revive that early state of perfection within Islamic society. *Salafis* may come from any of the four major schools of Sunni law, although they may not regard themselves as bound by earlier doctrines of those schools in their pursuit of what the forefathers did.

While they have much in common, these reformers have disagreed and do disagree on many particulars. Something as basic as the boundaries of the term *salafi*, from the *salaf*, or forefathers of Islam, isn't even agreed upon. Some limit the *salafs* to the generation of the Prophet, others to the era ending with the death of the last rightly guided caliph, and others are willing to stretch them almost to or as far as the time of ibn Hanbal.[429] Some would include thinkers of the 1800s like Muhammad Abduh and al-Sayyid Jamal al-Din al-Afghani as *salafis*, but others reject what can be understood as too liberal in their thought, and insist that real *salafis* are those holding the strict line of ibn Hanbal and ibn Taymiyah, and even there, some who think they are *salafi* aren't real *salafi*.[430]

These groups tried to carry out their missions under very different circumstances. Saudi Arabia wasn't colonized or occupied by the West, and the sacred and secular powers were left to strike the balance in the constitutional order on their own within an Islamic society. Mawdudi, al-Banna, and Qutb all lived and worked under Western occupation. It was probably clearer earlier in India than Egypt that the colonial regime was ending, but in these and other countries, reformist groups labored under the additional burden of fitting themselves into an alien legal and governing order. Implementing their programs could therefore look strikingly "modern".

The differences that matter most for the long term lie in what members of these groups are willing to do in order to reach the state of society their understanding of Islam requires. Wahhabis would tend to disagree with Muslim Brothers on the use of force against governments deemed *illegitimate*, and government actions considered incorrect. There is a spectrum of thought within the *salafi* tradition sometimes summed up in the words of *hadith* as involving the heart, the tongue, or the hand – signifying those who will keep a pure heart by not participating in what is wrong, those who will educate and persuade society around them to the right way, and those who will take up arms in their hands and use force.[431] Of course it is this last, and smallest, group which gets all the attention in news broadcasts.

Rejection of the West and Revival of Islam – Caused by Western Provocation?

Some argue that the *salafi* groups and ideology are a reaction against modernity. Western colonization and economic and cultural exploitation, or the harsh actions of a Middle Eastern secular state in repressing traditional Muslims, must be the cause of the troubles. There is truth in this argument that the shock of the Western advance from the 1800s on caused a reaction, but the *choice* of reaction and its intellectual content was not caused by the West. Kemalist Turkey adopted Western ideas and beat the West at its own game, but the vast majority of Muslims could not change so much, so fast. And some chose rejection of the West, and looked back into their own history, where they quickly found a line of scholars and strain of thought which supported their resistance to and rejection of the West.

Let me emphasize that I am not excusing or ignoring the rapacity of the Western imperial powers, chiefly Britain and France, in the Middle East. They did antagonize Muslims and Muslim thinkers and accelerate serious attempts at revival within Islam. All I'm saying is that the drive to purify Islam didn't begin only in reaction to Western dominance in the 1800s with thinkers like Muhammad Abduh or al-Sayyid Jamal al-Din al-Afghani. It had deep roots in the Islamic world, roots which had driven deep into the culture before Europeans as dominant powers appeared, far deeper even than al-Wahhab and his teachers in the early 1700s.

The great ibn Taymiyah, who lived from 1263 to 1328, was a follower of Ibn Hanbal. Ibn Taymiyah wanted to get back to true Islam, and was interested in offensive jihad against Muslims who were bad Muslims (or maybe not even Muslims at all). The Mongols claimed to be Muslims, but were not in his opinion, since they insisted upon retaining some of their customary laws.

> "Some would say that singling out heretics and schismatics had not been the spirit of early Islam. Arguments about the succession, yes; even bloody arguments. But Mohammed himself and the early Muslims in general tended to accept that people who wanted to be Muslims were Muslims. ("Hypocrites" – traitors pretending to be Muslims in order to undermine the community from within – were obviously a different case.) With all would-be Muslims accepted into the group, the group could sort out disagreements about

what "Muslim" meant. Ibn Taymiyah, however, insisted that there was one way to be a Muslim, and the main Muslim duty was to ascertain that one way and then follow it. Interpretation did not come into it, since everything a person needed to know about Islam was right there in the book in black and white."[432]

To many Muslims of the time, the Muslim Mongols would have been Muslims. But not to ibn Taymiyah, who insisted upon his strict interpretation of Islam. His thought cannot be ignored as a relic of long ago, since he "remains to this day the father figure of practically all Islamist fundamentalist movements."[433]

Ibn Taymiyyah of course had his own followers. Beside Taymiyyah himself, who al-Wahhab several hundred years later often referred to simply as "*the* Shaykh", Taymiyyah's disciple Jawziyya was cited by al-Wahhab in his own works.[434] When al-Wahhab himself was studying in Medina, his teachers were part of a re-emphasis of *hadith* and tradition which had been growing in Medina for roughly one hundred years. Part of this intellectual current "was an inclination to rehabilitate the ideas of Ahmad b. Hanbal (d. 241/855) and Ibn Taymiyya."[435]

Wahhab's teacher Muhammad Hayat al-Sindi taught themes that appeared later in al-Wahhab's own works. Al-Sindi "was the product of Islamic reformist currents that had begun to take shape with the rise of Ibrahim al-Kurani in the second half of the seventeenth century." Al-Sindi wrote a commentary on Hanbal's *Musnad*, and emphasized "the re-assertion of the position of *hadith* as a locus of religious authority and the precedence of *hadith* over the opinion of the *madhhab*" or school of law.[436]

"By the late 17th and early 18th centuries these earlier religious and political tendencies – Hanbalism, North African Sufism, Indian Naqshbandi Islam, and Ottoman conservative religious views found a common forum in Mecca and Medina (the *Haramayn*)."[437] From there, and later Cairo, these revivalist or reformist ideas could spread through the Islamic world. It looked to the reformers, in this time before the West had begun to make much of an impact on the Middle East, that Islam was in need of revival and reform.

The decay and disarray within the aging Ottoman, Safavid, and Moghul empires as we approach early modern times encouraged revival. In Istanbul in the early 1600s, Qadizade Mehmed Efendi used his best efforts to see Sufi lodges closed, Sufi leadership imprisoned, and enforcement of a stricter version of *shari'a*. Ahmad Sirhindi, who died in 1624, opposed the disorder during the Mughul Emperor Akbar's reign, and sought to strengthen and unify Islam. On the fringes of empire, movements like that of Abd al-Wahhab in Saudi Arabia, and Uthman don Fodio in Sudan, were well started before European colonization.[438] When that came, it only sped other revivalists on the same path.

This type of revivalist thinking isn't something which grew out of European colonization in the 1800s; it isn't something which grew out of the turmoil of WWI; not from the economic exploitation of the post-WWII world; or even the provocations of George Bush and the War on Terror. It is not Islam hijacked by some newly sprung-up radicals. It is the outgrowth of an accepted Sunni Islamic school of law which has been around for roughly one thousand, two hundred years. It cannot be easily reformed away, nor excused away by blaming Crusaders, the colonizing powers, or the modern oil-thirsty West.

It grew with Ahmad Ibn Hanbal and with the school that followed him. It matured with ibn Taymiyyah, and al-Wahhab found it full blown in Medina when he went to study there in the early 1700s. That way of thinking flourished from the time *when Islam was at what some would argue was its peak.* It continued in response to disasters like the Crusaders, then the Mongol invasion, then Tamerlane's. It went on with an internal struggle against Sufi mystics, although some of them would later drive revivalist thinking of the 1700s on[439], and in reaction to syncretism that crept in as Islam itself expanded to new horizons, and the decay of aging empires just mentioned.

It is a choice of interpretation of the Islamic corpus made by the scholars of Islam triumphant, when the Islamic empire spread from the borders of India to the Atlantic. It is a choice made at a time when Western Europeans were clearly less wealthy, less powerful, and most Christians were less cultured than the Muslims of that Islamic empire. That choice of interpretation was given a modern twist by al-Banna, Mawdudi, Qutb, and others, but all looked back to Hanbal, Taymiyyah, and al-Wahhab for inspiration. It is a choice which a significant and vocal minority of Muslims still makes today.

Chapter 11 - Lands of Confusion

Most Middle Eastern countries in modern times have spent generations freeing themselves from Western domination. Once freedom was theirs, they struggled to define social expectations and structures somewhere between traditional and historic Islamic ideas and the newer ideas from the West. This process has been so difficult that even where the answer different countries arrived at looks clear, as in Turkey or Saudi Arabia, it isn't. Significant minority groups arguing against the status quo exist in these two countries, both in and out of government. In other countries where the choice of models for society is even less clear, the argument rages too.

All over the Middle East, populations are in internal conflict as they try to live or live with different sets of ideas that don't fit well together. Does law come from the State? Does it come from God only as the *shari'a*? Is there a mix of the two that might work? Is democracy a man-made system offensive to God and true believers? What of Western notions like free speech, freedom of religion, or gender equality? Can they – should they – work under Islamic law or some mix of Western and Islamic law? Does a word like "freedom" mean different things in Europe and the Middle East?

Most people in the Middle East don't want to blow up or kill those who disagree with them. Most do not have routine exposure to violent terrorist acts. The small minority of terrorists within Islamic societies, or different interpretations of Islam used as pretexts for violence, grab the headlines and obscure what real people in the Middle East experience every day. But what real people endure every day may be more exhausting and frustrating than one sharp terrorist attack, because it simply goes on, day after day after day.

Listen to these different voices from Muslim-majority countries arguing about the shape of society, and look at the price they pay for doing so. I've selected mainly Egyptian, Saudi, and Turkish voices, since most of the material covered so far has come from these countries. These ideas, people, and events have counterparts all through the countries of the Middle East, and could be multiplied many thousands of times.

In Saudi Arabia, Raif Badawi, a young father and husband, established a blog called the "Saudi Free Liberals Forum" to air his thoughts. Some of his statements reported in the West included:

> "As soon as a thinker starts to reveal his ideas, you will find hundreds of fatwas that accused him of being an infidel just because he had the courage to discuss some sacred topics. I'm really worried that Arab thinkers will migrate in search of fresh air and to escape the sword of the religious authorities."

> "States based on religious ideology ... have nothing except the fear of God and an inability to face up to life. Look at what had happened after the European peoples succeeded in removing the clergy from public life and restricting them to their churches."

> "Finally, we should not hide that fact that Muslims in Saudi Arabia not only disrespect the beliefs of others, but also charge them with infidelity to the extent that they consider anyone who is not Muslim an infidel, and, within their own narrow definitions, they consider non-Hanbali Muslims as apostates. How can we be such people and build ... normal relations with six billion humans, four and a half billion of whom do not believe in Islam."

> "For me, liberalism simply means, live and let live. This is a splendid slogan."[440]

By Western standards, pretty tame stuff. I can imagine my Western friends and acquaintances, especially the self-identified liberals, saying that he's right, and agreeing that religion is a drag on the progress of society. I can imagine quite a few of my Turkish friends saying the very same things.

Raif Badawi didn't make those statements in the West though, but in Saudi Arabia. So he was arrested in 2012, and after trial sentenced to 10 years in prison, a 1,000,000 riyal fine (several hundred thousand dollars) and 1,000 lashes.[441] His website was shut down. The public whippings remain set at 50 per week on Friday at the Mosque. As of late 2015, he has undergone one set of 50 lashes, and due to his poor health there is a current suspension of further whipping.

A harsh sentence and softer implementation are not unusual practice in Saudi law. A convicted murderer may be sentenced to death by beheading, but frequently the practice of "blood money" payment by his family to the murder victim's family is an agreed resolution and there is no execution. I hope you will object that that is a practice under criminal law, that Raif Badawi didn't murder anyone, and ask why Raif's statements are treated and punished in the same way as a crime.

Maybe the pause in the beatings is the result of world-wide publicity and protest. His wife and little children fled the country after death threats started coming in, and today a website - www.raifbadawi.org - has been started by his wife, Ensaf Haidar, with support from friends, family, and many concerned citizens scattered through the world, to work for his release. It's worth looking at the website to see the number of awards for free speech Raif has been awarded by many supporting organizations. Or, try a quick internet search and look at the enormous number of "hits" for stories about Raif Badawi.

Raif Badawi is far from the only Saudi to express thoughts like that. He is not the only Saudi in prison for doing so. The website set up by his wife mentions others, and even a cursory search of English-language blogs yields yet other Saudis expressing similar ideas. But if they're not as famous as Raif, what then? What sentences will they receive?

Turkish pianist Fazil Say, who has performed with symphony orchestras worldwide, was sentenced in Istanbul to 10 months, for the crime of blasphemy. The court suspended the sentence – not an unusual practice in Turkey – which means that should Mr. Say choose to tweet or post something similar in the future, the sentence may be implemented against him right away. He was convicted of "insulting religious values of a part of the population" of Turkey, in April of 2013.[442]

His offenses? Say tweeted some verse of Omar Khayyam, 12th century Persian intellectual, (some argue they are not authentic works of the poet): "You say its rivers will flow in wine. Is the Garden of Eden a drinking house? You say you will give two houris to each Muslim. Is the Garden of Eden a whorehouse?" At another time, he sent out: "I don't know whether you have noticed or not but wherever there is a stupid person or a thief, they are believers in God. Is this a paradox?"

I don't follow Fazil Say on twitter (nor anyone else, for that matter). I don't know how many followers he had in Turkey when he sent those two comments, but I'm quite willing to bet that not many of them were conservative Muslims. So then, why the criminal prosecution? More problematic yet, Turkey has a Constitution not based on the Koran and *sunna* as is the basic law of Saudi Arabia, but on the secular principles of the Atatürk revolution. It contains several provisions resembling modern Western constitutional rights:

> Article 26: "Everyone has the right to express and disseminate his/her thoughts and opinions by speech, in writing or in pictures or through other media, individually or collectively. This freedom includes the liberty of receiving or imparting information or ideas without interference by official authorities....
>
> The exercise of these freedoms may be restricted for the purposes of national security,

public order, public safety, safeguarding the basic characteristics of the Republic and the indivisible integrity of the State with its territory and nation, preventing crime, punishing offenders, withholding information duly classified as a state secret, protecting the reputation or rights and private and family life of others..."

You might argue that Fazil Say can't be punished for freely expressing his thoughts. Or, you may object that Turkey has made it a crime to insult the religious feelings of others, so that Fazil Say's case falls under the "preventing crime" clause in Article 26. But *if* his comments are admitted to be insulting to religion, does that override his own right to express what he thinks?

Turkey has also joined the Convention for the Protection of Human Rights and Fundamental Freedoms, an international treaty to which all EU members and approximately twenty other countries are parties. Cases for violations of this treaty are heard in the European Court of Human Rights. As a result, issues of rights under the Turkish Constitution, the laws and court cases developing under it, can provide *more* liberty and freedom in the area of freedom to associate and speak than law under the Convention and cases decided in the European Court of Human Rights, but not *less*.

The Convention states:

Article 10: "1) Everyone has the right to freedom of expression. This right shall include freedom to hold opinions and to receive and impart information and ideas without interference by public authority and regardless of frontiers....

2) The exercise of these freedoms, since it carries with it duties and responsibilities, may be subject to such formalities, conditions, restrictions or penalties as are prescribed by law and are necessary in a democratic

Page 233

society, in the interests of national security, territorial integrity or public safety, for the prevention of disorder or crime, for the protection of health or morals…"

So, to be properly convicted of an insult to religion for sending those tweets, three conditions must be satisfied: One - Fazil Say must have been convicted for a crime set out in the Turkish law. Two - restriction of his right to free expression by this law must be found "necessary in a democratic society". Three – for a good reason like the prevention of crime, etc.

No argument with factor one – there is a law on the books (ill-advised as it might be). But factors two and three - "necessary in a democratic society", and, prevention of "disorder or crime"? Was there really disorder or crime in Istanbul, or anywhere in Turkey because of these two tweets? Did those two tweets so crush the rights of others that it was a crime to send them? Is it so likely that those two tweets, or more like them, would cause disorder, crime, or such serious damage to the rights of others that Fazil Say is to be forbidden to send them? What of Fazil Say's right to express his own opinion? Isn't vigorous public debate of ideas part of a democratic society? Doesn't his conviction trouble you given both the Turkish and International laws which apply? Given those laws, how can this prosecution have taken place?

Freedom of speech or criminal insult to religion? In which category do the website and tweets of Raif Badawi and Fazil Say belong? The law of Saudi Arabia makes the answer clear for Raif Badawi. The law of Turkey on the books is clear, but its application to the real case of Fazil Say is quite muddy – if not clearly backward. Understanding what the law in Saudi Arabia clearly *is*, and what it requires of Raif Badawi, is easy but not the same as the argument about what the law *ought* to be. Understanding what the law in Turkey clearly *is* is not an easy answer, nor what the law *ought* to be.

The argument about what the law *is* rages in Turkey. The argument about what the law *ought* to be burns on in both

Turkey and Saudi Arabia. Since these cases have both received wide publicity, many organizations and individuals in the West have commented freely. But these are arguments carried on by Muslims, by citizens of Turkey and Saudi Arabia, not by foreigners. They can't be dismissed as contamination of Middle Eastern Islamic cultures by Western ideas, *unless* you're willing to argue that Raif Badawi and Fazil Say cannot be allowed to think and say what they have, or that they are somehow not authentic Muslim people if they say what they have said.

If it *is* a crime for a Muslim to say what Raif Badawi has said, or what Fazil Say has said, then the law should be clear about it. If it *ought* to be a crime, then likewise that desire should be clear. And if these positions are so clear, then the governments of the West ought to stop pretending otherwise.

But is this only a one-way street, with "bad" religiously observant Muslims persecuting "good" non-religious or secular Muslims? What of denial of rights to religiously observant Muslims within Middle Eastern countries? That happens too, though today, less often than in the past given exhaustion of attempts to base national life on secularism, socialism, or nationalism instead of the traditional Islamic rules. This is shown most easily in stories from Turkey, the "secular" Muslim-majority state of the Middle East.

I worked at two Turkish universities while I lived in Istanbul with my family. At one university, a female student in one of my classes had hair that always looked the same – no new style, no new color or cut, ever. As bad at noticing these things as I am, I finally realized that there was no change because she was wearing a wig. She was religiously observant, and she was not allowed to "cover" or wear the headscarf, so the wig was an acceptable substitute. Other times, as I walked through university gates, I saw female students remove their headscarves, fold them away in their purses or backpacks, and enter the university grounds as modern, Western-looking young women. What was going on here?

The headscarf is a form of traditional Islamic covering for women, and has been a focus of contention in Turkey for decades. The early Republic wanted a modern look as part of its leap into Western modernity, so men were to wear the hat, not the fez or turban, and women were to uncover their heads. But time went on, and the secularism of the early Republic began to relax, and bans on wearing headscarves in public institutions, including universities, were inconsistently enforced. During the late 70s and 80s, the number of young women wanting to wear headscarves began to climb, and the official stance hardened.

After the military coup of 1980, the Higher Education Authority of Turkey issued an order in December 1982, banning headscarves in lecture halls. That rule was upheld in a judgment given December 13, 1984, by the Supreme Administrative Court, which stated that "Beyond being a mere innocent practice, wearing the headscarf is in the process of becoming the symbol of a vision that is contrary to the freedoms of women and the fundamental principles of the Republic."

Yet in December of 1988, transitional Section 16 of the Higher Education Law came into force, and stated that "...A veil or headscarf covering the neck and hair may be worn out of religious conviction." That law was promptly overturned by a ruling of the Turkish Constitutional Court given March 7, 1989, where the Court found that allowing the headscarf would violate principles of secularism, equality, and freedom of religion. Its judgment made clear that a strong secularism not allowing the headscarf was a hedge against the organization of political life on religious lines. It was in fact, a guarantor of freedom and individual conscience. Otherwise, individuals might feel themselves under compulsion, or there might be a serious risk to order.

In another judgment given in 1991, the Constitutional Court reaffirmed its ruling that the headscarf could not be worn in universities, reciting many of the same reasons. Universities during this time tried to clarify their rules in reaction to continuing protests for the right to wear the headscarf, among them, Istanbul University, whose administration published rules in 1994 and again in 1998.

In March of 1998, a young medical student named Leyla Şahin tried to enter into a hall at Istanbul University for her oncology exam. She was denied entry since her head was covered, contrary to university rules. She was subsequently refused admission to other exams and lectures, and was refused enrolment for classes.

On March 19, 1999, the university rules were upheld by the Istanbul Administrative Court, which dismissed her case, stating that the university could make rules regulating students' dress to maintain order within the university. In April of 2001, the Supreme Administrative Court refused an appeal. Meanwhile, Ms. Şahin had enrolled at university in Vienna to continue her studies.

Certainly anticipating that she would lose her case in the Turkish Court System, Ms. Şahin also petitioned the European Court of Human Rights, claiming that refusal to let her wear the headscarf was a denial of her rights to respect for private and family life, to freedom of thought, conscience and religion, to her freedom of expression, and was discriminatory against her. She lost on all grounds in a decision made by a Chamber of the Court on June 29, 2004.

Decisions in the European Court of Human Rights are most often made by rotating Chambers of Judges, chosen according to fixed procedure, each Chamber having seven judges to hear a case. In event of a serious question regarding the Convention, or a serious issue that may apply widely, an appeal can be made to a Grand Chamber of the Court, triggering a re-hearing of the case before a panel of seventeen judges.[443] Leyla Şahin promptly appealed.

The Grand Chamber, in its November 2005 opinion, recited the long history of her case as given above, and the background to the headscarf rules, summarizing the problem, that "[t]hose in favour of the headscarf see wearing it as a duty and/or a form of expression linked to religious identity. However, the supporters of secularism, who draw a distinction between the *başörtüsü* (traditional Anatolian headscarf, worn loosely) and the *türban* (tight, knotted headscarf hiding the hair and the throat), see the Islamic headscarf as a symbol of a political Islam."[444]

The Grand Chamber concluded that there was a law against wearing the headscarf that Ms. Şahin could or should have known of before trying to attend her exam wearing one; that the law against the headscarf "primarily pursued the legitimate aims of protecting the rights and freedoms of others and of protecting public order"; and that the law was "necessary" to protect those rights and freedoms (including the right to practice no religion at all). Ms. Şahin lost.

The Grand Chamber recognized that an area such as this is quite difficult for legal doctrine, and emphasized appropriate deference to national authorities making prior legal decisions, and the efforts of the university to react proportionately to the problem it faced. Only one of seventeen judges dissented, and that was only to part of the decision, agreeing with the majority that the insistence on secularism was "undoubtedly necessary for the protection of the democratic system in Turkey."[445]

But Leyla Şahin's losing court case didn't end the argument. In 2008, the Justice and Development Party (AKP), with support from other Turkish parties, moved to amend Articles 10 and 42 of the Constitution so that wearing the headscarf would be allowable. The main opposition party, the Republic People's Party (CHP) requested that the Constitutional Court rule on the constitutionality of the amendments, since the CHP thought the principle of secularism in the 1982 Constitution would be violated by the amendments. The Turkish Constitutional Court reviewed the law, and relying in part on the earlier Şahin decision, found that lifting the ban was unconstitutional, in order "to protect the rights of others in a Muslim majority country".

One sunny Spring day in 2009, a lot of my students skipped a late afternoon class – some things seem to be true universal values – and only about eight or ten female students attended. Since none of the male students were there, and since the headscarf issue had been in the news recently, I asked them what would happen if the rules were changed, allowing headscarves on campus. They all said that they would have to cover, since the young men "would make us". The pressure, comments, and shaming would be too much to resist.

But as the AKP gained strength within the government, and began to change rules, and began to see boards and commissions filled with its own appointees, the ban was lifted. "In a memorandum sent to Istanbul University, the Council of Higher Education (YÖK), the administrative body in charge of institutions of higher education, declared that students wearing headscarves should not be forced to leave classes under any circumstances." Soon after, in 2013, "the AKP lifted the ban on headscarves for women working in government offices." It remains in place in limited circumstances, including the police forces and the military.

So what is this headscarf debate really? Is it all about a harmless religious practice any woman ought to be free to follow, or is it about an establishment of religion, that will then force its way on others? Are the rights of observant Muslims being improperly limited in places like Turkey? I think the European Court of Human Rights has been clear. I know what the young Turkish women in my university class thought. How are Muslim women in Turkey to dress, and cover – and who decides? Government? Community pressure?

On June 12, 2012, the Hurriyet Daily News, an English-language daily, republished a story it had picked up about an event in Istanbul, titling it "Turkish woman barred from public bus by religious fanatics". Here it is:

> A Turkish woman claimed she was prevented from boarding a public bus by a group of Islamists because her outfit would "cause them to sin," according to a report by daily Evrensel.
>
> Yağmur Yılmaz, 21, said she left home on June 3 to go to work, wearing a pair of sweatpants and a T-shirt.
>
> Yılmaz said she walked to a stop in Istanbul's Edirnekapı

district to get on a bus going to Fatih district, where she worked. A group of around 15 men and women clad in burqas, cloaks and turbans who were on the bus blocked Yılmaz's path, saying she could not get on the vehicle. Yılmaz said she told the group it was everybody's right to board the bus, to which the women from the group replied, "We would sin if you get on this bus, you are causing us to sin."

The men in the group also harassed Yılmaz, she claimed, saying: "Look at her. Her head is not covered, shame!"

"Nobody in the bus did anything about it, not even the driver," Yılmaz said. "There were other 'uncovered' women waiting at the stop, but they just stood by idly."

Yılmaz told Evrensel that she had been using the same bus route for a long time and that it was the first time that she encountered such an incident. "I was wearing sweatpants and a T-shirt because it was a Sunday [when many workers can wear more casual clothes], but no one would have the right to do such a thing even if I were wearing a skirt or a dress."

Yılmaz said she was startled by the incident, meaning that she was unable to take the bus' license plate number to file a complaint. "I wanted the public to learn about it," she said. "It was a shameful act and should not have happened in the first place."

Maybe the European Court of Human Rights was correct in the Şahin case. Maybe the increasingly-worried secular Muslims of Turkey are right to be increasingly worried.

Confusion and Competition in Islamic Societies

There are so many stories and incidents that show the bitter internal argument of Islamic societies today. Are they to model themselves on the "good old days", or are they to look more like Western societies? Is there a possible compromise in the middle? Everywhere, in the Middle East in Muslim-majority countries, as well as in the West, where they are small minorities, Muslims are asking these questions and growing increasingly vocal.

Consider Mona Eltahawy, born in Egypt, who has lived in several countries of the Middle East, and West. Her website, http://www.monaeltahawy.com, lists some of her considerable achievements as a columnist and writer, and provides links to articles. Ms. Eltahawy describes herself on her website as "...a proud liberal Muslim." Links provided as I write this include articles like: *"Mona Eltahawy: 'All religions are obsessed with my vagina '"*, the Guardian, May 10, 2015; *"Egypt-born writer: 'We're more than our headscarves and hymens'"* CNN interview with Christiane Amanpour, April 22, 2015; and *"Egypt's War on Atheism",* an op-ed in the New York Times, January 27, 2015. There are many more, and I encourage a look at her website.

What about the Muslim fellow in France who in November of 2012 planned to open a Mosque for gay men? He stated that he realized the need within Islamic society for a Mosque for gay men, since in the usual Mosque "gay men are afraid of both verbal and physical aggression..."[446] In Toronto Canada there is a similar Mosque with location available only through its website. "The El-Tawhid Juma Circle Mosque is an LGBTQ friendly mosque where attendees have equal status regardless of their gender or sexual orientation."[447]

But what of the Koranic verses like 7:80, 26:165, and others, that state regarding homosexuals: "We rained down on them a shower (of brimstone)." And that's not even looking at the *hadith* on the subject! Al-Azhar in Egypt, among the foremost, if not the foremost center for traditional Islamic education, responded to legalization of same-sex marriage, and published a statement on its Facebook page reading in part: "Al-Azhar condemns the calls to legalize sexual deviancy, and stresses the following: These dubious calls actualize a satanic plan to destroy the system of human morals and values..."

How can these competing desires and statements by Muslims be reconciled? All of these statements are from people who say they are Muslims. Which is wrong? Are they both wrong? In a brief vignette from Omid Djalili's 2010 comedy film *The Infidel*, about a British Muslim who finds after his mother's death both that he's adopted, and that his birth parents were Jewish, a "liberal" Imam misunderstands what kind of secret Djalili is trying to come to terms with (his ethnicity, not his sexuality) and reinterprets fire and brimstone as an internal event. Is it possible outside a comedy film, and in seriousness, to interpret those verses figuratively and find a middle way?

Nuray Mert, Turkish academic and columnist, wrote on Western reactions to the Charlie Hebdo killings in Paris in the Hurriyet Daily News of January 26, 2015[448], that "I am sick and tired of all those 'well-intentioned' Western liberals and leftists who constantly pose as the most understanding of 'the oppressed Orientals,' especially because I was one years ago." Ms. Mert, who identified herself as having a Western education, wrote that she realized that her own "effort to find excuses for all the shortcomings of Islamists/conservatives was quite "patronizing" in the sense that I was not seeing them as equals but as "oppressed victims."

She noted the discourse of "'oppression,' 'exclusion,' 'alienation,' 'traumatic memories of Western imperialism' and the like", but continued that these views had basic assumptions of "Orientalism and Western supremacism." She argued that assuming that Muslims are members of a "timeless and coherent community" is just plain wrong, as is failing to identify wrong or evil actions. "...Muslims, their politics and indeed the politics of their states should be scrutinized in critical ways in the same way that Westerners, their politics and the politics of their states are held responsible for evil outcomes. Therefore,

Islamists should be invited to political debate rather than being reduced to being the subjects of anthropological understanding."

In Saudi Arabia, on September 27 of 2011 a Saudi woman was sentenced to ten lashes with the whip for driving a car. The AP story dated September 28 noted the usual practice that "police just stop female drivers, question them and let them go after they sign a pledge not to drive again. But dozens of women have continued to take to the roads since June in a campaign to break the taboo." This sentence was particularly distressing to many in Saudi Arabia (though undoubtedly pleasing to others), since in other areas the King had promised advancement in women's rights – participation in municipal elections, and the possibility of women's representation on the King's Shura council. Some viewed this as a backlash to the King from the Wahhabi scholars and their establishment. "Asked if the sentencing will stop women from driving, Maha al-Qahtani, another female activist, said, 'This is our right, whether they like it or not.'"[449]

Even in seemingly neutral places where you're not even aware an issue exists, there is an argument going on. One morning in 2008, I arrived at the university early, and headed up to my office, only to hear Mozart or perhaps Beethoven (I can't remember what was playing) wafting through the empty halls from the office of a Turkish professor. I stuck my head in and said something like "I really like that piece," and we chatted briefly, the professor casually delivering the line, that "you know, the party (AKP) doesn't like this music."

I hadn't given the matter any thought before that incident, but Western music, even as seemingly harmless as a beautiful classical piece, isn't acceptable in some Islamic circles. Try this: Do a quick internet search, using exactly this line "can a good Muslim listen to classical music", and marvel at the number and variety of responsive arguments.

And I haven't even touched disapproval of popular music, and what it might carry with it to the detriment of Muslim youths - just last Fall seven Iranians were sentenced to up to one year in prison for posting the video they'd made of themselves dancing to Pharrell Williams' song "Happy" from the Disney movie *Despicable Me 2*.[450] Try watching the 2009 Iranian film *Nobody Knows About Persian Cats* for an inside look at young people who love unapproved popular music.

Consider Sheikh Ibrahim al-Mardini in Lebanon, who despite his advanced degree, has no mosque or madrasa position, but must work in a pharmacy to support his family, because of his position that "secular music, including rock and heavy metal, is not prohibited by Islamic law." It isn't even that he is a fan of hard rock (he isn't), but "[f]or him, support or opposition to music represents the fault line between an Islam that is open to the world and tolerant, and one that is not. As he explained to me, 'There is nothing in the Qur'an that says music should be prohibited. In fact, it can play a positive role in society as long as it's not insulting or offers views against Islam.'" He continued that "A musical culture is necessary for people to develop themselves; any limitations on the arts will encourage the opposite of what a healthy religious system should call for, because culture is something owned by everyone, and not something that a few persons should decide upon."[451]

Or what about this? During 2012 and 2013 one of the issues the Turkish government wrestled with was whether within Islam it was permissible to establish a breast milk bank, for the babies of mothers who wanted to nurse their children but could not. The Health Ministry put that question to the Directorate of Religious Affairs, and received a positive response. The Health Minister went on to state that "the breast milk would be taken from people of different religions but added that *there would be no problem on the issue provided the families' permission is first taken*."[452] Enough said.

Or what about jihad? Is it a real physical battle with blood, wounds, and killing, or an inner struggle, or both – the "greater" and "lesser" jihads? Should there be blasphemy laws on the books as there are in many Islamic countries? What do we do about education of girls? Should every university have at least one Mosque on its grounds? How about bonus points for the private school the Education Ministry has just inspected if it has a prayer room on its grounds? The list could go on and on. These are only a few of the stories, deliberately picked only from English-language sources. There are many more, and you may find them easily.

As I write this, the offices of the French satirical weekly Charlie Hebdo were recently attacked (again) by terrorists "punishing" the paper and its staff for its treatment of the Prophet and Islam. As two attackers drove up, a young French bicycle policeman, Ahmed Merabet, a Muslim himself, drew his weapon and fired. He was cut down by automatic weapons immediately. One of the attackers walked up to him as he lay bleeding on the sidewalk and asked if he wanted to kill them, and the officer replied calmingly that "no, it's alright chief." He was shot dead on the spot. A short time later, Belgin Akaltan wrote a column in Turkey's Hurriyet Daily News that:

> "I think we are all like him. When I say we, I mean the modern Muslims of the world, the moderate Muslims, or maybe the non-practicing Muslims of the world. Those who have been born to a Muslim family and have that identity given to them, the one we pass on to our children; not bothering to question it much… Especially if you are in a once-secular country like Turkey, you can live your entire life being a non-practicing Muslim. You have a Muslim identity; you believe in the goodness of the religion, but seeing how it is you are distanced from the currently practiced faith, caught in a dilemma between modern times and medieval practices. We are trying to tell the world something, even with the last breath we take, we are sure of it; we are afraid, we are dying, we are injured; we have something to say. We want to cry it out loud…But it is not heard. It hits the wall of terror. It kills us…[o]ur combination of moderate Islam and modernism is dead."[453]

Is There an Answer?

Is this it? For Muslims is there only a choice between the sternest and starkest strains of law in Islamic jurisprudence, or Western secular modernity? If these are the only two options, then the answers to Raif Badawi's internet postings, Fazil Say's tweets, Leyla Şahin's headscarf, or even Ms. Yilmaz's T-shirt and sweats, are easy. Are these issues of free speech or blasphemy? Free speech or provocation? Are these actions the exercise of a human right, or vile sins? From either end of the spectrum, the answers are easy, and there is no reason to waste time on a discussion.

Western society in our time seems particularly ill-trained to even have a serious discussion on these points. The lines of thought (if I can call it that), for the modern educated Westerner run something like this: Pointing out a difference in belief or practice that might cause negative effects will cause the ignorant among us to rise up and attack or kill anyone who is different, so therefore, to keep peace in our time we must declare all cultures, behaviors, and cultural standards equally valid and ignore their differences that spur very different acts in the world by those who take those beliefs seriously. If we choose this way of thinking, than we'd better be honest and admit that we have no ground for protest and can only look away from poor Raif Badawi's bleeding back because it turns our delicate stomachs.

On the other hand, if we accept the notion that some cultural behaviors might be wrong, but then paint the whole culture with that brush instead of identifying one particular practice (you know that "those Muslims" are all the same…), and treat all Muslims as if they wanted to overthrow governments and establish a universal Caliphate where Muslims will lord it over the oppressed Christian, atheist, or other non-Muslim, then the majority of Muslims, who want nothing more than to live a quiet life with the family, to work, to pray at the Mosque when they wish, will be mistreated and persecuted.

Is it possible to have a reasonable discussion about values like free speech, or justice, or whether some things are right or wrong, and find common ground? Yes, but both Western and Islamic cultures have to rise above simplistic ways of understanding each other. For example, some argue with a straight face that Muslims are more religious than people in the West, so Westerners must adjust their behavior accordingly. The Pakistani cartoonist Sabir Nazar poked fun at this type of thinking a few years ago:

> "European tourists who come to Al-Absurdistan shall wear *shalwar kameez [loose trouser and shirt worn by Pakistani men]*, and should not drink or kiss in public as that would hurt the sensibilities of Al-Absurdistanis [i.e. the Pakistanis]. But a ban on the veil in Europe is against human rights and symbolic of Islamophobia in the West."[454]

Try turning that formula around for a moment. That's a start. Now do you see more clearly the need for a real discussion? Or do you cling tightly and bitterly to the school of thought which has Western society changing to accomodate strict Islamic sensibilities only – and not the other way round?

Are Western and Islamic cultures really this monolithic? Is there *nothing* good to take from the East, or from the West? "The problem is that we're educating young people to see 50 Cent and think that he's the West. We've managed to get all the bad values of the West without any of the good ones, which makes it pretty hard to bring the two cultures into harmony."[455]

Is there any wonder that the blood and terror this argument for self-definition causes within Middle Eastern countries has managed to spill over the borders? Is it any wonder that those unleashing terror sometimes aim at the West without which (they feel) these disasters wouldn't be happening? And what of the violence, suffering, and pervasive petty indignities (worse for their very pettiness) which citizens of conflicting cultural/religious camps experience within their own Middle Eastern countries?

For some Muslim people, the experience has been so bad that they've even wished for the return of the old colonial powers. For others, it is obvious that secularism or nationalism has failed, and that the only realistic solution is to get back to the practices of the forefathers of Islam. Many people in Muslim nations have become deeply cynical and see their leaders – despite whatever form of government they claim to endorse or rule by – as being nothing but greedy, corrupt, and driven by the goal of monopolizing power for themselves.

Is there no other way forward than to end up with a winner and a loser between the Islam of the Wahhabis, the Muslim Brothers, and their even more radical fellows or the rudderless modernity of the West where seemingly anything goes?

Chapter 12 – The Muslim Voices of an Islamic Reformation

So now that we've seen the state of confusion, dissension, dislike, hatred and prejudice the coming of modern times to the Islamic Middle East helped provoke, is there an answer better than the either-or of the last chapter? Are we stuck between either secularizing the Middle East or turning it back to the pristine Islam of the Prophet's day? The internet, ease of travel, emigration, refugees fleeing the Middle East, growing international trade in goods and services and other qualities of globalism push the peoples of the world more closely together whether they like it or not, heightening this conflict and forcing a consensus that something's got to be done. But is a middle path possible? Is it possible for Islam to reform itself?

I've arranged a sample of different proposals below. These are not voices from the West, but Muslim voices, since if Islam is to reform, it must do so itself, by its own volition, in its own manner, and at its own pace. Most of those mentioned are still living and working in the Middle East, although a few are recently deceased, and a few are living in the West. There are many more who could be mentioned, from earlier within the last century all the way back to the 1800s, and Sufi voices are omitted, since I'm trying to focus on official Sunni Islam.

There is a very rough spectrum, from those who would demand the least amount of change, to those who would demand radical change within Islam. Some Muslims would say plainly that those on the far end of the spectrum are not real Muslims at all, and in reply liberal Muslims would accuse the first school of narrowing and harshening Islam to the point of choking it. Those seeking a middle road will of course be figuratively or literally shot at from both ends of the spectrum.

culture and they were individuals who were outside the [Islamic] mainstream. They were and continue to be unrecognized in our culture. We even burned their books, harassed them, [and] warned against them, and we continue to look at them with suspicion and aversion."

Like al-Ansari, al-Buleihi demands the difference between Islam and historical acts be recognized. "We sharply distinguish between Islam in itself and what people do in its name. The great principles of Islam and its sublime doctrines that emphasize and uphold human value and dignity have not had a chance throughout history to establish themselves. Ever since the end of the period of the rightly-guided Caliphs, man's individuality was eradicated in Arab history and his value has been linked to his political, religious, regional, or tribal affiliation..."

Abdennour Bidar, a French Muslim philosopher, whose books include *Self Islam: A Personal History of Islam*, *Islam without Submission: Muslim Existentialism*, and *A History of Humanism in the West*, in a 2014 newspaper essay argued that the Muslim world needed reform, implementing values like freedom of thought, freedom of religion, equality, and respect for others through education.[460]

Bidar argues that the problems of Islam do not lie in the West. Self-examination within Islam is necessary since "[t]he root of this evil that today steals your face is within yourself; the monster emerged from within you. And other monsters, some even worse, will emerge as well, as long as you refuse to acknowledge your sickness and to finally tackle the root of this evil!" This is something the West often fails to see, since it has forgotten the power of religion. The challenge of the West that began in earnest in the 1800s was met with exactly the wrong reaction – a return to the past and the strict Wahhabi interpretations of Islam.

He sees within Islam a "great multitude of men and women who are willing to reform Islam, to reinvent its genius beyond its historical forms...", but not enough yet, and not with enough power behind their words - yet. "Dear Muslim world: I am but a philosopher, and as usual some will call the philosopher a heretic. Yet I seek only to let the light shine forth once again – indeed, the name that you have given me commands me to do so: Abdennour, Servant of the Light. If I did not believe in you, I would not have been so harsh in this essay."

Mustafa Akyol, Turkish columnist, also sees the cure for Islam as a return to what is right about Islam and the worship of God, carefully avoiding the wrong turns taken by many in the last century that have turned Islam from the worship of God to the worship of a perfect system of politics, society and life. His *Islam Without Extremes: A Muslim Case for Liberty*, makes the argument, that in Turkey at least we are witnessing, "the growing acceptance and advocacy of liberal political ideas by the country's practicing Muslims."[461]

In part, the call for liberalism (meaning a movement back toward the center from the end of the spectrum) grew from what this group felt as repression from hard-line secularists in the early Turkish Republic. Couldn't an idea like "freedom of religion" benefit Muslims – and not just the dominant Sunnis, as well as Christians, Jews, and others? It seemed so. Even the Diyanet, the State religious structure, began to sponsor and publish reformist material, distinguishing between historical and religious qualities in Islamic thought. Context and custom, and their changes, could be discussed, but all of this was a change driven by the people more than the leadership.

This call for interpretation and separation of history and culture from religion, leaving pure religious principles free to express themselves in new ways, is at the core of Akyol's argument. This discussion can be carried out within the context of a democratic system. Indeed, this allows a more pure Islam, since the choice of adherence becomes that of an individual, not an Islam or an Islamic law imposed by the State. "What Muslims really need from the state, in other words, is not religion but freedom of religion."[462]

The AKP government which started in 2002 promoted this successful synthesis of liberalism with Islam, and did have significant public support. Sadly though, authoritarian leadership began to assert itself after several years in power, doing in some cases exactly what it had complained of from its opponents. The dream faded, with the AKP taking a sound beating in national elections in June of 2015 as a result. Whether a turn back to what was a positive direction within Turkish society can be made is an open question.

Iyad Jamal al-Din, an Iraqi Shi'ite cleric and politician, born in Najaf and a descendant of the Prophet himself, first called for a separation of religion and state, and freedom within the state from religion, the turban and other symbols before Saddam Hussein was driven from power. He was a member of Parliament from 2005-2010, though he left in 2009 to form his own political party. His call for a secular state is not to reduce the role of religion in life, but like Mustafa Akyol, rather to free religion from the pressures which heavy state involvement brings to bear upon it: "The holy Koran has been kidnapped by the Islamic state because it is the state that interprets it, and we have to save the religion from the clutches of the state."[463]

He accepts that Islam has varying interpretations, but is against a "bloodthirsty" way of understanding Islam. . "Al-Zarqawi was not born evil," he told an audience in Washington D.C., "but learned to be evil in the mosque. He was taught there to hate the whole world, and so he became ready to carry out acts of suicide." He has called for an interpretation of Islam closer to humanity – even calling for the bars and liquor stores of Baghdad to stay open. He certainly wouldn't go to those places himself, but thinks it is not right to impose that requirement upon others, who must be free to make that choice. The Baghdad government shut them all down later, in the name of imposing *shari'a*.

Ahmad Al-Qabbanji, an Iraqi Shi'ite, left Iraq when Saddam Hussein took power, and eventually ended up in Iran, where his brother had a prestigious position as the Friday prayer Imam of Najaf, and a member of the Iranian establishment. It wasn't long before his liberal ideas caused his own brother to issue a *fatwa* against him, stating that Al-Qabbanji's ideas were distorted, un-Islamic, and part of the war the enemies of Islam are waging. They must be dangerous ideas indeed.

So what are the ideas? Al-Qabbanji demands first, that reason be applied, and if something can't pass the test of reason, it must be rejected, even if it is part of the Koran itself. This is the *fiqh al-maqasid*, or jurisprudence of the meaning. Meaning is to be put before the words of the text. For example,

> "It is like a man who has a lantern. His friend wants to light his cigarette and asks him: 'Do you have a lighter?' The man answers: 'No, I don't.' It is true that he doesn't have a lighter, but, using reason, he could let his friend light his cigarette with the lantern. A reasonable man would understand that what the man wanted was a light, not a lighter. The Wahhabis and most clerics say: No, we must adhere to the text."[464]

A principle like this would allow changes in interpretation. Distilling general rules and exceptions from the text, instead of applying only a narrow textual rule, would allow concepts like justice to stay up to date. With reason in front, the Koran and *sunna* may then be examined, and a decision made whether there is a general rule applicable to us here and now, or whether something reported there was particular to a historic place and time.

He doesn't reject the Prophet, and believes that he created a Koran, driven by God – so that the book is still something which is divine, though it is the Prophet's own interpretation of the divine. Refusal by traditional *ulama* to grasp the leeway for interpretation this understanding of the Koran and *sunna* makes possible is what keeps Islam backward. Some of his statements have been even more radical, and it shouldn't be surprising that he was arrested in Iran on February 18, 2013.

Gamal al-Banna (1920-2013) was the younger brother of Muslim Brotherhood founder Hasan al-Banna. During a long life in Egypt, he wrote a great number of books and articles.

While he respected his older brother, he could not himself be a member of the Brotherhood, and thought that had his older brother lived he would have been a moderating influence on the organization. He thought the organization should stay out of politics, and stick with its goal of influence through teaching.[465]

He addressed a great number of social issues, such as prisoners' rights, and trade union issues, as well as women's rights. His books include *The Muslim Woman between the Emancipation of the Quran and Jurist-made Constraints*. He challenged the idea that states of the Middle East must be Islamic, in his book *Islam is a Religion and an Ummah, not a Religion and a State*. Other books include *The Appeal to an Islamic Revival*, and *The Revolutionization of the Quran*.

Al-Banna accepted the idea of criticism within the vast body of *hadith*, (note his 2008 *The Cleansing of Bukhari and Muslim from useless Hadiths*). He argued that Umayyad and Abbassid leaders in particular had corrupted *hadith* about leadership and rebellion to consolidate their own rule. He couldn't go so far as to apply the same tools of source and textual criticism to the Koran itself. He preferred to stay closer to traditional methods of interpretation and argument. On the other hand, some of the interpretations of the Koran were open to challenge, such as the juridical doctrine whereby later verses in the Koran in effect cancel out earlier. He was unwilling to accept that doctrine, stating that seemingly contradictory positions on issues like *jihad* appeared in the Koran so that they could be applied differently, in different times and place. Religion was to look forward, not backward.

In his last interview with the Arab-West Report, Al-Banna "call[ed] for an Islam that evolves with the times and stays abreast of developments, so that religion continues to be a relevant and potent force within the daily life of both the individual and society."[466]

Bahraini liberal **Dhiyaa Al-Musawi** wants to change the way Islam is thought and taught by the dominant culture in Arab countries. He has appeared on many television channels throughout the Arabic-speaking world. He calls for education, for reading, to an opening of the mind of the Arabic world to beauty, and to not reject a language or dialogue that seeks common ground with others. He states that religious thinking needs to be reformed, and reshaped, and asks why Islam talks only of judgment and the last day, instead of the balance of both hell and paradise contained in the Koran.

He blames this type of thinking for misleading young people who lack education. Instead, he asks, why couldn't the DNA of someone like Gandhi be implanted into Arab youth? Why not listen to beautiful music that develops the spirit of man and humbles him? He listens to Beethoven, though the interviewer in this clip *http://memritv.org/clip/en/1363.htm* asks whether the Arab public is ready to accept a cleric who does things like this.

His home has pictures of Dr. Martin Luther King, Jr., on the wall, along with a picture of Jesus, which opens worlds of peace and love before him when he looks at it. Yet Jews or Christians are called the sons of apes and pigs by his surrounding culture. Al-Musawi hopes that someday, someday, it will be possible to gather in love around the table of humanity.

King Mohammed VI and the government of Morocco, reacting to suicide bombings by Islamic radicals, introduced an unprecedented reform experiment, the subject of a recent film, "Casablanca Calling"[467]. Women are enrolled in a year-long training program, and then assigned to a Mosque. As "Morchidat", their role seems a combination of spiritual leader, social worker, and counsellor. They don't work only in the Mosques, but in neighborhood outreach in schools, prisons, workplaces, homes and hospitals – wherever people in need are found.

The focus is on women, and the problem of separating what the culture of an Islamic country demands, and what Islam itself actually demands. For example, could young women or girls actually have the right to wait for marriage, or have some role outside the home? The Morchidat help encourage education and staying in school, directly confronting cultural norms. Because they are Muslims, working within the Islamic tradition, they are not seen as the threat they would be if they were Westerners.

Ayaan Hirsi Ali is well known in the West, as is the story of her journey from Somalia to the Netherlands, and her outspoken rejection of the Islam she had experienced. Her 2007 book *Infidel* recounted that journey, but her recent work in her new home in the U.S., *Heretic: Why Islam Needs a Reformation Now*, is a little more nuanced. There is an air of regret in a few places in the book, of a wish that she could have remained a Muslim, a wish that there were room within Islam for a faith shaped as she would have liked.[468]

Ali is quite clear that Muslims aren't all violent, that "there are many millions of peaceful Muslims in the world. What I do say is that the call to violence and the justification for it are explicitly stated in the sacred texts of Islam."[469] The challenge is confronting the problems with the text and traditional interpretation, and repudiating the intolerance and violence they allow. She identifies five steps necessary for reform within Islam, so that Muslims are not either forced to leave Islam, or become one of the radicals themselves.

Literal reading of the Koran and an almost semi-divine status of the Prophet must be changed; life here and now instead of in paradise must be emphasized; *Shari'a* and jurisprudence must reform; the individual practice of forcing others to meet commands of the law; and the practice of jihad as physical aggression, all must reform or be rejected.[470] She closes her book with a short review of many different reformers of Islam, (some mentioned here) both within Islamic societies and in the West, and argues that their existence is proof that reformation has begun.

Dr. Bassam Tahhan is a Syrian-born French professor of Arabic literature in Paris. He calls for a "rationalist" reading of the Koran[471], saying that "[t]o be a rationalist is to accept that each era, with its [particular] methods and discoveries, presents its own reading of the Koran..." He rejects what he sees as rigidity in the system of Islamic law, and wants the freedom to go back to the Koran alone to question and interpret – noting that there are different versions and variant readings of parts of the Koran. Admitting this would be the beginning of a broader approach to Islam, and within Islam for Muslims.

> "As a Protestant Muslim, I do not merely challenge the over-application of the Shari'a. I believe that basing Islam [only] on the Five Pillars is a narrow approach. I say that Islam has many dimensions: the judicial dimension which deals with ethics, the theological dimension that has to do with philosophy, and the mystical dimension which has to do with socio-psychology and spirituality. I wish that the training of theologians in Muslim countries would consider all these various dimensions. When you limit religious teaching to the Shari'a, you impoverish it."

His idea of a "Protestant Muslim" is a person who is not content to rest with *hadith*, but digs and criticizes sources to ferret out what is authentic, and rejects the inauthentic. He may claim to be a Protestant Muslim, but is still without question a Muslim. "Why should I be considered a less devout Muslim if I follow the directives of Al-Tabari (a brilliant exegete who was murdered by obscurantists) rather than those of [Ibn] Hanbal? God granted me freedom of thought and I intend to make use of it!"

Ahmed Vanya, an immigrant in the late 1970s from Myanmar (Burma) has spent a long career as an engineer in Silicon Valley, and has lately been speaking out on Islamic issues. He published an advertisement in the New York Times on January 11, 2015, signed by twenty or so other Muslim thinkers, based on his essay at http://www.gatestoneinstitute.org/4894/beautifying-islam.

His argument there was that "[r]eligious traditions have changed and evolved over time, therefore it is the duty of us Muslims, using reason and common sense, to reinterpret the scriptures to bring about an Islam that affirms and promotes universally accepted human rights and values." If Islam went wrong within the first few hundred years, coming to rely on military conquest, and "developed a massive doctrine and theology of intolerance" then the other traditions within Islam need to be reawakened – Sufi traditions that reach toward core principles common to all humanity; or the kind of Islam that produced the society of Andalusia and other places where non-Muslims were treated well.

Vanya blames the problems of Islam today on the tradition which won and developed after the Mihna:

> "This mainstream, legalistic, text-bound, literalist Islam -- now the dominant strain and controlled by the traditional Muslim scholars -- is a mixture of both humanistic ethical values, combined with supremacist ethos, as it developed throughout the centuries. Due to its literalist tradition, it does not have the flexibility or the ability to overcome interpretations of the scriptures that are inimical to pluralistic and humanistic values."

Vanya points to the interpretations of this Islamic mainstream as the way forward – if that school of thought in Islam is only the winning interpretation, might there not be others? "But is it not possible that God wanted humans to use their brains and rational faculties, and that He did not provide step-by-step instructions for all the questions in life simply to be obeyed by humans without reflection or questioning?" There must be a way to balance revelation and reason within Islam. The result of the *Mihna* was that revelation was declared supreme, and the reason which the Mu'tazilites championed was subservient to that revelation. Vanya would come down on the side of the Mu'tazilites.

Egyptian philosopher **Murad Wahba** also points to the necessity of rational criticism for society to progress. Secularism within the state is a way to secure the possibility of rational criticism. Rational criticism is only possible where secularism preserves a structure and an understanding of Islam which prevents it from combining too much power within one institution, or eliminating debate. He criticized Turkey as relying too much on the army to impose and preserve secularism, and failing to plant this idea securely within the intellectuals in society.[472]

Shaker al-Nabulsi, author of somewhere over sixty books, left Jordan for fear of his life and moved to the U.S., where he died in 2014. His works focused on the political, religious, and social reform of the Arabic world, and he was optimistic that a secular view, separating state and religion, would win the day. He pointed to the gradual changes in the legal order – the end of the Ottoman Empire, the abolishing of *shari'a* courts, of Islamic criminal penalties, and growth of secular courts as signs that progress in the right direction was happening, even though it might be slow, as in Saudi Arabia.

He saw in today's opposition the indicator to a coming victory: "[These threats] reveal the bankruptcy of terrorist religious fundamentalism, [which cannot] counter arguments with arguments [...], and a word with a [different] word, but instead deals with words by means of the sword [...], and with life through death."[473]

Lafif Lakhdar (1934-2013) was a French-Tunisian lawyer, leftist thinker and writer, author of a great number of books, articles, and newspaper columns. He was very critical of today's movements back to the forefathers of Islam, tracing contemporary movements back to the 1800s, and the birth of Pan-Islamism, with "its famous old rubbish about the need for a just despot modelled on the second caliph, 'Umar, who would impose on his subjects a bovine discipline for 15 years before guiding them step by step to the age of reason."[474]

He blamed the weakness of contemporary Arab states on Islam: "Its denominational character, since Islam is proclaimed the state religion, prevents it to date from creating a true national cohesion." The lack of a real secularism along with this means that states must remain divided along confessional lines. Worse, "[i]n the Arab world, those who think for themselves and are capable of elaborating a criticism of all the sacred or profane mystifications come up against the political and religious censorship of the present Arab state — a censorship which is infinitely worse than that of the caliphate state."[475]

The *salafi* movements are no answer. Lakhdar pointed out quite rightly that the fabled golden age to which these movements appeal was never quite so golden in fact as it is in today's stories. "Apart from its exemplary punishments, Islamic archaism has nothing new to offer. It appears to me to be part of the process of the break-up of the state in a world which is becoming ungovernable."[476] A separation of the state and religion, reform of the treatment of women, and full admission to citizenship and nationality of all, regardless of religious confession, are all required for success.

Educational reform is critical. "Open religious rationalism--subjecting the religious text to rational investigation and research--ought to become the core of the aspired religious education in the Arab-Islamic region, since it is absurd to believe the text and deny reality."[477] He points out that the only state even attempting this is Tunisia. For real reform in the state and society, correct education of the young must come first. Religion may be part of this, but a religion which realizes the difference between history and religion – between Koranic verses suited to a time and place, and applying these to all people for all time.

M. Zuhdi Jasser, son of Syrian immigrants, medical doctor, and proud former officer of the U.S. Navy, started thinking more deeply about what he states is wrong within Islam after the 9/11 New York terrorist attacks. He was outraged by published reactions in his local paper that blamed 9/11 on America itself, or that tried to ignore traditions within Islam that were responsible. "I had no such struggle in my life between being American and Muslim, and questioned why were there no Muslims like me included in the article…"[478] Eventually this led Jasser to found with a few others the AIFD (American Islamic Forum for Democracy).

The platform of AIFD includes calls for law based on the Constitution and reason, for pluralism and moderation, will make no justification for terrorism, and rejects what it calls

"Islamism" forced upon and equated to Islam itself. Jasser too, calls for modernizing the interpretation of Islam, and harmonizing it with concepts such as liberty as understood in the U.S. system. The Koran itself must be examined closely, and "...we must turn away from the narrow Wahhabi practices of Islam..."[479] He demands recognition that there is a difference between the faith of Islam itself, and the cultural positions of the Islamists that they claim are Islam.

This path has led Jasser on to what was for him, unexpectedly, almost a second career beyond medical practice, involving refutation of Islamic organizations in the U.S. that advocate fiercely, and sometimes very much under the radar, for precisely what he is against. But Jasser has worked on despite adversity, stating that "[t]he Muslim ideas and thinkers devoted to modernity, reform, and liberty are out there; they just need our unwavering support, clarity, and perseverance."[480] That would include substantial leadership and support by the U.S. government, support Jasser clearly feels is lacking - where it is not altogether absent.

Abdullahi Ahmed An-Na'im has written a thoughtful book which he regards as "the culmination of my life's work, the final statement I wish to make on issues I have been struggling with since I was a student at the University of Khartoum, Sudan, in the late 1960s. I speak as a Muslim in this book because I am accountable for these ideas as part of my own religion and not simply as a hypothetical academic argument."[481]

He argues that Islam may reform itself to be compatible with the ideas and structures of modern, democratic, societies. This reform will not involve Islam losing part of itself, but will instead improve Islam, since, "[i]n order to be a Muslim by conviction and free choice, which is the only way one can be a Muslim, I need a secular state."[482] A secular state neither favoring nor penalizing any particular religion may allow free choice of religion, and makes compulsion or lying about one's religion less likely.

Separation of politics and the state means that civil society within the state will carry on a dialogue about which principles to enforce in law, and by participating in politics sincere Muslims may see that Islamic principles may make their way into public life. The state must ensure that it does not enforce *shari'a*, but maintains a separation of itself and religion, something that "is not easy, because the state must necessarily regulate the role of religion to maintain its own religious neutrality, which is required for its role as a mediator and an adjudicator among competing social and political forces."[483] This can work where Muslims are either the majority of the population, or the minority, and over time this secular state allowing the political process will create a body of civic thought – certain basics all in society can agree upon.

The principles of constitutionalism, human rights, and citizenship are necessary as "an integrated framework for regulating the practical way secularism works to negotiate the tension between the religious neutrality of the state and the connectedness of Islam and public policy."[484] Constitutionalism includes things like majority respect for minority rights, limitations and controls on government in dealing with its own citizens to secure their rights, and the rule of law, all working through state institutions and within the broader culture in a continuing process. "The whole principle of constitutionalism and its various institutions and processes is dependent on the willingness and the ability of citizens to uphold this principle for the public good of all rather than for the narrow self-interest of one segment of the population."[485]

This is all possible, he argues, without doing violence to Islam, since "there is nothing to prevent the formation of a fresh consensus around new interpretative techniques or innovative interpretations of the Qur'an and Sunna, which would become a part of *shari'a*, just as the existing methodologies and interpretations came to be a part of it in the first place."[486] If the ideas of the secular state, the separation of state and religion, a healthy regard for constitutionalism, human rights, and the privileges and responsibilities of citizenship were understood, it

Page 264

would be safe (or perhaps possible) for Muslims to take on this reform task.

This could be done with an approach like that of his own predecessor, **Mahmoud Mohammed Taha**, who substituted earlier Mecca verses for later Medina verses, "the rationale for this proposed shift is that earlier revelations represented the universal message of Islam, while the later ones were specific responses to the historical context of human societies at the time."[487]

He closes the book by emphasizing the use of "negotiation", in the sense of a long, gradual, and continuous process of dialogue and formation to reach this goal.

Finally, (no doubt controversially for some) the **Egyptian President, Abdel Fattah el-Sisi**, also called for reform in the way Islam thinks about itself in a speech given January 1, 2015.[488]

> "I am referring here to the religious clerics. We have to think hard about what we are facing—and I have, in fact, addressed this topic a couple of times before. It's inconceivable that the thinking that we hold most sacred should cause the entire umma [Islamic world] to be a source of anxiety, danger, killing and destruction for the rest of the world. Impossible!
>
> That thinking—I am not saying "religion" but "thinking"—that corpus of texts and ideas that we have sacralized over the centuries, to the point that departing from them has become almost impossible, is antagonizing the entire world. It's antagonizing the entire world!
>
> Is it possible that 1.6 billion people [Muslims] should want to kill the rest of the world's inhabitants—that is 7 billion—so that they themselves may live? Impossible!

I am saying these words here at Al Azhar, before this assembly of scholars and ulema—Allah Almighty be witness to your truth on Judgment Day concerning that which I'm talking about now.

All this that I am telling you, you cannot feel it if you remain trapped within this mindset. You need to step outside of yourselves to be able to observe it and reflect on it from a more enlightened perspective.

I say and repeat again that we are in need of a religious revolution. You, imams, are responsible before Allah. The entire world, I say it again, the entire world is waiting for your next move... because this umma is being torn, it is being destroyed, it is being lost—and it is being lost by our own hands."

In an interview shortly afterward with Spiegel online, President el-Sisi emphasized again that what he was talking about was bad interpretation – not Islam itself – and that change would take time.[489] No matter what one may think of his rise to the Presidency, he is reputed to be sincere and thoughtful when it comes to Islam and the modern world. I doubt that anyone could put the need for reform any more starkly than this.

A Liberal Islamic Consensus for Reform?

This chapter opened with the contention that modernization and globalization are forcing the issue of reform. It seems to be happening. "In unprecedentedly large numbers, the faithful—whether in the vast cosmopolitan city of Istanbul, the suburbs of Paris, or in the remote oases of Oman's mountainous interior—are examining and debating the fundamentals of Muslim belief and practice in ways that their less self-conscious predecessors in the faith would never have imagined."[490]

"Voicing such [liberal] concerns can be dangerous in some countries, and proponents of this tradition have suffered for their beliefs..."[491] Reform thought in the Islamic world must not be confused with Western liberalism, but recognized as an Islamic form of liberalism, in an Islamic context. That sometimes means categorization of thought by the method used in approaching the sources. The Koran and *sunna* may mandate a liberal position; or the *shari'a* developed from those basic sources may be silent, allowing adoption of liberal positions; or a liberal position may be found through different modes of interpretation of the Koran and *sunna*. Each method naturally has different strengths and weaknesses when arguing with the tradition-minded.[492]

Besides methods of liberal criticism, common substantive threads appear in the statements and thoughts of these Muslim intellectuals. The struggle for primacy, or even balance between reason and revelation in thinking about the issues of Islam, is one. Many of these reformers mention the Mu'tazilites within their works. They understand that the issue of the *Mihna* – the balance within Islam between the dictates of revelation and the freedom to apply reason to life issues, must be reopened if reform is to happen.

The question of reason versus revelation is tied closely to the need for change in education. In both these areas, there must be a distinction between what history and culture indicate Islam is, and what the Koran and *sunna* say Islam is (a subset of this distinction is scholarly criticism of *hadith* both for authenticity and also upon the basis of reason). There is room within the broad Islamic tradition for diversity and difference in practice and life.

The Koran itself may even be questioned, according to those who call for application of rules of interpretation to distinguish between commands binding in all times and places, and those given in the time of the Prophet for circumstances or events particular to that day. Many of the reformers desire to strip away negative additions, and get back to a cleaner Islam, and that will require examining history, culture, and context of statements in both the Koran and the hadith.

The old acceptance within Islam of the plurality of faith, and tolerance of those within other traditions of the book, must reappear. With this plurality, Islam must also not fear to borrow what is good from the West, and adapt it for Islamic cultures. Acceptance of modern forms of governance like democracy with its required tolerance, even protection, of minorities goes along with this. This requires Islam to engage in serious and sustained self-reflection and self-criticism, and not take the easy way out of blaming current negative qualities within Islamic societies upon the West (though again, the West certainly did accelerate the growth of negative qualities already present in Islamic thought with its challenge to modernize).

Several of these modern reformers are quite critical about a negative culture existing within dominant forms of Islamic practice today, and want a presentation of Islam which is more affirming of what they see as the good things in life. Islam has allowed itself to become too narrow under the influence of doctrines like those of the Salafis, Wahhabis, or Muslim Brothers. And yet none of these Muslim reformers is demanding that Muslims desert Islam. Even Ayaan Hirsi Ali, who did leave loudly and publicly, seems now to regret at least a little a choice in effect forced upon her.

It is difficult to draw out the lines of an ideological structure of moderate or reform Islam. Without a unified body of thought, "it is more accurate to refer to *moderate Muslims* than to *moderate Islam*." A claimed moderate Islam cannot be set up (yet) as the opposite of the extremists, since it "…has no systematic doctrine and no organizations acting in its name. It has meager financial support and no governmental backing."[493]

An organization to unify the reformers is lacking, and given the wide array of problems they see as needing reform, this shouldn't be a surprise. Islam has usually been so close an ally as to seem part of the organization of the state itself. Reform demands an opposition against that relationship and state support of religion, and that is something that Islam in general does not have much practice in doing. An effective reform organization requires at least a basic agreement on enough specific issues to allow a group big enough to have significant social effect to coalesce.

Liberal Saudi journalist Mansour Al-Hadj, among others, has recognized these problems, and recently called for formation of an organization that is to include Muslim people with a broad set of reform-agenda items. "I fully realize the difficulty of this task, and what criticism to expect from different groups. But I am wagering on the voices of the silent majority – who are the victims of terrorism and also the ones most dishonored by it. Since extremist rhetoric is an integrated idea, it must be countered with a comprehensive Islamic idea, supported by millions of ordinary Muslims who want to practice their religion freely..."[494]

It is true that the reformers, with notable exceptions like the women Morchidats in Morocco, for the most part have little or no financial backing or state support. Again, this shouldn't be a surprise, since the dominant schools within Islam have typically been in a close partnership with the machinery of the state. But does reform demand strong state support? A Westerner, thinking of Martin Luther, would be tempted to answer yes, but that assumes a Western-shaped reform, and why would reform within Islam look like reform within Christianity? And again, within Islamic societies, reform will in many cases be *against* the state and what it supports.

No agreement on the method to be used in finding space for reforming ideas within the Islamic tradition; no unified body of substantive reform doctrine; and no organization broad enough to unite the many reformers within the Islamic world. But yet, considering the many thousands of books, articles, websites, video and audio clips, from those mentioned above, and the many others who exist, it seems that a "Muslim Reformation" is upon us.

Must it have a coherent ideological structure, agreed method of thought, or a unified organization in order to be a successful reform movement? What exactly can we expect a "Muslim Reformation" to look like?

Chapter 13 - The Shape of the Islamic Reformation

Voices all over the Islamic world are calling for a "Muslim Reformation", and looking for a "Muslim Martin Luther." But the Middle East lacks the institutional structures and intellectual heritage that made the Reformation possible in Europe. European society, religion, and state re-formed based on the particular historical experience with institutional structures and intellectual substance in the conflict that culminated in the Papal Revolution. The different history of the Islamic world means that if reform comes, then we should expect to see a reformation process sharply different from the Western experience.

Challenges to the place and weight of the faith itself in society were easier in the West in the Reformation (but still bloody and long lasting!) since law and religion had already substantially diverged in the Papal Revolution. The authority structure in one area of society could be challenged without upsetting the authority of all of society. Different sources of authority and strong enough bodies of secular law to preserve social order had already developed by the time of the Reformation. Luther himself supported state power when over-enthusiastic peasants went too far in reform.

It is no accident that the great era of European royal power and royal power in law followed closely after the Reformation. The intellectual base upon which to construct needed laws apart from the Church helped the state grow strong. After the Reformation Christianity, while still a powerful social influence, began to shift its character to private piety and worship, away from an institution active in ordering society through law.

defined it as wrong, how are we to choose between the two? Consensus, *ijma*, of the community is the answer, and that means that reform demands intellectual consensus before it can proceed.

The appeal of the reformers within Islam may be directed only to a great and diffuse body of scholars, both those now alive and those long dead, who hold the position the reformer complains against. The task of persuasion becomes that much more difficult, since were one *ulama* member to be persuaded that the reformer is right about something like letting women drive alone in cars, he will suddenly find himself on the outside of a circle of faces looking with disapproval at him, when they even bother to turn around to notice him. That really brilliant man in the small Egyptian village might remain the local imam his entire life.

Martin Luther and other reformers were bothered by abusive practices of the Church like the sale of indulgences, and, supported by the separate and secular hierarchy of the state, appealed to the hierarchy of the Church to put an end to these practices. Since the Church had a hierarchical authority structure with the Pope at its apex, the appeal could be ultimately directed to one person, with the power to reform an institution. At the very least, the Pope had the authority to direct a strong start to a process of reformation, which could then falter or succeed based on the strength of anti-reform resistance and the personal power of the Pope himself.

The reformers of the Islamic world have a more difficult time defining what it is that is wrong and needs to be reformed. Is it treatment of women? Education? And what is it, even, in those issues that ought to be reformed? The target in reform of Islamic knowledge and practice has not been defined, nor is there one dominant voice for reform. As noted in the last chapter, several scholars have pointed out the lack of coherence in reform proposals, their wide diversity, and by implication the many different voices calling for reform instead of one strong voice. Reform within Islam does not involve a doctrine or set of doctrines over which a hierarchy has authority and the ability to

Page 276

order change. Instead there is the authority of scholarship, spread over many centuries and many countries, in several competing schools of law, all of which are legitimately Islamic.

The lack of an obvious gap between the sacred and secular in society like Martin Luther experienced, and the different challenges of a widely distributed intellectual hierarchy as against a centralized hierarchy of offices, makes the Muslim Reformation that much more difficult than that of Europe. If what is to be reformed can be defined, then the difficulty is finding authority to which complaint can be made, and from which a remedy may be sought. Both the content of thought to be reformed, and the power to do the reforming, are diffuse and decentralized within Islamic cultures. It is far easier to reform a structure than a body of knowledge. Martin Luther and his methods would not succeed in the Islamic world.

Yet the calls by Muslims for reform continue: Blind following of earlier thought must change, along with intolerance of change and condemnation of it as "innovation" (Sheikh 'Adel Al-Kalbani). Friday sermons filled with repression, prohibition, and hate must change (Abdul Hamid al-Ansari). Individuality and independent thought can improve Islamic cultures (Ibrahim Al-Buleihi). Values like freedom of thought, freedom of religion, equality, and respect for others must come through education (Abdennour Bidar). Separation of history and culture from religion, leaving pure religious principles free to express themselves in new ways is needed (Mustafa Akyol). Freeing religion from the pressure of the state will allow it to improve (Iyad Jamal al-Din). Reason must be applied to the study of Islam, not only traditions of the past (Ahmad Al-Qabbanji). The doctrine of Islam must change over time, and not be dictated by past history (Gamal al-Banna). Education, reading, dialogue, and opening the mind to beauty are necessary (Dhiyaa Al-Musawi). Women religious workers? "Yes" say the Morchidat. Protestant Muslims? Mosques which are gay-friendly? Intolerance of other viewpoints, forcing Muslims to comply with doctrines they don't like, and on, and on…

If there were agreement on what needed to be reformed within Islam, or a grand coalition to promote it, as Lafif Lakhdar hoped to see and Mansour Al-Hadj recently called for, how could reformers make real change happen within the diffuse intellectual hierarchy of Islam? I think there are three major routes or methods of reform: Changing the intellectual content of Islamic law and reforming the constitutional structure of society, defining differently what it is to be a Muslim, and adopting different educational content and methods. These all overlap with one another, and promote each other.

Reform in Legal and Constitutional Structures

Law changes over time, since if it refuses to change it risks becoming irrelevant as people and practices in society change. At the same time, it must not change too fast, because people make plans in both personal and business life relying on "what the law is". Law has developed a set of tools to help manage the pace of change, and focusing on these tools of interpretation and precedent is critical in discussing the probability of reform within the content of Islamic law.

Just how are we to understand, or interpret, a text? Some tools don't seem too controversial: Understanding the language of the text means understanding words in their usually accepted meanings, unless the text specifies a limited or special understanding of the term used. Words of the same kind should be interpreted as consistent with the rest of the group. For example, in: "pistols, revolvers, derringers, or other dangerous weapons," the term "dangerous weapons" would be interpreted as another firearm, or perhaps narrowly as only meaning another handgun. Textual tools include interpreting different parts of a body of law as consistent with one another, giving effect to all the words used, and not ignoring inconvenient clauses. It means rules of construction like a specific norm prevailing over a more general norm.

But then the tools of legal interpretation become more controversial. Interpretation departs for more speculative areas when it begins to ask questions such as what the intent behind a law is, and seeks an interpretation of the law that will best carry out the intent of the law. One possibility here is a re-opening of the Mu'tazilite controversy which appeared settled by Ibn Hanbal's ideological victory: the place and authority of reason versus revelation in understanding the substance of Islamic law. The modern *salafis* are willing to question the conclusions of those who came before them, but only along a strict Hanbalite line of revelation, refusing the appeal to a wider use of reason which the modern Mu'tazilites pursue.

Legal text may also be interpreted by focusing on the result desired, not the means used in attaining it. A provision of law that would inhibit the desired result can be distinguished away, or de-emphasized so that it does not rule in the case at hand. Closely related is the idea that the end result is part of an overall ideology or is a human right, or something mandated by God. If the argument between reason and revelation to interpret what God desires is a dead end, is there another way?

There might be an opportunity to inquire into the conditions at the time the rule was given, and may allow distinguishing between social conditions in our time, and social conditions of the time in which the law was made. For reform aiming toward a more universally acceptable body of law "[i]t would have to distinguish, more radically than has hitherto been done, between the essential principles of its divinely-given code of conduct and the temporary applications, and work out fresh applications to novel circumstances."[497] But how to decide which commands of the law of God apply to all people in all places and times, and which applied only at a specific time and place?

Applying too much reason in interpreting a text is certain to bring conflict between the partisans of reason and those who state that revelation and tradition are enough and that clear words ought not be questioned. Applying too little means that reform won't come. Trying to refine this inquiry by narrowing it to universally applicable rules versus contextual rules limited by space and time might narrow the field of argument a bit, but only leads back to the weight reason and revelation are to be assigned in deciding the question.

In discussing the need to strike the balance between reason and revelation, Taha Akyol quoted Mehmet Görmez (President of the Diyanet – the Turkish Presidency of Religious Affairs). Görmez, speaking of Al-Azhar University and Saudi Arabia's Islamic University and others, said, "'The Islamic world should discuss what kind of an education they have received at which sharia faculty.' He also warned that 'instead of solving problems, scholars educated in these places are becoming problems themselves in many areas.'"[498] But who can open that discussion? There is no more caliph to call for *Mihna II.* The lack of a centralized authority to which appeal for reform can be directed makes this limited task of deciding on the interpretation of Islamic law very difficult.

Finally, there is the idea of precedent. How have the thinkers and judges of the past understood the text or command we're examining? This is not only an aid to interpretation, but the idea of precedent in itself is important enough to be understood as the second major tool for handling change within law.

A precedent is an opinion given in the past, revolving around the same legal text or same question of law as the one confronting us in the present. Lawyers usually distinguish precedent into two kinds, binding (strong) precedent or persuasive (weak) precedent. But it is a little more complicated than this. If confronted with a legal question, on the same legal text and with the same facts as a case of the past, under a binding precedent scenario, a judge *must* decide the current case to produce the same result as in the old case. In a weak precedent scenario, the judge, *if persuaded* that the precedent is correct, should rule in the same way as the old case was decided. That allows continuity and predictability in the law, but leaves open the possibility for change where appropriate.

But some have no doubt noticed that troublesome little clause "with the same facts" when discussing applying a precedent to the case at hand. What cases in law have exactly the same facts? How different must they be before a judge may decide that the precedent really doesn't apply to the case at hand? In other words, just how binding is even a binding precedent? A judge may easily say he or she hasn't been persuaded that the precedent applies, given different facts. On the other hand, hundreds of years of either persuasive or binding precedent on an issue revealed in the Koran or *sunna* that is part of the *shari'a* cannot be lightly overturned.

And what if one group of judges decide that a precedent applies, but another group decides that it does not? Remember that in Sunni Islam alone there are four major schools of law, and no supreme court or supreme council to decide between their competing rulings. At the end of the day the consensus of the community is supposed to control, but how long will it take to reach that consensus? Nearly as soon as the Prophet had died, the Kharijites argued for a strict reading of the Koran and exclusion of tradition to solve the problems of the *ummah*, and kept arguing that point, weapons in hand, even as a small minority in the Islamic society of the day.

Even if Muslim reformers were to evolve coherent bodies of doctrine around interpretation and precedent to explain why their views ought to be dominant within mainstream Sunni Islam, and even if their views were to actually gain majority support, then what? The constitutional issue, the place or weight of Islam in society is still to be resolved. What is to be the character of the *shari'a* itself? Is it to be normative and binding, or aspirational and encouraging? Will the *ulama* give legal judgments, or will they tell judges – civil servants of the state – what the *ulama* think the right result should be? What constitutional structure of society will allow for reform?

Islam has been and is carrying on a debate about democracy – whether democracy is compatible with Islam, whether it is not, or whether it is simply a vehicle Islam may use, and from which to alight and leave empty when the destination of an Islamic society is reached. The form of government of the state is not so important though, as the relationship between the state and Islam itself. Professor An-

privatization of religion."[501] Hardly a result the more strict interpreters of Islam would welcome, even if the reformers would.

I think that this is already happening within Islamic societies. In the previous chapter, we've seen reformers like Iyad Jamal al-Din in Iraq stating that religion should be independent of the State, so that it can actually be free. Mustafa Akyol and Abdullahi Ahmed An-Na'im both argued in their books that religion is more of a real choice if it is not the law of the State, but something an adherent clings to by positive choice. *Shari'a* has indeed lost its place as constitution-in-fact in nearly all of the countries of the Middle East (Saudi Arabia is the exception). A change from public law and compliance, even where *shari'a* is still very important as a source of law, leaves us with a wider scope for private choice within religion as well as reform.

These are of course strong means of explaining the faith in the other two great Abrahamic religions, Judaism and Christianity. Neither of these religions have disappeared (despite predictions) in modern times, and both still have many dedicated adherents globally. They have managed to thrive and survive without law as the dominant way of explaining faith. Islam has without doubt a rich and deep enough tradition that other qualities may be emphasized more strongly as law declines, if the reform process continues.

A privatization trend in religion may also pick up speed even when an ostensibly religious government wishing to raise "pious generations" is involved. The sheer number and breadth of goals a modern government is able to promote may cause the definition of religion to drift. Turkish journalist Taha Akyol (Mustafa Akyol's father), was interviewed by Today's Zaman, the published interview appearing June 9, 2014 under the title "AKP is secularizing religious people". The AKP is the Turkish party widely viewed as bringing religion and Islam to the forefront of Turkish politics since its rise to power in the 2002 elections. Akyol sees this as ultimately harmful to Islam:

"The politicization of Islam paves the way for it being emptied of content. Without being politicized and by remaining a set of moral, spiritual and cultural values, Islam is more resistant to secular values. However, when Islam is politicized, religiosity starts to be perceived as a political attitude. And if politicians' moral and cultural impoverishment of religiosity continues in Turkey, Turkish society will become a highly secularized community where religious values are extremely ineffective, as is the case in Europe."[502]

He went on to explain that while society may appear more religious, there seems to be a stronger appetite and greed for power on the part of religious politicians. While people appear more religious, they want to earn more money. Akyol identified those desires as secular attitudes. Religion, after all, urges people to control such urges. "Religious people are leading more secular lives, but not in a hypocritical manner. They give religion a new interpretation so that they don't believe their lives to be conflicting with religion." Secularization as Akyol discussed it in the interview is "…the process in which worldly values come to be seen as more important." Those values, such as earning more money, amassing more power, are becoming more important because they are precisely what AKP policies are aimed toward.

Sociological study of Turkish society had already pointed toward a changing definition of Islam in daily life. In a newspaper interview two years before Akyol's own interview, Professor Ersin Kalaycıoğlu, of Sabancı University in Istanbul, talked about findings from a field survey for the International Social Survey Program (ISSP) that he helped conduct with his colleague Professor Ali Çarkoğlu of Koç University in Istanbul. The study revealed that Turks preferred to live the way they chose, and that theological or moral aspects of religion were not really internalized by a large majority of people, even those who identified as religiously conservative. "You worship, so you are religious. Once you worship, you can do whatever you want:

That's the major perception of the people. Religiosity in Turkey is reduced to worship."[503]

That's a very modern idea of what religion is. Patricia Crone argued in her *Pre-Industrial Societies* that with the coming of modernity, the definition of religion would in fact change and narrow, as more complex social life and the growth of knowledge allowed an appeal to multiple sources of authority to explain and manage different parts of life. Where money and earning money is talked of in terms of the economy, or fiscal policy, and where power is talked of in terms of the State, and of bureaucracy, then we can expect to see the authority of religion in such areas displaced. Not with a hostile intent, nor even consciously, but as Taha Akyol described, through a process of re-definition of what religion means and what it means to be religious, so that we end up with precisely what Professor Kalaycıoğlu found: religiosity reduced to worship.

If a reforming Islam no longer clings to *shari'a* as a public legal presentation of what Islam itself is, but accepts the coming of modern society with multiple categories of authority for life decisions, growth of the State, secularization, a diminished role for law, and the secondary codings of morality and salvation or damnation to explain faith, then it seems that Islam will indeed become a private matter of worship by the individual. These things are happening not only in Turkey, but all over the Middle East. While there is not yet an organized and comprehensive "moderate" Islamic ideology (in the sense of modern and private religion), there are in practice many moderate Muslims. Official ideology just has to catch them.

Reform in Education

Finally, different educational content and methods (and the personnel willing and able to implement them) are necessary for reform. Traditionally, education was in the *madrassa*, the school of law, but starting with the Western challenge to modernize, the trend in education has been to broaden from only the *madrassa*, to primary and secondary schools organized on

Western lines. Within those schools, teachers and professors educated in non-religious disciplines are the norm. Widening the educated and teaching class from only traditionally-trained *ulama* members to those with a secular education or at least a partial secular education has enormous potential for change, if seized by those who want change.

There is no question that broader content of education was introduced throughout the Islamic world in answer to that first Western challenge. Different ways of thinking, and different sources of intellectual authority for decision-making, remove the *shari'a* law from its primary place within the educational world. But knowledge of the law itself, and the content of law, is also an arena for wider discussion as a result of changes in education. I hope you noticed that several of the reformers in the last chapter talked about how law was to be interpreted, *and* that the majority of those men were not members of the *ulama*.

The role of education in preparing people to question their own ideas, to be open to inquiry, and not to be hostile to others who differ from them cannot be neglected. A study titled "Religiosity in Turkey - An International Study", conducted in 2009 revealed that of those who joined the study, 66% said that members of other religions should not be allowed to expound their ideas by organizing meetings open to the public. A further 62% responded that they should not even be allowed to give out books that explain their views. Professor Çarkoglu said the results of the study could be attributed to the Turkish educational system, which mandates religious studies for both junior high school and high school students – classes where Christians and Jews "are not even mentioned" or are portrayed as "the others." "That instills in these students a severe point of view of intolerance," he added.

But if the personnel of education evolve away from traditionally-trained teachers, (and it certainly has done so in Turkey) there is a greater chance of curriculum changes, or different influences upon the students in the classroom. The idea of tolerance of others could be aired in that Turkish classroom, but that requires reform in the content of education, not just a change in teachers. Lafif Lakhdar thought that educational reform was critical for real change within the Islamic world, and focused specifically on the content taught.

Education isn't only conducted in schools and colleges, but in public talks on television, radio, and internet platforms, as well as in newspapers and magazines. Journalists, academics and others are on the cutting edge of the intellectual reform endeavor here. If the character of the educational system has changed from one which emphasized personal approval of a student's progress and thought to one where journalists or academics have a greater independence and don't require a jurists' certificate to hold forth, then those intellectuals will be more free to question their society.

Technology has an impact upon education as well. Those throughout the Islamic world with web access can find challenging ideas, presented by Muslims – not just by Westerners - that they would likely have never heard within the traditional *madrassa* mode of education, or from the traditional *ulama* member in charge of the lecture. Control of education by teachers who follow a strict construction of Islam can dramatically slow or stop reform. Control and censorship of public modes of teaching can do the same. But as we're all aware, it is difficult to keep people from finding what they'd like to find on the internet.

Involvement of the State with Reform

The state cannot escape being involved in most, if not all, of these primary paths of reformation, so what is the place of the state within a Muslim Reformation? It must be remembered first that Islam is not the law of the state, rather, the state formed around the law accepted by the *ummah*, to assist in carrying those ideas forward. "…Islam is unique among the great civilizations in the extent to which the state has ceased to embody public norms…"[504] which shouldn't surprise us if we reflect upon history in Islamic lands.

Page 288

Islam expanded rapidly to the East and the West, but dynasties changed. Regional families and dynasties ruled parts of the Islamic lands, but not the whole. States within the Islamic world came and went, but they rested on something stable that didn't change very quickly – the *shari'a* and its social norms, the communal prayers at the mosque, education in the schools of law within Islam, the way of life – all of life - of which an individual was either a member or was not. This communal identity is the distinctive quality of Islam to this day. In short, Islam needs the state much less than the Middle Eastern state needs Islam.

Where the Middle Eastern state in the last century has tried to squeeze Islam into the mold of a Western-like religion limited to personal piety and worship, without the adoption of a Western-modeled robust civil society through which to resist state actions contrary to Islam, the result has almost invariably been repression of dissent, corruption, and the accumulation of power into too few hands. "In terms of Islamic political theory, what subsequently happened was what was supposed to happen. Theory predicted that rulers freed from the bonds of the sharia would seek absolute power, and they regularly lived up to that expectation."[505] Think of Saddam Hussein's Iraq, Syria under the Assads, the Shah's Iran, and lighter forms of the same story in Egypt and Turkey. Eventually, that pressure and repression contributed to a resurgence of more traditional forms of Islam.

The state's role then, is not to try to change the place of Islam within society by itself, since that has not worked, but to push or pull along with those within Islam who want to change it. That role of assistant doesn't necessarily work to support reform, though. Saudi Arabia funds Wahhabi global missions with an astonishing amount of money. But Morocco is willing to try the experiment of the Morchidat, and Turkey through its Diyanet funds a variety of scholarly research and writing into a reforming Islam.

Some states make life difficult for reformers, or fail in their duties to police and keep order such that reformers may speak. Others at the very least let reformers appear on the television, or in radio shows, or refrain from arresting them, or censoring the books they'd like to publish. Constitutions may refer to Islamic law as "a source of law" within the state, and may staff their judicial institutions with *ulama*, while at the same time pulling back from the position of states like Saudi Arabia, which has only a basic law since the Koran and the *Sunna* are explicitly its constitution.

The content of those constitutional orders is still an open question. Would it be the legal and social program of the *salafis*, or that of the reformers I've mentioned? As many of the reformers make clear, a certain amount of liberalism and acceptance of "the other" would need to be present in such a state-sponsored order to avoid persecution of minorities. That idea of liberalism cannot come from only the state, but from within the ranks of those arguing about the shape of Islam itself, both traditional *ulama* and upstart non-*ulama* intellectuals.

When we consider the Muslim Brothers, the *salafi* and Wahabbi doctrines, and groups like ISIS, we cannot but conclude that significant parts of Islam would be happy to take on the role of the State itself (or come quite close to it). If it is the state which is fighting to push these ideologues out of what it considers its own sphere, then what we're witnessing is something closer to the Papal Revolution than Vatican II, and some new iteration of the two powers theory of the West must be articulated. If it is the intellectual establishment of Islam or the vast majority of Muslims reforming, then we're witnessing an internal social dialogue closer to Vatican II.

Would we Know an Islamic Reformation if it Bit Us?

For an outside observer it is difficult to see a reformation. After all, should we be expecting something that looks like the European Reformation, the Papal Revolution, Vatican II, or something completely different? There is no one Martin Luther to watch. There can't be. Instead, the Western onlooker must trace reform efforts in a dizzying variety of areas, conducted by many people, in different ways, in different locations throughout the Islamic world. This can lead us to miss the Muslim Reformation altogether.

For example, not long ago I went to a lecture at an area college, where a visiting professor from the U.K. talked about events in Egypt in the Arab Spring and afterward – the overthrow of Hosni Mubarak, the election of Morsi, and then the military intervention and subsequent election of President al-Sisi. Al-Sisi and the army were cast only and exclusively in the bad guy role, since a "democratically elected" ruler (Morsi) had been overthrown. No mention of the Islamizing work by Morsi once he took power. No acknowledgment that the military had stepped out of power after the initial upheaval of the Arab Spring when Morsi was elected, nor acknowledgment that the military had sided with the people against one of their own (former air chief marshal Mubarak) in the beginning.

The significant developments seemed only the failure in the democratic process and military interference, and how closely those resembled (or didn't) the standards of Western Europe. President al-Sisi and his election were branded embarrassing and ugly failures by the liberal standards of a Western university professor. I was taken aback, even though I had expected that conclusion.

Within the context of the traditional Islamic constitutional order and Egypt's long struggle to reconcile with the challenges of Western modernity and to reconcile yet again with the violent counter-reactions to modernity, the rise of the al-Sisi government, warts and all, is actually a positive step. The people of Egypt – civil society – didn't want *either* extreme, but something, somewhere, near the middle – and that was not recognized at all by the Western intellectual! How closely does the Western onlooker demand reform attempts in the Islamic world resemble model Western behavior before giving approval?

We should also reflect on the fact that the Reformation in Europe didn't happen everywhere. Large portions of Europe stayed determinedly Catholic. I think it is reasonable to expect the same within Islam, if we don't already see it. For example,

North African countries like Morocco or Tunisia are certainly more willing to experiment with reform proposals than is Saudi Arabia, which remains firmly within the Wahhabi orbit. Other countries and regions seem to be moving back toward a strict Salafi Islam.

Just as Christianity weathered multiple splits within the Church along national or cultural lines even before the great divide between Orthodox and Catholic, and then later the Reformation which produced Protestant Christianity, Islam has already been long accustomed to the split between Shia and Sunni, and many variations within both of these main branches of Islam, along with the Sufi movement. Islam is not so monolithic as popular Western accounts tend to portray it, nor must it be. I think it can grow accustomed to yet another split into a Reformed Islam. Not all European reformers were the same, and I don't know why we would expect Muslim reformers to be the same or to have a common program.

And if a Muslim Reformation really is underway, why would we expect to see its end? "All established religions tend to be conservative and to dislike change; but Islam is characterized by an extreme degree of resistance to change..."[506] Reaction to reformation has risen, and will continue to rise. It is very likely that things will get much worse before they get better. If the Western Reformation was as painful as it was, even working off the strong base provided it by the Papal Revolution, than we'd better anticipate a very long and painful process in the Islamic world, where brother will continue to fight against brother. How bitterly would Hasan and Gamal al-Banna eventually have fallen out with one another?

Since the major factor in kicking off reaction and reform within Islam was the shock of the Western invasion from the 1800s on, why would the West expect not to see violent reactions continually directed toward us? After all, many within the Islamic world think that the West is either totally or partially responsible for the flaws in Islam which need reform.

Conclusion

The struggles within Islam will rage on during our lifetimes. They will and must center around what are the most contentious areas within Islam: the question of a reasonable balance between reason and revelation; the question of the separation of the Koran and *hadith* (if possible) from culture and history; the question of interpretation and change in the vast mass of Islamic law that now exists; the role of the *ulama* in thwarting or promoting change[507]; the question of whether reform will be driven by leaders with possible state allies; or whether reform will come from the bottom up as Muslims ignore or quietly reject the harsh formulations of the *salafis,* the Wahabbis, and the Muslim Brothers.

The history of Islam means this will be difficult: the formation of Islam as a total culture excluding those outside as far back as the *hijra* from Mecca to Medina; the creation of a vast and comprehensive legal system supporting that total society; the *Mihna* and its consequences of tying state leaders and *ulama* together in a tight mutual relationship and promoting Islamic legal science as the highest and best knowledge; the defensive position the modernity of the West has placed Islamic heartlands in; and the confusing and contradictory reactions to the West in modern times.

I think that reform in the Islamic world will be driven primarily by everyday people as a bottom-up process, and will make a painful and costly progress. Some constitutional and intellectual positions will continue to be explained and written about and kicked off by intellectuals. But for the majority of Muslims, reform will be experienced as a lived behavior, without even articulating the "whys" behind it. The freedom produced by recasting the view of religion from primarily legal/illegal to moral good/bad, or salvation/damnation is attractive, and doesn't mean that Islam must disappear. Many Muslims would like to see that freedom within Islam and are staking their lives on it.

I hope they succeed.

Afterword

So what am I, or you, to make of all this? I have deliberately avoided drawing some of the conclusions I could have, because it is important for all of us to arrive at our own conclusions and apply them in the public and private realms of our own lives. That means some hard thinking about the differences which exist between Christianity and Islam as they began, as they developed, and as they cope with modern times.

For example, if Christianity and Islam both answer the questions of how life is to be lived in the here-and-now, and point toward our destinations in the afterlife, but answer those questions in different orders, or emphasize one question over the other, that seems important. If the Papal Revolution helped split Church from State in Christian societies in the West, while the *Mihna* helped Islam seem even more like a unitary system, that might help explain things. If law now comes from the State, and not from God, that might help explain some differences.

If we make no attempt to understand even a little history, it is easy to have a conversation of mutual incomprehension like this:

"Questions of law undoubtedly seem more important to Muslims than Christians. I have more than once witnessed a conversation between an Evangelical Christian and a Muslim in which the Evangelical urged the Muslim to consider his status as a sinner. What was supposed to happen was that the Muslim realized that he was a sinner, unable to please God on his own, beg to be told how he could restore himself to divine favor, hear the good news that Christ will bear his sin for him, and so on. What actually happens is that the Muslim says yes, he sins but he also obeys, and at the final reckoning, God will generously let each act of obedience outweigh many sins. He goes away wondering why Christians are so morbidly obsessed with sin. Conversely, I have often been asked by Muslims how Christians divide inherited property. What is supposed to happen is that I realize I have a religion that does not provide for elementary demands of life, beg to be told how I may know what to do, and then hear that I need only convert to Islam and follow the Qur'an and God's Prophet. What actually happens is that we both go away wondering at the other's complacency. This mutual incomprehension comes about, at least in part, because Christians are used to thinking first of theology and Muslims of law."[508]

Realizing even one basic difference like this in how most people from Christian-background, or Islamic-background societies think, might help us to build more constructive relationships. At the very least, it might instruct us on the reasons we keep failing.

Or consider this example of the three basic group reactions within Islam to the coming of modernity and the West, and its implications for migrants or refugees:

As I write, it looks as if 2016 will be another record year for refugees fleeing the Middle East. They're running from bombs dropping from Russian, U.S., and Syrian warplanes. They're running from bombs, guns and knives used all too willingly by an alphabet-soup mix of Islamic/nationalist/ideological/ethnic/tribal and other groups. I don't blame them. I'd take my family and run too if I'd lost faith that the West would do more than just talk a good game, and would actually intervene to calm the turmoil inside my own country.

Europe and the West have been generally receptive to refugees, but they're quickly becoming less so. Western political leaders are responsible for this. Some want to close the borders and keep out all Muslims. Others equate Muslims to Western Christians and ask why we can't all just worship freely in our own way. I hope after reading this book that you can see why these simplistic and simple-minded statements from politicians and political candidates are so wrong.

The secular/atheist/agnostic group of Muslims coming to the West doesn't want to overthrow Western government and Western ways of life. Those Western ways and their own convictions fit together quite well.

The large group of somewhat observant Muslims coming to the West is content to fit in with the Western structure of the State and culture. That group is satisfied with being good Muslims within their own homes and families, or in the Mosque on Fridays, or filtering their moral beliefs through civil society so that elected representatives may make law for the State. That's the group functionally reforming Islam while Islamic theory and law lag behind.

Then there is that last group that hates everything the West stands for, and longs for purification of Islam and defeat of the enemy it blames for bringing humiliation and shame to the heartlands of the Muslims. This group definitely does not worship like Western Christians after the long evolution of Western Christianity. It isn't interested in an evolving Islam either. It expects *shari'a* law to govern Muslims and rejects the legal systems of the West even while living in Western States. It doesn't hesitate to use guns and bombs against Western enemies. To pretend that this group doesn't exist within Islam, isn't Islamic, or clings to the ideas it does because of Western "provocations" like obscure you-tube movies seen by nobody until Western politicians have brought them to public attention, only enables aspiring terrorists in the West.

Worse, it utterly devalues the lives of the many good and decent people of the Middle East who identify as Muslims. Don't forget that the vast majority of the victims of the violence of *salafi* and other Islamist groups are other Muslims. Western fantasizing that a centuries-deep thread of strict Islamic legal positions supporting these *salafis* isn't really there allows the aspiring terrorist in the West breathing room to organize and plan.

In the Middle East, it confirms to the majority of Muslims that they shouldn't count on the West for help. Bombs in Paris are a big deal, but in the ancient and storied cities of

Damascus, Istanbul, or Baghdad only part of normal life? Are those Muslim lives that cheap to the West? Bombs in Brussels are reported upon extensively while a bombing just days before in Istanbul passes without comment in the West.

A deliberate refusal to recognize the differences in beliefs of groups of Muslims so that Muslims in the West won't be "discriminated against", only makes it more likely that Muslim people in general will suffer. That is mental depravity on the part of our leaders.

Recognizing and Thinking about Differences Means...?

Most of us do not have the public recognition to bring these subjects up for public discussion. But we can write, and e-mail, and vote, and donate money to get the attention of politicians. We can form civil society organizations to assist the silent majority of Muslim people who need our help. Maybe most importantly, we can respond on individual and family levels.

We can try to articulate to ourselves answers to questions many Western Christians and many traditional Muslims would answer differently:

Is religion something I use to privately beat myself up for yet another failing, or something that brings comfort in my life when things get bad? Or is it a matter of a legal code that governs my life, a code more important than the law of the State, and about whether or not I belong to a group (publicly at least) so that I'm accepted by my neighbors?

What do I expect the place of religion in society to be? Is it an aspirational role calling me on to be better and look for better things in life, or a set of legal norms to which my behavior must conform if I expect to escape without penalty?

How free am I to even speculate about these matters?

Can there be both revelation and reason in matters of religion?

How have these different visions of religion shaped the societies in which they are set?

Why might a Westerner unconsciously see religion as a consumer product to take from the supermarket shelf while many in the Islamic world see it as the only serious central point of legal, public and group identity?

As a Westerner, do you understand a little more the strains under which societies in the Middle East function? Do you understand why those exist?

If we understand some of the differences between the cultures formed from Christian and Islamic backgrounds, we should use that knowledge. When that Muslim moves into the neighborhood, or that Westerner moves into the neighborhood, what will you do?

Will you try to join with what is best in humanity, or will you ignore the great questions being asked within and about the Islamic world today?

Will you respond even though you must change?

Respondeo etsi mutabor

If you have serious comments or questions, please e-mail me.

If you think that I've missed a critical point in this discussion, let me know.

If you'd like to hear more about a certain topic, contact me.

Blaque@MissingTheMuslims.com

Sources Consulted

BOOKS

Akçam, Taner, *A Shameful Act: The Armenian Genocide and the Question of Turkish Responsibility*, (New York: Henry Holt and Company, 2007)

Akyol, Mustafa, *Islam Without Extremes: A Muslim Case for Liberty*, (New York: W.W. Norton & Company, 2011)

Ali, Ayaan Hirsi, *Heretic: Why Islam Needs a Reformation Now*, (New York: HarperCollins Publishers, 2015)

Andrae, Tor, *Mohammed: The Man and his Faith*, translated by Menzel, Theophil, (New York: Harper & Brothers, 1960)

An-Na'im, Abdullahi Ahmed, *Islam and the Secular State: Negotiating the Future of Shari'a*, (Cambridge, Massachusetts and London: Harvard University Press, 2008)

Ansaray, Tamim, *Destiny Disrupted: A History of the World Through Islamic Eyes*, (New York: PublicAffairs/Perseus Books Group, 2010)

Armstrong, Karen, *Islam: A Short History*, (New York: Random House, Inc., 2002)

Berkes, Niyazi, *The Development of Secularism in Turkey*, (Montreal: McGill University Press, 1964)

Berkey, Jonathan P., *The Formation of Islam: Religion and Society in the Near East, 600-1800*, (New York: Cambridge University Press, 2003)

Berman, Harold J. *Faith and Order: The Reconciliation of Law and Religion* (Grand Rapids, MI: William B. Eerdmans Publishing Company, 2000)

Berman, Harold J. *The Interaction of Law and Religion*, (New York: Abingdon Press, 1974)

Berman, Harold J., *Law and Revolution I: The Formation of the Western Legal Tradition*, (Cambridge, Mass: Harvard University Press, 1983)

Birdal, Murat, *The Political Economy of Ottoman Public Debt*, (London: I.B. Tauris, 2011)

Brockelmann, Carl, *History of the Islamic Peoples*, translated by Carmichael, Joel, and Perlmann, Moshe, (London: Routledge & Kegan Paul, 1980)

Bulliet, Richard W., *The Case for Islamo-Christian Civilization*, (New York: Columbia University Press, 2004)

Calvert, John, *Sayyid Qutb and the Origins of Radical Islamism*, (New York: Columbia University Press, 2010)

Cheng-Hsiang, Hsu, *The First Thirty Years of Arabic Printing in Egypt, 1238-1267 (1822-1851): A Bibliographical Study with a Checklist by Title of Arabic Printed Works*, (Doctoral Thesis, University of Edinburgh, January 1985)

Clement *Miscellanies* V.109.3: fr. 15 [KRS 169], in Malcolm Schofield, "The Ionians" in C.C.W. Taylor, editor, *Routledge History of Philosophy Volume 1: From the Beginning to Plato*, (London: Routledge, 1997)

Commins, David, *The Wahhabi Mission and Saudi Arabia*, (New York: I.B. Tauris, 2009)

Crone, Patricia, *Meccan Trade and the Rise of Islam*, (Piscataway, NJ: Gorgias Press, 2004)

Crone, Patricia, *Pre-Industrial Societies* (Oxford and Cambridge, Mass.: Blackwell, 1989)

Crone, Patricia, *Slaves on Horses: The Evolution of the Islamic Polity*, (Cambridge: Cambridge University Press, 2003)

Crone, Patricia, and Hinds, Martin, *God's Caliph: Religious authority in the first centuries of Islam*, (Cambridge: Cambridge University Press, 2003)

Curtis, William Eleroy, *The Turk and His Lost Provinces*, (New York: Fleming H. Revell Company, 1903)

Dagron, Gilbert, *Emperor and Priest – The Imperial Office in Byzantium*, translated by Birrell, Jean, (New York: Cambridge University Press, 2003)

Dahmus, Joseph, *A History of the Middle Ages*, (New York: Doubleday & Co, 1968)

Eco, Umberto, *Baudolino*, translated by Weaver, William, (New York: Harcourt, 2002)

El-Fadl, Khaled Abou, *The Great Theft: Wrestling Islam from the Extremists*, (New York: HarperCollins, 2007)

Esposito, John L., *The Islamic Threat: Myth or Reality?* 3rd edition (New York: Oxford University Press, 1999)

Feldman, Noah, *The Fall and Rise of the Islamic State*, (Princeton: Princeton University Press, 2008)

Finucane, Ronald C., *Soldiers of the Faith: Crusaders and Moslems at War*, (New York: St. Martin's Press, 1983)

Fox, Robin Lane, *Alexander the Great – A Biography*, (New York: The Dial Press, 1974)

Frend, W. H.C., *The Rise of the Monophysite Movement: Chapters in the History of the Church in the Fifth and Sixth Centuries*, (Cambridge: Clarke, 2008)

Fromkin, David, *A Peace to End all Peace: The Fall of the Ottoman Empire and the Creation of the Modern Middle East*, (New York: Henry Holt and Company, LLC, 1989)

Gibb, H.A.R., *Arabic Literature – An Introduction*, 2nd edition, (Oxford: Oxford University Press, 1974)

Gibb, H.A.R., *Mohammedanism*, 2nd edition (New York: Oxford University Press, 1962)

Goldziher, Ignaz, *Introduction to Islamic Theology and Law*, translated by Hamori, Andras and Hamori, Ruth, (Princeton: Princeton University Press, 1981)

Grant, Michael, *From Alexander to Cleopatra: The Hellenistic World*, (London : Weidenfeld & Nicolson, 1982)

Heer, Friedrich, *The Medieval World: Europe 1100-1350*, translated by Sondheimer, Janet, (London: Weidenfeld & Nicholson, 1990)

Hourani, Albert, *A History of the Arab Peoples*, (Cambridge, Mass.: Belknap, Harvard University Press, 1991)

Hurvitz, Nimrod, *The Formation of Hanbalism: Piety into Power*, (New York: Routledge/Taylor & Francis Group, 2002)

Imber, Colin, *Ebu's-Su'ud: The Islamic Legal Tradition*, (Stanford: Stanford University Press, 1997)

Ishaq, Muhammad Ibn., *Life of Muhammad: A translation of Ishaq's "Sirat Rasul Allah"* translated by Guillaume, Alfred, (Oxford: Oxford University Press, 1955)

Isocrates, *Panegyricus* 50, quoted on introductory page of Harry Brewster, *Classical Anatolia: The Glory of Hellenism*, (London: I.B.Tauris & Co Ltd, 1993)

Jasser, M. Zuhdi, *A Battle for the Soul of Islam: An American Muslim Patriot's Fight to Save His Faith* (New York: Threshold Editions/Simon & Schuster, Inc., 2012)

Johnson, Paul, *A History of Christianity*, (New York: Atheneum, 1976)

Kinross, John Patrick Douglas Balfour, Baron, *Atatürk: The Rebirth of a Nation*, (Nicosia, Northern Cyprus: K. Rustem & Brother, 1981)

Kinross, John Patrick Douglas Balfour, Baron, *The Ottoman Centuries*, (New York: Perennial/HarperCollins, 2002)

Krejči, Jaroslav, *The Paths of Civilization – Understanding the Currents of History* (New York: Palgrave Macmillan, 2004)

Kuran, Timur, *Islam & Mammon: The Economic Predicaments of Islamism*, (Princeton: Princeton University Press, 2004)

Kuran, Timur, *The Long Divergence: How Islamic Law Held Back the Middle East*, (Princeton: Princeton University Press, 2011)

Kurzman, Charles, editor, *Liberal Islam: a Sourcebook*, (New York: Oxford University Press, 1998)

Lacey, Robert, *Inside the Kingdom – Kings, Clerics, Modernists, Terrorists, and the Struggle for Saudi Arabia,* (New York: Viking/Penguin Group, 2009)

LeVine, Mark, *Heavy Metal Islam: Rock, Resistance, and the Struggle for the Soul of Islam,* (New York: Three Rivers Press, 2008)

Lewis, Bernard, *Islam and the West* (New York: Oxford University Press, 1993)

Lewis, Bernard, *The Arabs in History,* (Oxford: Oxford University Press, 1958)

Lewis, Bernard, *The Jews of Islam,* (Princeton: Princeton University Press, 1984)

Lewis, Bernard, *The Middle East and the West,* (New York: Harper & Row, Publishers, 1966)

Maine, Henry Sumner, *Ancient Law,* (New York: H. Holt, 1908)

Makal, Mahmut *A Village in Anatolia,* translated by Deedes, Sir Wyndham, edited by Stirling, Paul; combining *Bizim Köy,* 1950, and *Köyümden,* 1952, (London: Vallentine Mitchell, 1954)

Makdisi, George, *The Rise of Colleges: Institutions of Learning in Islam and the West,* (Edinburgh: Edinburgh University Press, 1981)

Mango, Andrew, *Atatürk: The Biography of the Founder of Modern Turkey,* (New York: The Overlook Press, 2000) 193-195

Mango, Andrew, *The Turks Today,* (London: John Murray, 2004)

Marsot, Afaf Lutfi Al-Sayyid, *A Short History of Modern Egypt*, (Cambridge: Cambridge University Press, 1985)

Mazower, Mark, *Salonica: City of Ghosts*, (New York: Vintage Books/Random House, 2004)

McDowall, David, *A Modern History of The Kurds, 3rd edition*, (London: I.B. Tauris, 2007)

Meddeb, Abdelwahab, *The Malady of Islam*, translated by Joris, Pierre and Reid, Ann, (New York: Basic Books/Perseus Books Group, 2003)

Melchert, Christopher, *Makers of the Muslim World: Ahmad Ibn Hanbal*, (Oxford: Oneworld Publications, 2006)

Muller, Herbert J., *Freedom in the Western World: From the Dark Ages to the Rise of Democracy*, (New York: Harper & Row, 1963)

Murphy, Francis X., *Politics and the Early Christian*, (New York: Desclee Company, Inc., 1967)

Nasr, Seyyed Hossein, *Science and Civilization in Islam*, (Cambridge, Mass.: Harvard University Press, 1968)

Nasr, Seyyed Vali Reza, *Mawdudi & The Making of Islamic Revivalism*, (New York: Oxford University Press, 1996)

O'Shea, Stephen, *Sea of Faith: Islam and Christianity in the Medieval Mediterranean World*, (London: Profile Books, Ltd., 2007)

Patton, Walter M., *Ahmed ibn Hanbal and the Mihna*, (Leiden: Brill, 1897)

Pope, Nicole, and Pope, Hugh, *Turkey Unveiled: A History of Modern Turkey*, (New York: The Overlook Press, 2004)

Raissouni, Ahmed, *Islamic Waqf Endowment: Scope and Implications*, translated by Behhallam, Abderrafi, (Mohammedia, Morocco: Islamic Educational, Scientific and Cultural Organization, 2002)

Rogan, Eugene, *The Arabs – A History*, (New York: Basic Books/Perseus Books Group, 2011)

Rosenstock-Huessy, Eugen, *Out of Revolution: Autobiography of Western Man*, (New York: Morrow, 1938)

Schaff, Philip, *History of the Christian Church*, (New York: Charles Scribners' Sons, 1910)

Stark, Rodney, and Finke, Roger, *Acts of Faith: Explaining the Human Side of Religion*, (Berkeley and Los Angeles, CA: University of California Press, 2000)

Stein, Peter, *Roman Law in European History*, (Cambridge: Cambridge University Press, 1999)

Taheri-Iraqi, Ahmad, *Zandaqa in the Early Abbasid Period with Special Reference to the Poetry*, (April 1982 doctor's thesis, University of Edinburgh)

Tellenbach, Gerd, *Church, State and Christian Society at the Time of the Investiture Contest*, translated by Bennett, R.F., (New York: Harper & Row, Publishers, Inc., 1970)

Trimingham, J. Spencer, *Christianity among the Arabs in Pre-Islamic Times*, (London: Longman Publishing Group, 1979)

Trimingham, J. Spencer, *The Sufi Orders in Islam*, (Oxford: Clarendon Press, 1971)

VanCleve, Thomas C., *The Emperor Frederick II of Hohenstaufen Immutator Mundi*, (Oxford: Oxford University Press, 1972)

Watt, W. Montgomery, *Islamic Political Thought, the Basic Concepts*, (Edinburgh: Edinburgh University Press, 1968)

Watt, W. Montgomery, *Islam and the Integration of Society*, (London: Routledge & Kegan Paul, 1961)

Wheatcroft, Andrew, *The Enemy at the Gate: Habsburgs, Ottomans, and the Battle for Europe*, (New York: Basic Books, 2010)

Wickham, Carrie Rosefsky, *Mobilizing Islam: Religion, Activism, and Political Change in Egypt*, (New York: Columbia University Press, 2002)

Williams, Charles, *The Descent of the Dove: A Short History of the Holy Spirit in the Church*, (Vancouver, BC: Regent College Publishing, 2002)

Witte, John Jr., and Alexander, Frank S., editors, *Christianity and Law: An Introduction*, (New York: Cambridge University Press, 2008)

Witte, John Jr., *God's Joust, God's Justice: Law and Religion in the Western Tradition*, (Grand Rapids, MI: Eerdmans, 2006)

Zaman, Muhammad Qasim, *The Ulama in Contemporary Islam: Custodians of Change*, (Princeton: Princeton University Press, 2002)

Zernov, Nicolas, *Eastern Christendom: A Study of the Origin and Development of the Eastern Orthodox Church*, (New York: G. P. Putnam's Sons, 1961)

JOURNAL ARTICLES

Abrahamov, Binyamin, "Ibn Taymiyya on the Agreement of Reason with Tradition," *The Muslim World* LXXXII, no. 3-4 (1992) 256-273

Afsah, Ebrahim, "Contested Universalities of International Law. Islam's Struggle with Modernity," *Journal of the History of International Law* 10 (2008) 259-307

Akoğlu, Kerime Sule, "Piecemeal Freedom: Why the Headscarf Ban Remains in Place in Turkey," *Boston College International and Comparative Law Review* 38, no. 2 (2015) 277-304

Arjomand, Sa'id Amir, "The Constitution of Medina: A Sociolegal Interpretation of Muhammad's Acts of Foundation of the Umma," *International Journal of Middle East Studies* 41, (2009) 555-575

Barnard, Laurette, "The Criminalisation of Heresy in the Later Roman Empire: A Sociopolitical Device?" *The Journal of Legal History* 16, no. 2 (1995) 121-146

Barnwell, P.S., "Emperors, Jurists and Kings: Law and Custom in the Late Roman and Early Medieval West," *Past & Present* 168, (2000) 6-29

Bazzano, Elliot A., "Ibn Taymiyya, Radical Polymath, Part 1: Scholarly Perceptions," *Religion Compass* 9, no. 4 (2015) 100-116

Berman, Harold J., "Religious Foundations of Law in the West: An Historical Perspective," *Journal of Law and Religion* 1, no. 1 (1983) 3-43

Berman, Harold J., "Religious Freedom and the Challenge of the Modern State," *Emory Law Journal* 39, (1990) 149-164

Berman, Harold J. "The Background of the Western Legal Tradition in the Folklaw of the Peoples of Europe," *The University of Chicago Law Review* 45, no. 3 (1978) 533-597

Berman, Harold J., "Why the History of Western Law is not Written," *University of Illinois Law Review* 1984, no. 3 (1984) 511-520

Berween, Mohamed, "Al-Wathiqa: The First Islamic State Constitution," *Journal of Muslim Minority Affairs* 23, no. 1 (2003) 103-119

Beyer, Peter, "The Religious System of Global Society: A Sociological Look at Contemporary Religion and Religions," *Numen* 45, no. 1 (1998) 1-29

Blumenthal, Uta-Renate, "Pope Gregory VII and the Prohibition of Nicolaitism" in *Medieval Purity and Piety: Essays on Medieval Clerical Celibacy and Religious Reform*, edited by Frassetto, Michael, (New York and London: Garland Publishing, Inc., 1998) 239-267

Brock, S. P., "Early Syrian Asceticism," *Numen* 20, no. 1 (1973) 1-19

Bulliet, Richard W., "The Shaikh Al-Islām and the Evolution of Islamic Society", *Studia Islamica* 35 (1972) 53-67

Cameron, Alan, "Gratian's Repudiation of the Pontifical Robe," *The Journal of Roman Studies* 58, Parts 1 and 2 (1968) 100-114

Cantoni, Davide, and Yuchtman, Noam, "Medieval Universities, Legal Institutions, and the Commercial Revolution," *The Quarterly Journal of Economics* 129, no. 2 (2014) 823-887

Casanova, José, "Civil Society and Religion: Retrospective Reflections on Catholicism and Prospective Reflections on Islam," *Social Research* 68, no. 4 (2001) 1041-1080

Cetinsaya, Gökhan, "Rethinking Nationalism and Islam: Some Preliminary Notes on the Roots of "Turkish-Islamic Synthesis" in Modern Turkish Political Thought," *The Muslim World* 89, no. 3-4 (1999) 350–376

Çizakça, Murat, "The Evolution of Domestic Borrowing in the Ottoman Empire," in *East Meets West – Banking, Commerce and Investment in the Ottoman Empire,* edited by L. Cottrell, Philip L., (Aldershot: Ashgate Publishing Limited, 2008) 1-10

Clark, David S., "The Medieval Origins of Modern Legal Education: Between Church and State," *The American Journal of Comparative Law* 35, no. 4 (1987) 653-719

Coates, Simon, "Venantius Fortunatus and the Image of Episcopal Authority in Late Antique and Early Merovingian Gaul," *The English Historical Review* 115, no. 464 (2000) 1109-1137

Cobban, Alan B., "Medieval Student Power," *Past & Present* 53, no. 1 (1971) 28-66

Cook, Michael, "On the Origins of Wahhābism," *Journal of the Royal Asiatic Society, Third Series* 2, no. 2 (1992) 191-202

Cooperson, Michael, "Baghdad in Rhetoric and Narrative," *Muqarnas* 13 (1996) 99-113

Cooperson, Michael, "Two Abbasid Trials: Ahmad Ibn Hanbal and Hunayn B. Ishaq," *Al-Qantara XXII* 2 (2001) 375-393

Cotterrell, Roger, "The struggle for law: some dilemmas of cultural legality," *International Journal of Law in Context* 4, no. 4 (2009) 373-384

Crone, Patricia, "Quraysh and the Roman army: Making sense of the Meccan leather trade," *Bulletin of the School of Oriental and African Studies* 70, no. 1 (2007) 63-88

Dawisha, Adeed, "Requiem for Arab Nationalism," *Middle East Quarterly* 10, no. 1 (2003) 25-41

de Ste. Croix, G.E.M., "Why Were the Early Christians Persecuted?," *Past & Present* 16, (1963) 16-24

De Villiers, Pieter G.R., "Union with the transcendent God in Philo and John's Gospel," *HTS Teologiese Studies/Theological Studies* 70, no. 1 (2014)

Demichelis, Marco, "Between Mu'tazilism and Syncretism: A Reappraisal of the Behavior of the Caliphate of al-Ma'mūn," *Journal of Near Eastern Studies* 71, no. 2 (2012) 257-274

Denny, Frederick M., "Ummah in the Constitution of Medina," *Journal of Near Eastern Studies* 36, no. 1 (1977) 39-47

Drake, H.A., "Constantine and Consensus," *Church History* 64, no. 1 (1995) 1-15

Drake, H. A., "Lambs into Lions: Explaining Early Christian Intolerance," *Past & Present* 153, (1996) 3-36

Eickelman, Dale F., "The Coming Transformation of the Muslim-Majority World," *The Review of Faith & International Affairs* 7, no. 2 (2009) 23-26

El Fadl, Khaled Abou, "Constitutionalism and the Islamic Sunni Legacy," *UCLA Journal of Islamic & Near Eastern Law* 1, no. 67 (2001-2002) 67-101

El-Hibri, Tayeb, "Harun al-Rashid and the Mecca Protocol of 802: A Plan for Division or Succession?" *International Journal of Middle East Studies* 24, no. 3 (1992) 461-480

Endicott, Timothy A. O., "The Impossibility of the Rule of Law," *Oxford Journal of Legal Studies* 19, no. 1 (1999) 1-18

Fowden, Garth, "Bishops and Temples in the Eastern Roman Empire A.D. 320-435," *Journal of Theological Studies, N.S.*, xxix, pt. 1, (1978) 53-78

Frazee, Charles A., "The Origins of Clerical Celibacy in the Western Church," *Church History 57, Supplement: Centennial Issue* (1988) 108-126

Fueck, Johann, "The Role of Traditionalism in Islam" in *Studies on Islam*, translated and edited by Swartz, Merlin L., (New York: Oxford University Press, 1981) 99-122

Gibb, H.A.R., "The Evolution of Government in Early Islam," *Studia Islamic* 4 (1955) 1-17

Goldziher, Ignaz, *"Muslim Education"* in *The Formation of the Classical Islamic World, vol. 43: Education and Learning in the Early Islamic World*, general editor Conrad, Lawrence I., edited by Gilliot, Claude, (Farnham, Surrey: Ashgate Publishing Limited, 2012) 13-22

Goldziher, Ignaz, "The Attitude of Orthodox Islam Toward the 'Ancient Sciences'" in *Studies on Islam*, translated and edited by Swartz, Merlin L., (New York: Oxford University Press, 1981) 185-215

Gözaydın, İştar B., "A Religious Administration to Secure Secularism: The Presidency of Religious Affairs of the Republic of Turkey," Marburg Journal of Religion 11, no. 1 (2006) 1-8

Grant, Edward, "The Fate of Ancient Greek Natural Philosophy in the Middle Ages: Islam and Western Christianity," *The Review of Metaphysics* 61, no. 3 (2008) 503-528

Grendler, Paul F., "The Universities of the Renaissance and Reformation," *Renaissance Quarterly* 57, no. 1 (2004) 1-42

Griffel, Frank, "What do we mean by 'Salafi'? Connecting Muhammad Abduh with Egypt's Nur Party in Islam's Contemporary Intellectual History," *Die Welt Des Islams* 55 (2015) 186-220

Güriz, Adnan, "Sources of Turkish Law," in *Introduction to Turkish Law, 5th edition,* edited by Ansay, Tuğrul, and Wallace, Don Jr., (2004) 1-18

Hagner, Donald A., "The Vision of God in Philo and John: A Comparative Study," *Journal of the Evangelical Theological Society* 14 (1971) 81-93

Hallaq, Wael B. Hallaq, "Considerations on the Function and Character of Sunnī Legal Theory," *Journal of the American Oriental Society* 104, no. 4 (1984) 679-689

Hallaq, Wael B., "Juristic Authority vs. State Power: The Legal Crises of Modern Islam," *Journal of Law and Religion* 19, no. 2 (2003 - 2004) 243-258

Hanson, R.P.C., "The Reaction of the Church to the Collapse of the Western Roman Empire in the Fifth Century," *Vigiliae Christianae* 26, no. 4 (1972) 272-287

Henry, Patrick, "'And I Don't Care What It Is': The Tradition-History Of A Civil Religion Proof-Text," *Journal of the American Academy of Religion* 49, no. 1 (1981) 35-47

Hodgson, Marshall G. S., "How Did the Early Shî'a become Sectarian?" *Journal of the American Oriental Society* 75, no. 1 (1955) 1-13

Horii, Satoe, "Reconsideration of Legal Devices (Ḥiyal) in Islamic Jurisprudence: The Ḥanafīs and Their "Exits" (Makhārij)", *Islamic Law and Society* 9, no. 3 (2002) 312-357

Hourani, George F., "Islamic and Non-Islamic Origins of Mu'tazilite Ethical Rationalism," *International Journal of Middle East Studies* 7, no. 1 (1976) 59-87

Hurvitz, Nimrod, "Miḥna as Self-Defense," *Studia Islamica* 92 (2001) 93-111

Hurvitz, Nimrod, "Who is the Accused? The Interrogation of Ahmad Ibn Hanbal," *Al-Qantara* XXE, 2 (2001) 359-373

Hussain, Muzaffar, "The Islamic Polity of Abdul A'La Mawdudi," *VFAST Transactions on Islamic Research* 3:1 (2014) 13-21

Isaac, Steven, "The Ba'th of Syria and Iraq," in *The International Encyclopedia of Revolution and Protest: 1500 to the Present*, edited by Ness, Immanuel, (Malden, MA: Wiley-Blackwell, 2009)

Jackson, Sherman A., "The Alchemy of Domination? Some Asharite Responses to Mutazilite Ethics," *International Journal of Middle East Studies* 31:2 (1999) 185-201

Kinzig, Wolfram, "Non-Separation': Closeness and Co-operation between Jews and Christians in the Fourth Century," *Vigiliae Christianae* 45, no. 1 (1991) 27-53

Kirschner, Robert, "The Vocation of Holiness in Late Antiquity," *Vigiliae Christianae* 38, no. 2 (1984) 105-124

Kister, M.J., "Musaylima." *Encyclopaedia of the Qur'ān.* General Editor: Dammen, Jane, (Brill, 2009)

Koeppler, H., "Frederick Barbarossa and the Schools of Bologna," *The English Historical Review* 54, no. 216 (1939) 577-607

Lakhdar, Lafif, "Moving from Salafi to Rationalist Education," *Middle East Review of International Affairs* 9, no. 1 (2005) 30-44

Lakhdar, Lafif, *"Why the Reversion to Islamic Archaism?"* Forbidden *Agendas* from the Journal *Khamseen (1984)* 275-301

Landau-Tasseron, Ella, "The Status of Allies in Pre-Islamic and Early Islamic Arabian Society," *Islamic Law & Society* 13, no. 6 (2006) 6-32

Lapidus, Ira M., "Islamic Revival and Modernity: The Contemporary Movements and the Historical Paradigms," *Journal of the Economic and Social History of the Orient* 40, no. 4 (1997) 444-460

Lapidus, Ira M., "Separation of State and Religion in the Development of Early Islamic Society," *International Journal of Middle East Studies* VI (1975) 363-385

Lawson, M.K., "Archbishop Wulfstan and the Homiletic Element in the Laws of Æthelred II and Cnut," *The English Historical Review* 107, no. 424 (1992) 565-586

Layish, Aharon, "Saudi Arabian Legal Reform as a Mechanism to Moderate Wahhābī Doctrine," *Journal of the American Oriental Society* 107, no. 2 (1987) 279-292

Lehman, Warren Winfred, "The First English Law," *The Journal of Legal History* 6, no. 1 (1985) 1-32

Lewis, Bernard, "On the Revolutions in Early Islam," *Studia Islamica* 32 (1970) 215-231

Libson, Gideon, "On the Development of Custom as a Source of Law in Islamic Law," *Islamic Law and Society* 4, no. 2 (1997) 131-155

Lindgren, James, "Symposium: Why the Ancients may not have needed a System of Criminal Law," *Boston University Law Review* 76, no. 1-2 (1996) 29-56

Loseby, S.T., "Marseille – Late Antique Success Story?" *The Journal of Roman Studies* 82 (1992) 165-185

MacMullen, Ramsay, "Two Types of Conversion to Early Christianity," *Vigiliae Christianae* 37, no. 2 (1983) 174-192

Madden, M. Stuart, "Paths of Western Law after Justinian," *Widener Law Journal* 22, no. 3 (2013) 757-828

Makdisi, George, "Ashʿarī and the Ash'arites in Islamic Religious History I," *Studia Islamica* 17 (1962) 37-80

Makdisi, George, "Hanbalite Islam," in *Studies on Islam*, translated and edited by Swartz, Merlin L., (New York: Oxford University Press, 1981) 216-274

Makdisi, George, "Institutionalized Learning as a Self-Image of Islam" in *Religion, Law and Learning in Classical Islam,* (London: Variorum, 1991) 57-_____

Makdisi, George, "Muslim Institutions of Learning in Eleventh-Century Baghdad", in *Religion, Law and Learning in Classical Islam,* (London: Variorum, 1991) 1-56

Makdisi, George, "Scholasticism and Humanism in Classical Islam and the Christian West, " in *Religion, Law and Learning in Classical Islam,* (London: Variorum, 1991) _____-_____

Makdisi, George, "The Significance of the Sunni Schools of Law in Islamic Religious History," *International Journal of Middle East Studies* 10:1 (1979) 1-8

Mallat, Chibli, "From Islamic to Middle Eastern Law a Restatement of the Field (Part I)," *The American Journal of Comparative Law* 51, no. 4 (2003) 699-750

Marmor, Andrei, "The Rule of Law and Its Limits," *Law and Philosophy* 23, no. 1 (2004) 1-43

Massell, Gregory J., "Law as an Instrument of Revolutionary Change in a Traditional Milieu: The Case of Soviet Central Asia," *Law & Society Review* 2, no. 2 (1968) 179-228

McKitterick, Rosamond, "The Illusion of Royal Power in the Carolingian Annals," *The English Historical Review* 115, no. 460 (2000) 1-20

Melchert, Christopher, "Religious Policies of the Caliphs from al-Mutawakkil to al-Muqtadir, A H 232-295/A D 847-908," *Islamic Law and Society* 3, no. 3 (1996) 316-342

Melchert, Christopher, "The Adversaries of Aḥmad Ibn Ḥanbal," *Arabica*, T. 44, Fasc. 2 (1997) 234-253

Miller, Andrew C., "Jundi-Shapur, bimaristans, and the rise of academic medical centres," *Journal of the Royal Society of Medicine* 99 (2006) 615–617

Miller, Ruth A., "The Ottoman and Islamic Substratum of Turkey's Swiss Civil Code," *Journal of Islamic Studies* 11, no. 3 (2000) 335-361

Minnerath, Roland, "How Should State and Church Interact?" *The Jurist* 70 (2010) 473-486

Morden, John W., "An Essay on the Connections Between Law and Religion," *Journal of Law and Religion* 2, no. 1 (1984) 7-39

Morris, John, "Early Christian Orthodoxy," *Past & Present* 3 (1953) 1-14

Mueller, Wolfgang P. "The Recovery of Justinian's Digest in the Middle Ages," *Bulletin of Medieval Canon Law* 20 (1990) 1-29

Muhammad, Atta, "Mutazila-Heresy; Theological and Rationalist Mutazila; Al-mamun, Abbasid Caliph; Al-mutawakkil, Abbasid Caliph; The Traditionalists," *Middle-East Journal of Scientific Research* 12, no. 7 (2012) 1031-1038

Nadolski, Dora Glidewell, "Ottoman and Secular Civil Law," *International Journal of Middle East Studies* 8, no. 4 (1977) 517-543

Nafi, Basheer M., "A Teacher of Ibn Abd Al-Wahhab: Muhammad Hayat Al-Sindi and the Revival of Ashab Al-Hadiths Methodology," *Islamic Law & Society* 13 (2006) 208-241

Nasr, Seyyed Hossein, "Islamic Conception of Intellectual Life," in *Dictionary of the History of Ideas*, edited by Weiner, Philip P., (New York: Charles Scribner's Sons, 1973) II:639-652

Nasr, Seyyed Hossein, "The Meaning and Role of "Philosophy" in Islam," *Studia Islamica* 37 (1973) 57-80

Nawas, John A., "The Mihna of 218 A.H. / 833 A.D. Revisited: An Empirical Study," *Journal of the American Oriental Society* 116, no. 4 (1996) 698-708

Neff, Stephen, "Decline and Emergence: Roman law and the Transition from Antiquity to Feudalism," *The Journal of Legal History* 5, no. 2 (1984) 91-116

Orücü, Esin, "Judicial Navigation as Official Law Meets Culture in Turkey," *International Journal of Law in Context* 4, no. 1 (2008) 35-61

Paden, William E., "Universals Revisited: Human Behaviors and Cultural Variations," *Numen* 48, no. 3 (2001) 276-289

Paden, William E. "Elements of a New Comparativism," in *A Magic Still Dwells, Comparative Religion in the Postmodern Age*, edited by Patton, Kimberley C. and Ray, Benjamin C. (Oakland, CA: University of California Press, 2000) 182-192

Pears, Edwin, "The Campaign against Paganism A. D. 324," *The English Historical Review* 24, no. 93, (1909) 1-17

Peters, F.E., "The Quest of the Historical Muhammad," *International Journal of Middle East Studies* 23, no. 3 (1991) 291-315

Pitts, Lynn F., "Relations between Rome and the German 'Kings' on the Middle Danube in the First to Fourth Centuries A.D.," *The Journal of Roman Studies* 79 (1989) 45-58

Pixley, Michael M., "The Development and Role of the Şeyhülislam in Early Ottoman History," *Journal of the American Oriental Society* 96, no. 1 (1976) 89-96

Rahman, Asyraf Hj.A.B. and Ali, Nooraihan, "The Influence of Al-Mawdudi and the Jama'at Al Islami Movement on Sayyid Qutb Writings", *World Journal of Islamic History and Civilization* 2, no. 4 (2012) 232-236

Rives, J.B., "The Decree of Decius and the Religion of Empire," *The Journal of Roman Studies* 89, (1999) 135-154

Robinson, Francis, "Technology and Religious Change: Islam and the Impact of Print," *Modern Asian Studies*, 27:1 (1993) 229-251

Robinson, I.S., "Pope Gregory VII, the Princes and the Pactum 1077-1080," *The English Historical Review* 94, no. 373 (1979) 721-756

Sabra, A.I., "The Appropriation and Subsequent Naturalization of Greek Science in Medieval Islam: A Preliminary Statement," *History of Science xxv* (1987) 225-238

Sahas, Daniel J., "The seventh century in Byzantine-Muslim relations: Characteristics and forces," *Islam and Christian–Muslim Relations* 2, no. 1 (1991) 3-22

Schulze, Reinhard, "The Birth of Tradition and Modernity in 18th and 19th Century Islamic Culture – the Case of Printing," *Culture & History* (1997) 29-72

Serjeant, R.B., "The "Sunnah Jāmi'ah," Pacts with the Yat͟hrib Jews, and the "Taḥrīm" of Yat͟hrib: Analysis and Translation of the Documents Comprised in the So-Called 'Constitution of Medina'," *Bulletin of the School of Oriental and African Studies* 41, no. 1 (1978) 1-42

Sibley, Mulford Q., "Religion and Law: Some Thoughts on Their Intersections," *Journal of Law and Religion* 2, no. 1 (1984) 41-67

Smith, Huston, "Methodology, Comparisons, and Truth," in *A Magic Still Dwells, Comparative Religion in the Postmodern Age*, Kimberley C. Patton and Benjamin C. Ray, eds. (2000) 172-181

Smith, Sidney, "Events in Arabia in the 6th Century A. D.," *Bulletin of the School of Oriental and African Studies* 16, no. 3 (1954) 425-468

Spectorsky, Susan A. "Ahmad ibn Hanbal's Fiqh," *Journal of American Oriental Society* 102, no. 3 (1982) 461-465

Tetley, William, "Mixed Jurisdictions: Common Law v. Civil Law (Codified and Uncodified) ", *Louisiana Law Review* 60 (2000) 677-738

Voll, John, "Muḥammad Ḥayyā al-Sindī and Muḥammad ibn 'Abd al-Wahhab: An Analysis of an Intellectual Group in Eighteenth-Century Madīna," *Bulletin of the School of Oriental and African Studies* 38, no. 1 (1975) 32-39

Von Grunebaum, G.E., "Nationalism and Cultural Trends in the Arab Near East," *Studia Islamica* 14 (1961) 121-153

Watkin, Thomas Glyn, "Paul of Tarsus: A citizen of no mean city," *The Journal of Legal History* 9, no. 2 (1988) 119-141

Watson, William J., "İbrāhīm Müteferrika and Turkish Incunabula," *Journal of the American Oriental Society* 88, no. 3 (1968) 435–441

Weismann, Itzchak, "Genealogies of Fundamentalism: Salafi Discourse in Nineteenth-Century Baghdad," *British Journal of Middle Eastern Studies* 36, no. 2 (2009) 267-280

Whitney, J. P., "Gregory VII," *The English Historical Review* 34, no. 134 (1919) 129-151

Wickham, Chris, "The Other Transition: From the Ancient World to Feudalism," *Past & Present* 103 (1984) 3-36

Wiktorowicz, Quintan, "Anatomy of the Salafi Movement," *Studies in Conflict & Terrorism* 29, no. 207 (2006) 207–239

Zahniser, Mathias, "Insights from The Uthmaniyya of Al-Jahiz into the Religious Policy of al-Ma'mun," *Muslim World* 69, no. 1 (1979) 8-17

Zaman, Muhammad Qasim, "The Caliphs, the ʿUlamā', and the Law: Defining the Role and Function of the Caliph in the Early ʿAbbāsid Period," *Islamic Law and Society* 4, no. 1 (1997) 1-36

NEWSPAPER AND ONLINE ARTICLES

Akaltan, Belgin, *"We are like the cop shot on the pavement"*, Hurriyet Daily News, January 17, 2015, http://www.hurriyetdailynews.com/we-are-like-the-cop-shot-on-the-pavement.aspx?pageID=238&nID=77045&NewsCatID=469, accessed October 28, 2015

Taha Akyol, *"The founding of an Islamic university in Turkey"* Hurriyet Daily News, October 2, 2014,

http://www.hurriyetdailynews.com/the-founding-of-an-islamic-university-in-turkey-
.aspx?pageID=449&nID=72424&NewsCatID=458, accessed
November 8, 2015

Al-Banna, Gamal, *"The Muslim Brotherhood is strong, but weak to lead Egypt"* Oasis, December 5, 2012,
http://www.oasiscenter.eu/articles/arab-revolutions/2012/12/05/gamal-al-banna-the-muslim-brotherhood-is-strong-but-weak-to-lead-egypt, accessed October 28, 2015

Ankara - Anatolia News Agency, *"Religious leaders mull conditions for 'breast milk bank'"* Hurriyet Daily News, February 27, 2013,
http://www.hurriyetdailynews.com/religious-leaders-mull-conditions-for-breast-milk-bank.aspx?pageID=238&nID=41942&NewsCatID=341, accessed October 28, 2015

Badawi, Raif, *"From an Earlier Blog of Raif Badawi, Sentenced to 1000 Lashes, Jail, Fine in Saudi Arabia"*, Gatestone Institute, July 7, 2014, http://www.gatestoneinstitute.org/4393/raif-badawi, accessed October 28, 2015

Batha, Emma, *"Morocco's Islamic women preachers lead social revolution"* Reuters, May 19, 2015,
http://www.reuters.com/article/2015/05/19/us-morocco-women-morchidat-idUSKBN0O40MG20150519, accessed October 28, 2015

Bednarz, Dieter, and Brinkbäumer, Klaus, *"Interview with Egyptian President Sisi: 'Extremists Offend the Image of God"'* Spiegel online International, February 9, 2015,
http://www.spiegel.de/international/world/islamic-state-egyptian-president-sisi-calls-for-help-in-is-fight-a-1017434.html, accessed October 28, 2015

Black, Ian, "*A look at the writings of Saudi blogger Raif Badawi – sentenced to 1,000 lashes*", The Guardian, http://www.theguardian.com/world/2015/jan/14/-sp-saudi-blogger-extracts-raif-badawi, accessed October 28, 2015

Cairo – AP, "*Saudi woman sentence to 10 lashes for driving car*", Hurriyet Daily News, September 28, 2011, http://www.hurriyetdailynews.com/default.aspx?pageid=438&n=saudi-woman-sentenced-to-10-lashes-for-driving-car-2011-09-28, accessed October 28, 2015

"Casablanca Calling: Morocco's first female Muslim leaders set out to change their country" documentary film, accessed October 28, 2015, http://www.casablancacalling.com/

Couprie, Dirk, "Anaximander," *Internet Encyclopedia of Philosophy*, accessed October 28, 2015, http://www.iep.utm.edu/anaximan/

"Edict of Milan" *Internet Medieval Source Book*, accessed October 28, 2015 http://legacy.fordham.edu/halsall/source/edict-milan.asp,

Electa Draper, "*Legacy of Islamic revolutionary's hate haunts Greeley*" Denver Post, February 6, 2011, updated February 8, 2011, accessed October 28, 2015, http://www.denverpost.com/ci_17306551

El-Hennawy, Noha, "*Gamal al-Banna leaves behind a legacy of controversial views on Islam*" Egypt Independent, February 17, 2003, http://www.egyptindependent.com/news/gamal-al-banna-leaves-behind-legacy-controversial-views-islam, accessed October 28, 2015

Feltner, Yotam, "*Liberal Iraqi Shi'ite Scholar Sayyed Ahmad Al-Qabbanji Calls For Reason In Islamic Discourse and*

Jurisprudence", MEMRI, Inquiry and Analysis Series Report No. 937, February 21, 2013, http://www.memri.org/report/en/print7015.htm, accessed October 28, 2015

Gillis, Wendy *"Toronto mosque is gay friendly, mixed gender prayers led by a woman*" Toronto Star News, August 25, 2013 http://www.thestar.com/news/gta/2013/08/25/islamic_scholars_ experience_diversity_of_muslim_practices_at_u_of_t_summer_ program.html, accessed October 28, 2015

Graham, Daniel W., "Anaximenes," *Internet Encyclopedia of Philosophy*, accessed October 28, 2015, http://www.iep.utm.edu/anaximen/,

Ibrahim, Raymond *"Egypt's Sisi: Islamic 'Thinking' Is 'Antagonizing the Entire World'*", From the Arab World, translation by Michele Antaki, January 1, 2015, http://www.raymondibrahim.com/from-the-arab-world/egypts-sisi-islamic-thinking-is-antagonizing-the-entire-world/, accessed October 28, 2015

Istanbul – Doğan News Agency, *"Top appeals court reverses blasphemy decision against Turkish pianist Say*", Hurriyet Daily News, October 26, 2015, http://www.hurriyetdailynews.com/top-appeals-court-reverses-blasphemy-decision-against-turkish-pianist-say.aspx?pageID=517&nID=90336&NewsCatID=339, accessed October 28, 2015

Istanbul – Doğan News Agency, *"Turkish pianist Fazil Say sentenced to 10 months in prison for blasphemy in retrial*", Hurriyet Daily News, October 19, 2015, http://www.hurriyetdailynews.com/turkish-pianist-fazil-say-sentenced-to-10-months-in-prison-for-blasphemy-in-retrial.aspx?PageID=238&NID=54824&NewsCatID=341, accessed October 28, 2015

Lakhdar, Lafif, *"Vatican II as a model for Islamic reform"*, Almuslih.org, accessed November 6, 2015, http://almuslih.org/index.php?option=com_content&view=articl e&id=228:vatican-ii-as-a-model-for-islamic-reform&catid=38:obstacles-to-reform&Itemid=207

MEMRI – *"Egyptian Philosopher Murad Wahba: Secularism Is the Only Way to Emerge from Our Crisis of Lack of Rationality"* MEMRI, Special Dispatch No. 3446, December 14, 2010, http://www.memri.org/report/en/print4841.htm, accessed October 28, 2015

MEMRI – *"Former Imam Of Mecca's Grand Mosque: There Is No Escaping Reform To Bring Islam Back To Its Path Of Tolerance"*, MEMRI, Special Dispatch No.6063, June 2, 2015, http://www.memri.org/report/en/0/0/0/0/0/0/8593.htm, accessed October 28, 2015

MEMRI – *"In Open Letter To Muslim World, French Muslim Philosopher Says Islam Has Given Birth To Monsters, Needs Reform"*, MEMRI, Special Dispatch No.5873, November 5, 2014, http://www.memri.org/report/en/print8206.htm, accessed October 28, 2015

MEMRI – *"Liberal Writer Mansour Al-Hadj Proposes Founding An Independent Islamic Organization To Address Root Causes Of Violent Extremism, Promote Peaceful Aspects Of Islam"* MEMRI, Special Dispatch No. 6118, July 30, 2015, http://www.memri.org/report/en/0/0/0/0/0/0/804)/8681.htm, accessed October 28, 2015

MEMRI – *"Muslim Intellectual Calls for 'Protestant Islam'"*, MEMRI, Special Dispatch No.1198, July 6, 2006, http://www.memri.org/report/en/0/0/0/0/0/0/1734.htm, accessed October 28, 2015

MEMRI – *"Qatari Religious Scholar Calls for A Moderate and Modern Islam"* MEMRI, Special Dispatch No. 885, March 25, 2005, http://www.memri.org/report/en/0/0/0/0/0/0/1345.htm, accessed October 28, 2015

MEMRI – *"Reformist Author Dr. Shaker Al-Nabulsi: Recent Attacks by Islamists on Arab Liberals – A Sign of Distress and Imminent Defeat"* MEMRI, Special Dispatch No.1163, May 12, 2006 , http://www.memri.org/report/en/0/0/0/0/0/804/1688.htm, accessed October 28, 2015

MEMRI – *"Saudi Intellectual: Western Civilization Has Liberated Mankind,"* MEMRI, Special Dispatch No.2332, April 29, 2009, http://www.memri.org/report/en/print3264.htm, accessed October 28, 2015

Mert, Nuray, *"An open letter to some 'Western liberals and leftists',"* Hurriyet Daily News, January 26, 2015, http://www.hurriyetdailynews.com/an-open-letter-to-some-western-liberals-and-leftists.aspx?pageID=449&nID=77419&NewsCatID=406, accessed October 28, 2015

Milson, Menahem, *"Reform vs. Islamism in the Arab World Today"* MEMRI Special Report No. 34, September 15, 2004, http://www.memri.org/report/en/0/0/0/0/0/855/1220.htm, accessed October 28, 2015

Morin, Arzu Çakır, *"Mosque for gays to open in France"* Hurriyet Daily News, November 19, 2012, http://www.hurriyetdailynews.com/mosque-for-gays-to-open-in-france.aspx?pageID=238&nid=34981, accessed October 28, 2015

Nazar, Sabir, "Principle political standpoints in Al-Absurdistan", Dawn.com, August 29, 2012, http://www.dawn.com/news/745445/principle-political-standpoints-in-al-absurdistan, accessed October 28, 2015

Plato, *Laws*, 635b-674c, accessed October 28, 2015, http://www.perseus.tufts.edu/hopper/text?doc=Perseus%3Atext%3A1999.01.0166%3Abook%3D1%3Asection%3D635b

Raphaeli, Nimrod, *"Sayyed Ayad Jamal Al-Din – Liberal Shi'ite Cleric and Foe of Iran"* MEMRI, Inquiry & Analysis Series Report No.582, January 21, 2010, http://www.memri.org/report/en/print3920.htm, accessed October 28, 2015

"Republic of Turkey Presidency of Religious Affairs," www.diyanet.gov.tr, accessed October 28, 2015

Rouhani, Hassan, *"Iran 'happy' dancers get suspended sentences"*, Al-Jazeera, September 19, 2014, http://www.aljazeera.com/news/middleeast/2014/09/iran-happy-dancers-get-suspended-sentences-201491913331993392.html, accessed October 28, 2015

Slackman, Michael, *"A voice for 'new understanding' of Islam"* - Africa & Middle East - International Herald Tribune, in The New York Times, October 20, 2006, http://www.nytimes.com/2006/10/20/world/africa/20iht-profile.3237674.html?_r=1&, accessed October 28, 2015

Stalinsky, Steven, *"A Muslim Friend of America"*, The New York Sun, May 23, 2007, http://www.nysun.com/foreign/muslim-friend-of-america/55011/, accessed October 28, 2015

Tatli, Selma, *"AKP is secularizing religious people"* Today's Zaman, June 9, 2014, http://www.todayszaman.com/anasayfa_akp-is-secularizing-religious-people_349917.html, accessed November 8, 2015

Taylor, C.C. W. and Lee, Mi-Kyoung, "The Sophists," The
Stanford Encyclopedia of Philosophy (Fall 2015 Edition),
Edward N. Zalta (ed.), accessed October 28, 2015,
http://plato.stanford.edu/archives/fall2015/entries/sophists/

Vanya, Ahmed, *"Beautifying Islam"*, November 20, 2014,
http://www.gatestoneinstitute.org/4894/beautifying-islam,
accessed October 28, 2015

Yinanç, Barçın, *"I worship so I can do anything I like' is Turks'
lifestyle: Scholar"* Hürriyet Daily News, June 16, 2012,
http://www.hurriyetdailynews.com/i-worship-so-i-can-do-
anything-i-like-is-turks-lifestyle-
scholar.aspx?pageID=238&nID=23284&NewsCatID=338,
accessed November 8, 2015

**CONSTITUTIONS, LAWS, COURT RULES, and LEGAL
CASES**
Constitution of Egypt (1923),
http://www.constitutionnet.org/vl/item/egypt-constitution-1923,
accessed October 28, 2015

The Basic Law of Governance of Saudi Arabia (1992),
http://www.saudiembassy.net/about/country-
information/laws/The_Basic_Law_Of_Governance.aspx,
accessed October 28, 2015

The Constitution of Syria, September 5, 1950, in Peaslee, Amos
J., Constitutions of Nations, 2nd edition, vol. III, (1956), pp. 360-
382

Constitution of the Syrian Arab Republic (2012),
http://www.voltairenet.org/article173033.html
accessed October 28, 2015

The Ottoman Constitution (1876, with 1909 amendments), Boğaziçi University, Atatürk Institute of Modern Turkish History (The translator is unknown), http://www.ata.boun.edu.tr, accessed October 28, 2015

Constitution of the Republic of Turkey (1924, anayasa.gen.tr, links to Earle, Edward Mead, "*The New Constitution of Turkey*, 40 Political Science Quarterly 1, (1925)

Constitution of the Republic of Turkey (1961), http://www.anayasa.gen.tr/1961constitution-text.pdf, accessed October 28, 2015

Constitution of the Republic of Turkey (1982, as amended through 2011), https://www.constituteproject.org/constitution/Turkey_2011.pdf, accessed October 28, 2015

United States Constitution (1789, as amended through 1992, with commentary), S.PUB.103-21, http://www.senate.gov/civics/constitution_item/constitution.htm, accessed October 28, 2015

European Court of Human Rights, "*Rules of Court*", accessed October 28, 2015, http://www.echr.coe.int/Documents/Rules_Court_ENG.pdf

Plessy v. Ferguson, 163 U.S. 537 (1896), https://www.law.cornell.edu/supremecourt/text/163/537, accessed October 28, 2015

Brown v. Board of Education, 347 U.S. 483 (1954), http://caselaw.findlaw.com/us-supreme-court/347/483.html, accessed October 28, 2015

Leyla Şahin v. Turkey [GC], no. 44774/98, § 113, ECHR (2005), http://hudoc.echr.coe.int/app/conversion/pdf/?library=ECHR&id

=001-70956&filename=001-70956.pdf, accessed October 28, 2015

Notes

Forward

[1] Timur Kuran, *Islam & Mammon: The Economic Predicaments of Islamism*, (Princeton: Princeton University Press, 2004) 122

[2] Eugen Rosenstock-Huessy, *Out of Revolution: Autobiography of Western Man*, (New York: Morrow, 1938) 741

Chapter 1

[3] Charles Williams, *The Descent of the Dove: A Short History of the Holy Spirit in the Church*, (Vancouver, BC: Regent College Publishing, 2002) 2-3

[4] Matt. 22:21, JB

[5] b.Shab.31a, accessed October 28, 2015, http://www.come-and-hear.com/shabbath/shabbath_31.html

[6] Isocrates, *Panegyricus* 50, quoted on introductory page of Harry Brewster, *Classical Anatolia: The Glory of Hellenism*, (London: I.B.Tauris & Co Ltd, 1993)

[7] Jaroslav Krejčí, *The Paths of Civilization – Understanding the Currents of History* (New York: Palgrave Macmillan, 2004) 144

[8] Krejčí, 144

[9] Dirk Couprie, "Anaximander," *Internet Encyclopedia of Philosophy*, accessed October 28, 2015, http://www.iep.utm.edu/anaximan/

[10] Daniel W. Graham, "Anaximenes," *Internet Encyclopedia of Philosophy*, accessed October 28, 2015, http://www.iep.utm.edu/anaximen/,

[11] Clement *Miscellanies* V.109.3: fr. 15 [KRS 169], as quoted in Malcolm Schofield, "The Ionians" in C.C.W. Taylor, editor, *Routledge History of Philosophy Volume 1: From the Beginning to Plato*, (London: Routledge, 1997) 64

[12] C.C. W. Taylor, Mi-Kyoung Lee, "The Sophists," *The Stanford Encyclopedia of Philosophy* (Fall 2015 Edition), Edward N. Zalta (ed.), accessed October 28, 2015, http://plato.stanford.edu/archives/fall2015/entries/sophists/

[13] Plato, *Laws*, 635b-674c, accessed October 28, 2015, http://www.perseus.tufts.edu/hopper/text?doc=Perseus%3Atext%3A1999.01.0166%3Abook%3D1%3Asection%3D635b

[14] Michael Grant, *From Alexander to Cleopatra: The Hellenistic World*, (London : Weidenfeld & Nicolson, 1982) 124 *ff*

[15] Acts 16:37, JB

[16] Williams, 3-4

[17] Acts 2:46, 3:1, 3:11, JB

[18] Francis X. Murphy, *Politics and the Early Christian*, (New York: Desclee Company, Inc., 1967) 40

[19] Acts 2:5-12, JB

[20] Acts 10:9-36, JB

[21] Acts 17:23-29, JB, footnotes t., u., and v.

[22] Paul Johnson, *A History of Christianity*, (New York: Atheneum, 1976) 3-63

[23] Jonathan P. Berkey, *The Formation of Islam: Religion and Society in the Near East, 600-1800*, (New York: Cambridge University Press, 2003) 17

[24] Wolfram Kinzig, "Non-Separation': Closeness and Co-operation between Jews and Christians in the Fourth Century," *Vigiliae Christianae* 45:1, (1991) 36. Note that the sermons of Chrysostom are easily understood as anti-Semitic - he does use the term "Christ-killers".

[25] J. B. Rives, "The Decree of Decius and the Religion of Empire," *The Journal of Roman Studies* 89, (1999) 135

[26] G. E. M. de Ste. Croix, "Why Were the Early Christians Persecuted?," *Past & Present* 16, (1963) 7

[27] "Edict of Milan" *Internet Medieval Source Book*, accessed October 28, 2015 http://legacy.fordham.edu/halsall/source/edict-milan.asp,

[28] Murphy, 116 "...by 270 Porphyry in his attack on the church was concerned with the fact that it was a stronghold of the rich, many of whom, by giving their goods to the poor upon conversion, were upsetting the financial order and destroying sources of fiscal revenue."

[29] H.A. Drake, "Constantine and Consensus," *Church History* 64:1, (1995) 1*ff*

[30] Gilbert Dagron, *Emperor and Priest – The Imperial Office in Byzantium*, translated by Jean Birrell, (New York: Cambridge University Press, 2003) 181

[31] H.A. Drake, "Lambs into Lions: Explaining Early Christian Intolerance," *Past & Present* 153, (1996) *passim*

[32] Laurette Barnard, "The Criminalisation of Heresy in the Later Roman Empire: A Sociopolitical Device?," *The Journal of Legal History*, 16: 2, (1995) 126

[33] W. H. C. Frend, *The Rise of the Monophysite Movement: Chapters in the History of the Church in the Fifth and Sixth Centuries*, (Cambridge: Clarke, 2008) 52

Chapter 2

[34] Koran 6:163 Rodwell's translation

[35] Muhammad Ibn. Ishaq, *Life of Muhammad. A translation of Ishaq's "Sirat Rasul Allah"* translated by Alfred Guillaume, (Oxford: Oxford University Press, 1955) 111, 114

[36] Compare for example, Karen Armstrong, *Islam: A Short History*, Bernard Lewis, *The Arabs in History*, W. Montgomery Watt, *Muhammad at Mecca*, and Patrica Crone, *Meccan Trade and the Rise of Islam.*

[37] Bernard Lewis, *The Arabs in History*, (Oxford: Oxford University Press, 1958) 29-30

[38] Patricia Crone, "Quraysh and the Roman army: Making sense of the Meccan leather trade," *Bulletin of the School of Oriental and African Studies* 70:1, (2007) 65 *ff*

[39] Jonathan P. Berkey, *The Formation of Islam: Religion and Society in the Near East, 600-1800*, (New York: Cambridge University Press, 2003) 47

[40] Koran 12:2 Rodwell's translation

[41] M.J. Kister, "Musaylima." *Encyclopaedia of the Qur'ān.* General Editor: Jane Dammen, (Brill, 2009)

[42] Frederick M. Denny, "Ummah in the Constitution of Medina," *Journal of Near Eastern Studies* 36:1, (1977) 42

[43] Denny *passim*

[44] W. Montgomery Watt, *Islamic Political Thought, the Basic Concepts*, (Edinburgh: Edinburgh University Press, 1968) 27

[45] See, e.g, Sa'id Amir Arjomand, "The Constitution of Medina: A Sociolegal Interpretation of Muhammad's Acts of Foundation of the Umma," *International Journal of Middle East Studies* 41, (2009); R.B. Serjeant, "The "Sunnah Jāmi'ah," Pacts with the Yathrib Jews, and the "Taḥrīm" of Yathrib: Analysis and Translation of the Documents Comprised in the So-Called 'Constitution of Medina'," *Bulletin of the School of Oriental and African Studies* 41:1, (1978); or, Mohamed Berween, "Al-Wathiqa: The First Islamic State Constitution," *Journal of Muslim Minority Affairs* 23, (2003), among many others.

[46] Berween, "Al-Wathiqa" 103

[47] Patricia Crone, *Slaves on Horses: The Evolution of the Islamic Polity*, (Cambridge: Cambridge University Press, 2003) 87

[48] W. Montgomery Watt, *Muhammad at Medina*, (Oxford: Oxford University Press, 1956) 144

[49] Watt, *Islamic Political Thought*, 27

[50] Ishaq, 682-683

[51] W. Montgomery Watt, *Islam and the Integration of Society*, (London: Routledge & Kegan Paul, 1961) 90

[52] Tamim Ansaray, *Destiny Disrupted: A History of the World Through Islamic Eyes*, (New York: PublicAffairs/Perseus Books Group, 2010) 39

[53] Berkey, 99

[54] Nimrod Hurvitz, *The Formation of Hanbalism: Piety into Power*, (New York: Routledge/Taylor & Francis Group, 2002) 41

[55] H.A.R. Gibb, "The Evolution of Government in Early Islam," *Studia Islamic* 4 (1955) 5

[56] Berkey, 72

[57] Berkey, *The Formation of Islam*, 77

[58] Ella Landau-Tasseron, "The Status of Allies in Pre-Islamic and Early Islamic Arabian Society," *Islamic Law & Society* 13, no. 6 (2006) 13

[59] Bernard Lewis, "On the Revolutions in Early Islam," *Studia Islamica* 32 (1970) 217

[60] H.A.R. Gibb, "The Evolution of Government in Early Islam," *Studia Islamic* 4 (1955) 7

[61] Lewis, 226-227

[62] Watt, *Islamic Political Thought*, 33

[63] Patricia Crone and Martin Hinds, *God's Caliph: Religious authority in the first centuries of Islam*, (Cambridge: Cambridge University Press, 2003) 19

[64] Watt, *Islamic Political Thought*, 42

[65] Crone and Hinds, *God's Caliph*, 41-42

[66] Ibid. 64

[67] Johann Fueck, "The Role of Traditionalism in Islam" in *Studies on Islam*, translated and edited by Merlin L. Swartz, (New York: Oxford University Press, 1981) 100-101

[68] George Makdisi, "Institutionalized Learning as a Self-Image of Islam" in *Religion, Law and Learning in Classical Islam*, (London: Variorum, 1991) 75

[69] Crone and Hinds, *God's Caliph*, 51 *ff*

[70] Ibid. 74

[71] Ibid 74 *ff*

[72] Watt, *Islamic Political Thought*, 73

[73] Ibid. 75

[74] Noah Feldman, *The Fall and Rise of the Islamic State*, (Princeton: Princeton University Press, 2008) 34

[75] Fueck, 101

[76] Ignaz Goldziher, *"Muslim Education"* in *The Formation of the Classical Islamic World, vol. 43: Education and Learning in the Early Islamic World*, general editor Lawrence I. Conrad, edited by Claude Gilliot, (Farnham, Surrey: Ashgate Publishing Limited, 2012) 13

[77] Seyyed Hossein Nasr, "Islamic Conception of Intellectual Life," in *Dictionary of the History of Ideas*, edited by Philip P. Weiner, (New York: Charles Scribner's Sons, 1973) II:639-652

[78] Berkey, 26 *ff*

[79] George F. Hourani, "Islamic and Non-Islamic Origins of Mu'tazilite Ethical Rationalism," *International Journal of Middle East Studies* 7, no. 1 (1976) 65

[80] Hourani, 67

[81] Gibb, 17

[82] Fueck, 104

[83] Chibli Mallat, "From Islamic to Middle Eastern Law a Restatement of the Field (Part I)," *The American Journal of Comparative Law* 51:4, (2003) 724

[84] Mallat, 719

[85] Wael B. Hallaq, "Considerations on the Function and Character of Sunnī Legal Theory," *Journal of the American Oriental Society* 104:4 (1984) See also Gideon Libson, "On the Development of Custom as a Source of Law in Islamic Law," *Islamic Law and Society* 4:2 (1997)

[86] Hallaq, 687

[87] Satoe Horii, "Reconsideration of Legal Devices (Ḥiyal) in Islamic Jurisprudence: The Ḥanafīs and Their "Exits" (Makhārij)", *Islamic Law and Society* 9:3 (2002) 312-313

[88] *Hadith* of Muhammad, from al-Tirmidhi (4:2167), ibn Majah (2:1303) and others. Some varying wording exists.

[89] H.A.R. Gibb, *Arabic Literature – An Introduction*, 2nd edition, (Oxford: Oxford University Press, 1974) 29

[90] Gibb, 36

[91] Gibb, 36 *ff*

[92] Watt, *Islamic Political Thought*, 29 "There is indeed an Arabic phrase (*dini wa-dunyawi*) which is commonly translated 'religious and secular' but which properly means 'religious and this-worldly'. Moreover the connotations of the Arabic word *din* in Islamic countries, though it may be translated 'religion', are quite different from those of the English word 'religion'. *Din* may cover nearly the whole conduct of life."

Chapter 3

[93] If you have the time and inclination, Patricia Crone's short book *Pre-Industrial Societies* (Oxford and Cambridge, Mass.: Blackwell, 1989) is well worth reading.

[94] See, e.g., Henry Sumner Maine, *Ancient Law*, (New York: H. Holt, 1908) 33; James Lindgren, "Symposium: Why the Ancients may not have needed a System of Criminal Law," *Boston University Law Review* 76:29, (1996)

[95] Crone, *Pre-Industrial Societies*, 72 "The fact that the early Christians were bent on giving unto Caesar what was Caesar's in no way rendered them politically innocuous, nor was the fact that they refused to worship the Roman emperor the worst of their political sins. What really made them dangerous was their capacity to unite hitherto disparate masses in the name of an alternative vision and thus, whether this was intended or not, create an alternative power structure which the emperors ultimately preferred to have on their side rather than against them....As the Roman adoption of Christianity shows, rulers sometimes tried to cash in on horizontal linkages rather than to suppress them (although they usually tried to suppress them first). A monotheist religion such as Christianity offered the possibility of integration of the masses on a new scale..." Joseph Dahmus, *A History of the Middle Ages*, (New York: Doubleday & Co, 1968) 45-46 agrees, noting that the Jews who also had refused to worship Rome were a relatively small proportion of the empire's population, and so were given exemption from the civic cult of Rome, but the sheer number of the Christians didn't allow for this exemption and tolerance. See also Francis X. Murphy, *Politics and the Early Christian*, (New York: Desclee Company, Inc., 1967) 79 "...while the fact of being a professed Christian was considered a crime, it was not because of allegiance to a god foreign to roman belief. It was rather that, in refusing to participate in the honor given to the emperor and the state gods, they were considered obstinate fanatics who defied the power of the civil authority."

[96] Crone, 78

[97] The citations to several authors and works are omitted intentionally. There is no desire to take cheap shots at those who recognize a surface difference but miss an important underlying commonality in Christianity and Islam.

[98] Nicolas Zernov, *Eastern Christendom: A Study of the Origin and Development of the Eastern Orthodox Church*, (New York: G. P. Putnam's Sons, 1961) 84

[99] Jonathan P. Berkey, *The Formation of Islam: Religion and Society in the Near East, 600-1800*, (New York: Cambridge University Press, 2003) 58

[100] Jaroslav Krejči, *The Paths of Civilization – Understanding the Currents of History* (New York: Palgrave Macmillan, 2004) 155-156

[101] William E. Paden, "Elements of a New Comparativism," in *A Magic Still Dwells, Comparative Religion in the Postmodern Age*, edited by Kimberley C. Patton and Benjamin C. Ray, (Oakland, CA: University of California Press, 2000) *passim*

[102] Krejči, 155-156

[103] Charles Williams, *The Descent of the Dove: A Short History of the Holy Spirit in the Church*, (Vancouver, BC: Regent College Publishing, 2002) 2-3

[104] Francis X. Murphy, *Politics and the Early Christian*, (New York: Desclee Company, Inc., 1967) 42

[105] John 6:15 JB

[106] John Witte Jr., *God's Joust, God's Justice: Law and Religion in the Western Tradition*, (Grand Rapids, MI: Eerdmans, 2006) 10

[107] Mohamed Berween, "Al-Wathiqa: The First Islamic State Constitution," *Journal of Muslim Minority Affairs* 23, (2003) 103

[108] Ibid.

[109] Koran 4:11, Arberry's translation

[110] Luke 10:25-37, JB

[111] Chibli Mallat, "From Islamic to Middle Eastern Law a Restatement of the Field (Part I)," *The American Journal of Comparative Law* 51:4, (2003) 720 "Textually, it may be true that the Qur'an had "only" 500 legal verses out of more than 6000 in total, but this a significant proportion for a book of this nature, which compares favorably with the Pentateuch, the Bible's legal book par excellence. After all, the Qur'an is much shorter than the Bible, and this relatively large number of verses is further enhanced, for the purpose of legal reach, by the unusual length of the legal verses, especially in such areas as marriage and succession."

[112] Acts 2:46, 3:1 JB

[113] Acts 2:9-11 JB

[114] Thomas Glyn Watkin, "Paul of Tarsus: A citizen of no mean city," *The Journal of Legal History*, 9:2 (1988) 119-141

[115] See, e.g., Pieter G.R. De Villiers, "Union with the transcendent God in Philo and John's Gospel," *HTS Teologiese Studies/Theological Studies* 70:1, (2014) and Donald A. Hagner, "The Vision of God in Philo and John: A Comparative Study," *Journal of the Evangelical Theological Society* 14 (1971)

[116] Murphy, 89

[117] Paul Johnson, *A History of Christianity*, (New York: Atheneum, 1976) 8

[118] See discussion of this point throughout J. Spencer Trimingham, *Christianity among the Arabs in Pre-Islamic Times*, (London: Longman Publishing Group, 1979)

[119] W. Montgomery Watt, *Islamic Political Thought, the Basic Concepts*, (Edinburgh: Edinburgh University Press, 1968) 45 *ff*

[120] Berkey, 72

[121] Watt, 27

[122] Karen Armstrong, *Islam: A Short History*, (New York: Random House, Inc., 2002) p. xi

[123] See, e.g., Bernard Lewis, *The Jews of Islam*, (Princeton: Princeton University Press, 1984)

[124] Albert Hourani, *A History of the Arab Peoples*, (Cambridge, Mass.: Belknap, Harvard University Press, 1991) 62

Chapter 4

[125] Joseph Dahmus, *A History of the Middle Ages*, (New York: Doubleday & Co, 1968) 112

[126] So far as I can find, this term was first used by Eugen Rosenstock-Huessy, author of *Out of Revolution: Autobiography of Western Man*, (New York: Morrow, 1938) among other works. He held doctorates in both law and philosophy, and in Germany was a professor of legal history, concentrating on the Middle Ages, until the rise of the Nazis forced him to the US, first to Harvard and then Dartmouth. This term was used later by Harold Berman in his own work on Western law, the two volumes of his *Law and Revolution: The Formation of the Western Legal Tradition,* (Cambridge, Mass: Harvard University Press, 1983). It also goes by a number of other names in histories of the Middle Ages, such as the Investiture Controversy or Contest, or the Gregorian Reforms, though those terms limit and narrow the subject of this struggle too much. "The term 'Investiture Contest' is unfortunate, because it obscures the breadth of the controversy which centred round Gregory..." "Far from being concerned solely with the narrow issue of investitures, the Investiture Contest was in reality a conflict between two violently opposed conceptions of the nature of Christian society." Gerd Tellenbach, *Church, State and Christian Society at the Time of the Investiture Contest*, translated by R.F. Bennett, (New York: Harper & Row, Publishers, Inc., 1970) forward at xi.

[127] Lynn F. Pitts, "Relations between Rome and the German 'Kings' on the Middle Danube in the First to Fourth Centuries A.D.," *The Journal of Roman Studies* 79 (1989) 45-58

[128] S.T. Loseby, "Marseille – Late Antique Success Story?" *The Journal of Roman Studies* 82 (1992) *passim.*

[129] R.P.C. Hanson, "The Reaction of the Church to the Collapse of the Western Roman Empire in the Fifth Century," *Vigiliae Christianae* 26:4 (1972) 273

[130] Dahmus, *A History of the Middle Ages* 97

[131] Chris Wickham, "The Other Transition: From the Ancient World to Feudalism," *Past & Present* 103 (1984) 9 *ff*

[132] Stephen Neff, "Decline and Emergence: Roman law and the Transition from Antiquity to Feudalism," *The Journal of Legal History* 5:2 (1984) 103

[133] Dahmus, 36, see also Neff, 99

[134] Dahmus 189

[135] Garth Fowden, "Bishops and Temples in the Eastern Roman Empire A.D. 320-435," *Journal of Theological Studies, N.S.*, xxix, pt. 1, (1978) 53

[136] Dahmus, 59

[137] Hanson, "The Reaction of the Church" 280, also Dahmus, 90

[138] Fowden, 58

[139] Harold J. Berman, "The Background of the Western Legal Tradition in the Folklaw of the Peoples of Europe," *The University of Chicago Law Review* 45:3 (1978) 569

[140] Paul Johnson, *A History of Christianity*, (New York: Atheneum, 1976) 103

[141] Simon Coates, "Venantius Fortunatus and the Image of Episcopal Authority in Late Antique and Early Merovingian Gaul," *The English Historical Review* 115:464 (2000) 1133-4

[142] Gerd Tellenbach, *Church, State and Christian Society at the Time of the Investiture Contest*, translated by R.F. Bennett, (New York: Harper & Row, Publishers, Inc., 1970) 71

[143] Tellenbach, 73-4

[144] Coates, 1116-6

[145] Acts 8:9-24 JB records the confrontation of the disciple Peter with Simon Magus, who attempted to purchase spiritual gifts and authority.

[146] Tellenbach, 127

[147] Johnson, 134

[148] Warren Winfred Lehman, "The First English Law," *The Journal of Legal History* 6:1 (1985) 9-10. This appears in the dooms of Aethelbert I, probably written between 600-615 in Kent, though there is a strong argument that this was a later addition to the dooms.

[149] Johnson, 135

[150] Dahmus, 205

[151] M.K. Lawson, "Archbishop Wulfstan and the Homiletic Element in the Laws of Æthelred II and Cnut," *The English Historical Review* 107:424 (1992) 5-6

[152] Thomas C. VanCleve, *The Emperor Frederick II of Hohenstaufen Immutator Mundi*, (Oxford: Oxford University Press, 1972) 201

[153] Rosamond McKitterick, "The Illusion of Royal Power in the Carolingian Annals," *The English Historical Review* 115:460 (2000) 1

[154] Tellenbach, 69

[155] Johnson, 125-126

[156] Ibid.

[157] Dahmus, 219

[158] Ibid.

[159] Tellenbach, 84

Page 340

[160] Ibid. 128 *ff*

[161] Ibid, 131

[162] Ibid. 115

[163] Charles A. Frazee, "The Origins of Clerical Celibacy in the Western Church," *Church History 57, Supplement: Centennial Issue* (1988) 108

[164] Uta-Renate Blumenthal, "Pope Gregory VII and the Prohibition of Nicolaitism*"* in *Medieval Purity and Piety: Essays on Medieval Clerical Celibacy and Religious Reform*, edited by Michael Frassetto, (New York and London: Garland Publishing, Inc., 1998) 242. Even Gregory VII could not succeed in enforcing celibacy widely or uniformly. More legislation against clerical marriage came in the twelfth century at the first and second Lateran councils, held in 1123 (marriage of any person in higher orders invalid) and 1139 (no ordination of married men). It wasn't for several centuries afterward that celibacy came to be widely accepted and practiced in the Western church.

[165] Eugen Rosenstock-Huessy, *Out of Revolution: Autobiography of Western Man*, (New York: Morrow, 1938) 530

[166] This is the same Leo IX who is often remembered as the Pope who cited the spurious "Donation of Constantine" to the Eastern Church, causing what is usually referred to as "The Great Schism".

[167] Tellenbach, 109

[168] Ibid., 111

[169] Ibid.

[170] Dahmus, 227

[171] Tellenbach, 113

[172] Philip Schaff, *History of the Christian Church*, (New York: Charles Scribners' Sons, 1910) chapter II, section 16

[173] Tellenbach, 150. Rosenstock-Huessy went further: "The Papal Revolution of the eleventh century introduced the principle of dualism into the political world. Jesus had spoken of God and of Caesar, it is true; but God is not a visible institution. The dualism of institutions enables men to seek Him. In Western civilization, at least since Gregory VII, two sovereign powers have always balanced each other. This, and this alone, has created European freedom." *Out of Revolution,* 543

[174] Ibid. 156

[175] David S. Clark, "The Medieval Origins of Modern Legal Education: Between Church and State," *The American Journal of Comparative Law* 35:4 (1987) 669-670

[176] Ibid. 674

[177] Friedrich Heer, *The Medieval World: Europe 1100-1350*, translated by Janet Sondheimer, (London: Weidenfeld & Nicholson, 1990) 245

[178] Ibid. 246

[179] Ibid. 247-248

[180] Wolfgang P. Mueller, "The Recovery of Justinian's Digest in the Middle Ages," *Bulletin of Medieval Canon Law* 20 (1990) 1. It is hardly a coincidence that after Gregory VII's declarations the year before, and his own scholars' continuous search for precedents and authorities, that Roman law re-emerged in this year.

[181] Clark, 676

[182] Umberto Eco, *Baudolino*, translated by William Weaver, (New York: Harcourt, 2002) 59-60

[183] H. Koeppler, "Frederick Barbarossa and the Schools of Bologna," *The English Historical Review* 54:216 (1939) 58

[184] VanCleve, 261

[185] Ibid. 260

Chapter 5

[186] George F. Hourani, "Islamic and Non-Islamic Origins of Mu'tazilite Ethical Rationalism," *International Journal of Middle East Studies* 7, no. 1 (1976) 72

[187] Hourani, 76

[188] Hourani, 81

[189] Hourani, 86

[190] A. I. Sabra, "The Appropriation and Subsequent Naturalization of Greek Science in Medieval Islam: A Preliminary Statement," *History of Science xxv* (1987) 224-225

[191] Seyyed Hossein Nasr, *Science and Civilization in Islam*, (Cambridge, Mass.: Harvard University Press, 1968) introduction, *passim*

[192] Nasr, "Islamic Conception of Intellectual Life" 639 *ff*

[193] Andrew C. Miller, "Jundi-Shapur, bimaristans, and the rise of academic medical centres," *Journal of the Royal Society of Medicine* 99 (2006) 615–617

[194] Sabra, 226, 228

[195] Michael Cooperson, "Baghdad in Rhetoric and Narrative," *Muqarnas* 13 (1996) 99. He further notes the enduring legacy of Baghdad by pointing out that Ibn Batuta's visit was in 1326, after the city had been destroyed by the Mongols in 1258.

[196] Sabra, 228

[197] H.A.R. Gibb, *Arabic Literature – An Introduction*, 2nd edition, (Oxford: Oxford University Press, 1974) 65

[198] Gibb, 50

[199] Jonathan P. Berkey, *The Formation of Islam: Religion and Society in the Near East, 600-1800*, (New York: Cambridge University Press, 2003) 79

[200] Bernard Lewis, "On the Revolutions in Early Islam," *Studia Islamica* 32 (1970) 222

[201] Ignaz Goldziher, "The Attitude of Orthodox Islam Toward the 'Ancient Sciences'" in *Studies on Islam*, translated and edited by Merlin L. Swartz, (New York: Oxford University Press, 1981) 185

[202] Gibb, 67-68, quoting Duncan B. Macdonald, "Development of Muslim Theology, Jurisprudence and Constitutional Theory," in *Series of Handbooks in Semitics*, edited by James Alexander Craig (New York: Charles Scribner's Sons, 1903) 140

[203] Marco Demichelis, "Between Muʿtazilism and Syncretism: A Reappraisal of the Behavior of the Caliphate of al-Maʾmūn," *Journal of Near Eastern Studies* 71:2 (2012) 263

[204] Ignaz Goldziher, *Introduction to Islamic Theology and Law*, translated by Andras and Ruth Hamori, (Princeton: Princeton University Press, 1981) 90-91

[205] Goldziher, *Introduction* 88 and 92-94

[206] Goldziher, *Introduction* 88

[207] Karen Armstrong, *Islam: A Short History*, (New York: Random House, 2002) 58

[208] Goldziher, *Introduction* 85

[209] Hourani, 72

[210] Ahmad Taheri-Iraqi, *Zandaqa in the Early Abbasid Period with Special Reference to the Poetry*, (April 1982 doctor's thesis, University of Edinburgh) 56

[211] Ibid, 56, 59-60, 61, 62, 57-58

[212] Tamim Ansaray, *Destiny Disrupted: A History of the World Through Islamic Eyes*, (New York: PublicAffairs/Perseus Books Group, 2010) 105

[213] George Makdisi, *The Rise of Colleges: Institutions of Learning in Islam and the West*, (Edinburgh: Edinburgh University Press, 1981) introduction

[214] Goldziher, *Introduction* 54

[215] Goldziher, *Introduction* 62

[216] Gibb., 64

[217] Tayeb El-Hibri "Harun al-Rashid and the Mecca Protocol of 802: A Plan for Division or Succession?" *International Journal of Middle East Studies* 24:3 (1992) *passim*

[218] Walter M. Patton, *Ahmed ibn Hanbal and the Mihna*, (Leiden: Brill, 1897) 50-51

[219] Christopher Melchert, *Makers of the Muslim World: Ahmad Ibn Hanbal*, (Oxford: Oneworld Publications, 2006) 35

[220] Demichelis, 272

[221] Hurvitz, 117

[222] I'll use *Mihna* because for too many people using the word "inquisition", as *Mihna* is often translated, may cause confusion between what happened in Baghdad in the 800s and what took place in Spain several hundred years later. Those two historical events were very different.

[223] Patton, 68-70

[224] Melchert, 48

[225] Patton, 89

[226] Michael Cooperson, "Two Abbasid Trials: Ahmad Ibn Hanbal and Hunayn B. Ishaq," *Al-Qantara XXH*, 2 (2001) 375. Caliph al-Ma'mun had died only four months after the beginning of the Mihna, and al-Mutasim was his successor.

[227] Hurvitz, 131

[228] See, e.g., Patton, 104 *ff*, and Hurvitz, 131 *ff*

[229] Patricia Crone and Martin Hinds, *God's Caliph: Religious authority in the first centuries of Islam*, (Cambridge: Cambridge University Press, 2003) 1

[230] Ibid. 49

[231] Ibid. 51

[232] John A. Nawas, "The Mihna of 218 A.H. / 833 A.D. Revisited: An Empirical Study," *Journal of the American Oriental Society*, 116:4 (1996), *passim*

[233] Christopher Melchert, "The Adversaries of Aḥmad Ibn Ḥanbal," *Arabica*, T. 44, Fasc. 2 (1997) 235

[234] Hurvitz, "Who is the Accused? The Interrogation of Ahmad Ibn Hanbal" 361

[235] Ibid. 371

[236] Susan A. Spectorsky, "Ahmad ibn Hanbal's Fiqh," *Journal of American Oriental Society* 102:3 (1982) 463 *ff*

[237] Hurvitz, "Who is the Accused? The Interrogation of Ahmad Ibn Hanbal" 372

[238] Cooperson, 376

[239] Nimrod Hurvitz, "Miḥna as Self-Defense," *Studia Islamica* 92 (2001) 96

[240] Ira M. Lapidus, "Separation of State and Religion in the Development of Early Islamic Society," *International Journal of Middle East Studies* VI (1975), *passim*

[241] Berkey, 125

[242] Muhammad Qasim Zaman, "The Caliphs, the ʿUlamāʾ, and the Law: Defining the Role and Function of the Caliph in the Early ʿAbbāsid Period," *Islamic Law and Society* 4:1 (1997) 26

[243] Patton, 123

[244] Edward Grant, "The Fate of Ancient Greek Natural Philosophy in the Middle Ages: Islam and Western Christianity," *The Review of Metaphysics*, 61:3 (2008) 515, quoting Pervez Hoodbhoy, *Islam and Science: Religious Orthodoxy and the Battle for Rationality*, (London: Zed Books, 1991) 111. This was more severe than the beating given to Ahmad Ibn Hanbal, according to the sources quoted in Patton.

[245] Sabra, 242

[246] Grant, 514

[247] Grant, 512-513

[248] Grant, 514

[249] Goldziher, "The Attitude of Orthodox Islam Toward the ʿAncient Sciences'" 205-206

[250] Goldziher, "The Attitude of Orthodox Islam'" 186-187

[251] Sabra, 240

[252] Goldziher, "The Attitude of Orthodox Islam'" 199

[253] Grant, 507

[254] Hurvitz, *The Formation of Hanbalism: Piety into Power*, 104

[255] Ibid. 153

[256] Sherman A. Jackson, "The Alchemy of Domination? Some Asharite Responses to Mutazilite Ethics," *International Journal of Middle East Studies* 31:2 (1999) 190

[257] H.A.R. Gibb, *Arabic Literature – An Introduction*, 2nd edition, (Oxford: Oxford University Press, 1974) 121

[258] George Makdisi, "Ashʿarī and the Ash'arites in Islamic Religious History I," *Studia Islamica* 17 (1962) 46

[259] Ibid. 47

[260] George Makdisi, "The Significance of the Sunni Schools of Law in Islamic Religious History," *International Journal of Middle East Studies* 10:1 (1979) 3

[261] Ibid. 6

[262] Makdisi, *The Rise of Colleges, 9 ff*

[263] Ibid. 36

[264] George Makdisi, "Hanbalite Islam," in *Studies on Islam*, translated and edited by Merlin L. Swartz, (New York: Oxford University Press, 1981) 238

[265] W. Montgomery Watt, *Islamic Political Thought, the Basic Concepts*, (Edinburgh: Edinburgh University Press, 1968) 74

[266] Seyyed Hossein Nasr, "The Meaning and Role of "Philosophy" in Islam," *Studia Islamica* 37 (1973) 77

[267] Grant, 509

[268] Makdisi, "Ash'arī and the Ash'arites in Islamic Religious History I," 45

[269] Berkey, 215

[270] Ignaz Goldziher relates the delightful story of a fellow called "Hanfash", since he changed schools in progression from Hanbali, to Hanifa, to Shafi'i. See his *Introduction to Islamic Theology and Law*, 48

[271] George Makdisi, *The Rise of Colleges*, 146

[272] George Makdisi, "Scholasticism and Humanism in Classical Islam and the Christian West," in *Religion, Law and Learning in Classical Islam*, (London: Variorum, 1991) 176

Chapter 6

[273] George Makdisi, "Muslim Institutions of Learning in Eleventh-Century Baghdad", in *Religion, Law and Learning in Classical Islam*, (London: Variorum, 1991) 49

[274] George Makdisi, *The Rise of Colleges: Institutions of Learning in Islam and the West*, (Edinburgh: Edinburgh University Press, 1981) 32 *ff*

[275] Alan B. Cobban, "Medieval Student Power," *Past & Present* 53 (1971) 39-42

[276] David S. Clark, "The Medieval Origins of Modern Legal Education: Between Church and State," *The American Journal of Comparative Law* 35:4 (1987) 706

[277] Makdisi, *The Rise of Colleges*, 146 *ff*

[278] Makdisi, "Muslim Institutions of Learning in Eleventh-Century Baghdad" 49

[279] Ibid.

[280] Clark, 656

[281] Davide Cantoni and Noam Yuchtman, "Medieval Universities, Legal Institutions, and the Commercial Revolution," *The Quarterly Journal of Economics* 129:2 (2014) 10

[282] Umberto Eco, *Baudolino*, translated by William Weaver, (New York: Harcourt, 2002) 59

[283] H. Koeppler, "Frederick Barbarossa and the Schools of Bologna," *The English Historical Review* 54:216 (1939) 586 *ff*

[284] Ibid. 594 *ff*

[285] George Makdisi, "Institutionalized Learning as a Self-Image of Islam" in *Religion, Law and Learning in Classical Islam*, (London: Variorum, 1991) 77

[286] A.I. Sabra, "The Appropriation and Subsequent Naturalization of Greek Science in Medieval Islam: A Preliminary Statement", *Hist. Sci. xxv* (1987) 238

[287] Friedrich Heer, *The Medieval World: Europe 1100-1350*, translated by Janet Sondheimer, (London: Weidenfeld & Nicholson, 1990) 246

[288] Paul F. Grendler, "The Universities of the Renaissance and Reformation," *Renaissance Quarterly* 57:1 (2004), *passim*

[289] Makdisi, "Institutionalized Learning as a Self-Image of Islam" 58-59, citing Ibn Qudama, *Tahrim an-nazar fi kutub ahl al-kalam*, edited and translated, with introduction by G. Makdisi, *Ibn Qudama's Censure of Speculative Theology*, Gibb Memorial Series 23 (London: Luzac, 1962). [22 (English pagination), 32 (Arabic pagination), para.55.]

[290] Heer, 258

[291] Edward Grant, "The Fate of Ancient Greek Natural Philosophy in the Middle Ages: Islam and Western Christianity," *The Review of Metaphysics* 61:3 (2008) 515-516 See also James Hannam's *God's Philosophers: How the Medieval World Laid the Foundations of Modern Science*, (London: Icon Books, Ltd., 2009) for clarification of the role of the Church and growth of a free knowledge in Western Europe, including correction of some widely believed myths.

[292] Herbert J. Muller, *Freedom in the Western World: From the Dark Ages to the Rise of Democracy*, (New York: Harper & Row, 1963) 58

Chapter 7

[293] Rodney Stark and Roger Finke, *Acts of Faith: Explaining the Human Side of Religion*, (Berkeley and Los Angeles, CA: University of California Press, 2000) 1-14

[294] Patricia Crone, *Pre-Industrial Societies,* (Oxford and Cambridge, Mass.: Blackwell, 1989) 78

[295] Ibid. 191

[296] Starke and Finke, 55 They briefly discuss the findings of surveys of university professors that seem to indicate that "hard" scientists, in surveys conducted roughly 100 years apart, did not show the expected decline in the proportion of scientists having a religious faith.

[297] Patrick Henry, "'And I Don't Care What It Is': The Tradition-History Of A Civil Religion Proof-Text," *Journal of the American Academy of Religion* 49:1 (1981) 41.

[298] Binyamin Abrahamov, "Ibn Taymiyya on the Agreement of Reason with Tradition," *The Muslim World* LXXXII:3-4 (1992) 257

[299] Ibid. 258-261

[300] Elliot A. Bazzano, "Ibn Taymiyya, Radical Polymath, Part 1: Scholarly Perceptions," *Religion Compass* 9:4 (2015) 100-101

[301] Abrahamov, 272

[302] Bazzano, 103

[303] W. Montgomery Watt, *Islam and the Integration of Society*, (London: Routledge & Kegan Paul, 1961) 172

[304] Colin Imber, *Ebu's-Su'ud: The Islamic Legal Tradition*, (Stanford: Stanford University Press, 1997) 40

[305] Ibid, 71

[306] Michael M. Pixley, "The Development and Role of the Şeyhülislam in Early Ottoman History," *Journal of the American Oriental Society* 96:1 (1976) 95

[307] Imber, 7, see also Pixley, 89-91

[308] Imber, 14

[309] Albert Hourani, *A History of the Arab Peoples*, (Cambridge, Mass.: Belknap, Harvard University Press, 1991) 233

[310] Pixley, 94, footnote no. 32

[311] Richard W. Bulliet, "The Shaikh Al-Islām and the Evolution of Islamic Society", *Studia Islamica* 35 (1972) 53

[312] Pixley, 95

[313] Bulliet, 66-67

[314] Watt, 281

[315] Bernard Lewis, *The Jews of Islam*, (Princeton: Princeton University Press, 1984) 155

[316] It may be surprising and dismaying to the Western reader to learn how late some of the "disabilities" at law against minorities in society lingered into the modern era.

[317] Bernard Lewis, *Islam and the West* (New York: Oxford University Press, 1993) 136

Chapter 8

[318] Bernard Lewis, *The Jews of Islam*, (Princeton: Princeton University Press, 1984) 109

[319] Eugene Rogan, *The Arabs – A History*, (New York: Basic Books/Perseus Books Group, 2011) 61 *ff*

[320] Tamim Ansaray, *Destiny Disrupted: A History of the World Through Islamic Eyes*, (New York: PublicAffairs/Perseus Books Group, 2010) 160-161

[321] Afaf Lutfi Al-Sayyid Marsot, *A Short History of Modern Egypt*, (Cambridge: Cambridge University Press, 1985) 50-53

[322] Rogan, 80-81

[323] Hsu Cheng-Hsiang *The First Thirty Years of Arabic Printing in Egypt, 1238-1267 (1822-1851): A Bibliographical Study with a Checklist by Title of Arabic Printed Works*, (Doctoral Thesis, University of Edinburgh, January 1985) 6-7

[324] William J. Watson, "İbrāhīm Müteferriḳa and Turkish Incunabula," *Journal of the American Oriental Society* 88:3: (1968) 436

[325] Ibid., *passim* for discussion of the printed works.

[326] Cheng-Hsiang, 8

[327] Rogan, 85 *ff*

[328] Cheng-Hsiang, xxv

[329] Ibid, 41, 49, 51, 57

[330] Marsot, 57

[331] Rogan, 62-63

[332] Reinhard Schulze, "The Birth of Tradition and Modernity in 18th and 19th Century Islamic Culture – the Case of Printing," *Culture & History* (1997) 45

[333] Francis Robinson, "Technology and Religious Change: Islam and the Impact of Print," *Modern Asian Studies*, 27:1 (1993) 234

[334] Jonathan P. Berkey, *The Formation of Islam: Religion and Society in the Near East, 600-1800*, (New York: Cambridge University Press, 2003) 225

[335] Schulze, 48

[336] Schulze, 42 *ff*

[337] Robinson, 239

[338] John Patrick Douglas Balfour Kinross, Baron, *The Ottoman Centuries*, (New York: Perennial/HarperCollins, 2002) 210, 279

[339] Murat Çizakça, "The Evolution of Domestic Borrowing in the Ottoman Empire," in *East Meets West – Banking, Commerce and Investment in the Ottoman Empire,* edited by Philip L. Cottrell, (Aldershot: Ashgate Publishing Limited, 2008) 1

[340] Murat Birdal, *The Political Economy of Ottoman Public Debt*, (London: I.B. Tauris, 2011) 31

[341] Kinross, 480

[342] Birdal, 6

[343] Kinross, 508-509

[344] Birdal, 54

[345] Timur Kuran, *Islam & Mammon: The Economic Predicaments of Islamism*, (Princeton: Princeton University Press, 2004) 136 See also his essays in *The Long Divergence: How Islamic Law Held Back the Middle East*, (Princeton: Princeton University Press, 2011), for example those

dealing with the reluctance and delay prior to adopting the corporate form for conducting business.

[346] Rogan, 109 *ff*
[347] Lewis, 24 *ff*
[348] W. Montgomery Watt, *Islamic Political Thought, the Basic Concepts*, (Edinburgh: Edinburgh University Press, 1968) 49
[349] Tamim Ansaray, *Destiny Disrupted: A History of the World Through Islamic Eyes*, (New York: PublicAffairs/Perseus Books Group, 2010) 290
[350] Lewis, 184
[351] Kinross, 453 *ff*
[352] *"The Rescript of Gülhane"* (November 3, 1839), Boğaziçi University, Atatürk Institute of Modern Turkish History, the translator is unknown, accessed October 28, 2015 http://www.ata.boun.edu.tr,
[353] Dora Glidewell Nadolski, "Ottoman and Secular Civil Law," *International Journal of Middle East Studies* 8:4 (1977) 523
[354] Ibid., Appendix B
[355] Noah Feldman, *The Fall and Rise of the Islamic State* , (Princeton: Princeton University Press, 2008) 78
[356] Kinross, 503
[357] *"The Ottoman Constitution"* (1876, with 1909 amendments), Boğaziçi University, Atatürk Institute of Modern Turkish History, the translator is unknown, accessed October 28, 2015, http://www.ata.boun.edu.tr,
[358] Kinross, 557
[359] William Eleroy Curtis, *The Turk and His Lost Provinces*, (New York: Fleming H. Revell Company, 1903), *forward*

Chapter 9
[360] David Fromkin, *A Peace to End all Peace: The Fall of the Ottoman Empire and the Creation of the Modern Middle East,* (New York: Henry Holt and Company, LLC, 1989) 142
[361] Fromkin, 173 *ff*
[362] Afaf Lutfi Al-Sayyid Marsot, *A Short History of Modern Egypt*, (Cambridge: Cambridge University Press, 1985) 80-81
[363] Eugene Rogan, *The Arabs – A History*, (New York: Basic Books/Perseus Books Group, 2011) 158 *ff*
[364] Fromkin, 421-423
[365] Andrew Mango, *Atatürk: The Biography of the Founder of Modern Turkey*, (New York: The Overlook Press, 2000) 193-195
[366] G. E. Von Grunebaum, "Nationalism and Cultural Trends in the Arab Near East," *Studia Islamica* 14 (1961) 135

[367] Kinross, John Patrick Douglas Balfour, Baron, *Atatürk: The Rebirth of a Nation*, (Nicosia, Northern Cyprus: K. Rustem & Brother, 1981), p 340 *ff*
[368] Tamim Ansaray, *Destiny Disrupted: A History of the World Through Islamic Eyes*, (New York: PublicAffairs/Perseus Books Group, 2010) 303
[369] Niyazi Berkes, *The Development of Secularism in Turkey*, (Montreal: McGill University Press, 1964) 3-4
[370] Berkes, 137
[371] Esin Orūcū, "Judicial Navigation as Official Law Meets Culture in Turkey," *International Journal of Law in Context* 4:1 (2008) 40
[372] Mango, 297, 301, 313, 331, Kinross, 425 *ff*
[373] *"Constitution of the Republic of Turkey"* (1982, as amended through 2011), Article 174, accessed October 28, 2015, https://www.constituteproject.org/constitution/Turkey_2011.pdf
[374] Dora Glidewell Nadolski, "Ottoman and Secular Civil Law," *International Journal of Middle East Studies* 8:4 (1977) Appendix B
[375] *"Constitution of the Republic of Turkey"* (1924, http://genckaya.bilkent.edu.tr/1924constitution.pdf accessed November 2, 2015, links to Edward Mead Earle, "The New Constitution of Turkey," *Political Science Quarterly* 40:1 (1925), one of the first discussions of that initial document.
[376] Adnan Güriz, "Sources of Turkish Law," in *Introduction to Turkish Law, 5th edition*, edited by Tuğrul Ansay, and Don Wallace Jr., (The Hague: Kluwer Law International, 2004) 9
[377] Ruth A. Miller, "The Ottoman and Islamic Substratum of Turkey's Swiss Civil Code," *Journal of Islamic Studies* 11:3 (2000) 339
[378] See www.diyanet.gov.tr the website the Presidency of Religious Affairs of the Republic of Turkey
[379] İştar B. Gözaydın, "A Religious Administration to Secure Secularism: The Presidency of Religious Affairs of the Republic of Turkey," *Marburg Journal of Religion* 11:1 (2006) 1
[380] Noah Feldman, *The Fall and Rise of the Islamic State*, (Princeton: Princeton University Press, 2008) 78- 79
[381] Feldman, 79
[382] Nadolski, Appendix B
[383] Orūcū, 44-46
[384] Marsot, 80
[385] Rogan, 166
[386] Rogan, 192
[387] *"Constitution of Egypt"* (1923), accessed October 28, 2015, http://www.constitutionnet.org/vl/item/egypt-constitution-1923
[388] William Tetley, *"Mixed Jurisdictions: Common Law v. Civil Law (Codified and Uncodified)"*, *Louisiana Law Review* 60 (2000) 699-700

[389] Ibid.
[390] Ibid.
[391] Marsot, 96-97
[392] Rogan, 285 *ff*
[393] Von Grunebaum, 126
[394] Rogan, 304 *ff*
[395] Steven Isaac, "The Ba'th of Syria and Iraq," in *The International Encyclopedia of Revolution and Protest: 1500 to the Present*, edited by Immanuel Ness, (Malden, MA: Wiley-Blackwell, 2009) *passim*
[396] "*The Constitution of Syria, September 5, 1950,*" in Amos J. Peaslee, *Constitutions of Nations, 2nd edition*, (The Hague: M. Nijhoff, 1956) III 360-361
[397] Adeed Dawisha, "Requiem for Arab Nationalism," *Middle East Quarterly* 10:1 (2003) 31
[398] Ibid.
[399] "*Constitution of the Syrian Arab Republic*" (2012), accessed October 28, 2015 http://www.voltairenet.org/article173033.html
[400] W. Montgomery Watt, *Islamic Political Thought, the Basic Concepts*, (Edinburgh: Edinburgh University Press, 1968) 116

Chapter 10

[401] David Commins, *The Wahhabi Mission and Saudi Arabia*, (New York: I.B. Tauris, 2009) 71
[402] Ibid. 7 *ff*
[403] Ibid. 14
[404] Eugene Rogan, *The Arabs – A History*, (New York: Basic Books/Perseus Books Group, 2011) 68-71
[405] Commins, 62
[406] Ibid. 94
[407] Commins, 110. See also Robert Lacey, *Inside the Kingdom – Kings, Clerics, Modernists, Terrorists, and the Struggle for Saudi Arabia*, (New York: Viking/Penguin Group, 2009) 162-163, 235-236, and 238 for several examples.
[408] "*Plessy v. Ferguson*," 163 U.S. 537 (1896), accessed October 28, 2015, https://www.law.cornell.edu/supremecourt/text/163/537
[409] "*Brown v. Board of Education*," 347 U.S. 483 (1954), accessed October 28, 2015, http://caselaw.findlaw.com/us-supreme-court/347/483.html
[410] "*The Basic Law of Governance of Saudi Arabia*" (1992) accessed October 28, 2015, http://www.saudiembassy.net/about/country-information/laws/The_Basic_Law_Of_Governance.aspx

[411] Aharon Layish, "Saudi Arabian Legal Reform as a Mechanism to Moderate Wahhābī Doctrine," *Journal of the American Oriental Society* 107:2 (1987) passim

[412] Seyyed Vali Reza Nasr, *Mawdudi & The Making of Islamic Revivalism*, (New York: Oxford University Press, 1996) 3

[413] Nasr, 57

[414] Muzaffar Hussain, "The Islamic Polity of Abdul A'La Mawdudi," *VFAST Transactions on Islamic Research* 3:1 (2014) 21

[415] Nasr, 83

[416] Nasr, 92

[417] Nasr, 89

[418] Albert Hourani, *A History of the Arab Peoples*, (Cambridge, Mass.: Belknap, Harvard University Press, 1991) 348

[419] John Calvert, *Sayyid Qutb and the Origins of Radical Islamism*, (New York: Columbia University Press, 2010) see chapters 2 and 3

[420] Electa Draper, "*Legacy of Islamic revolutionary's hate haunts Greeley*" Denver Post, February 6, 2011, updated February 8, 2011, accessed October 28, 2015, http://www.denverpost.com/ci_17306551

[421] Calvert, 43

[422] Rogan, 281-282

[423] Calvert, 186

[424] Calvert, 199 *ff*

[425] Asyraf Hj.A.B. Rahman and Nooraihan Ali, "The Influence of Al-Mawdudi and the Jama'at Al Islami Movement on Sayyid Qutb Writings", *World Journal of Islamic History and Civilization* 2:4 (2012) 234-235

[426] Calvert, 220, cites in quote to Qutb's works omitted

[427] Lacey, 56-57

[428] Carrie Rosefsky Wickham, *Mobilizing Islam: Religion, Activism, and Political Change in Egypt,* (New York: Columbia University Press, 2002), passim

[429] Frank Griffel, "What do we mean by 'Salafi'? Connecting Muhammad Abduh with Egypt's Nur Party in Islam's Contemporary Intellectual History," *Die Welt Des Islams* 55 (2015) 197-198

[430] Quintan Wiktorowicz, "Anatomy of the Salafi Movement," *Studies in Conflict & Terrorism* 29:207 (2006) 212-217

[431] Wickham, 128

[432] Tamim Ansaray, *Destiny Disrupted: A History of the World Through Islamic Eyes*, (New York: PublicAffairs/Perseus Books Group, 2010) 163

[433] Itzchak Weismann, "Genealogies of Fundamentalism: Salafi Discourse in Nineteenth-Century Baghdad," *British Journal of Middle Eastern Studies* 36:2 (2009) 271

[434] Michael Cook, "On the Origins of Wahhābism," *Journal of the Royal Asiatic Society, Third Series* 2:2 (1992) 200

[435] Basheer M. Nafi, "A Teacher of Ibn Abd Al-Wahhab: Muhammad Hayat Al-Sindi and the Revival of Ashab Al-Hadiths Methodology," *Islamic Law & Society* 13:208 (2006) 214

[436] Ibid. 223-224

[437] Ira M. Lapidus, "Islamic Revival and Modernity: The Contemporary Movements and the Historical Paradigms," *Journal of the Economic and Social History of the Orient* 40:4 (1997) 456

[438] Lapidus, *passim*

[439] J. Spencer Trimingham, *The Sufi Orders in Islam*, (Oxford: Clarendon Press, 1971) 105

Chapter 11

[440] Ian Black, "A look at the writings of Saudi blogger Raif Badawi – sentenced to 1,000 lashes", *Guardian*, January 14, 2015, accessed October 28, 2015 http://www.theguardian.com/world/2015/jan/14/-sp-saudi-blogger-extracts-raif-badawi

[441] Raif Badawi, "From an Earlier Blog of Raif Badawi, Sentenced to 1000 Lashes, Jail, Fine in Saudi Arabia", on *Gatestone Institute*, July 7, 2014, accessed October 28, 2015, http://www.gatestoneinstitute.org/4393/raif-badawi

[442] Doğan News Agency, "Turkish pianist Fazil Say sentenced to 10 months in prison for blasphemy in retrial", *Hurriyet Daily News*, (Istanbul) October 19, 2015, http://www.hurriyetdailynews.com/turkish-pianist-fazil-say-sentenced-to-10-months-in-prison-for-blasphemy-in-retrial.aspx?PageID=238&NID=54824&NewsCatID=341 As of October 26, 2015, his conviction has been overturned on appeal. Once the appellate court issues its opinion (it hasn't yet), the original trial court must either disagree or agree with it. If that court agrees, the acquittal will stand. If it does not, the process will continue. See Doğan News Agency, "Top appeals court reverses blasphemy decision against Turkish pianist Say", *Hurriyet Daily News*, (Istanbul) October 26, 2015, http://www.hurriyetdailynews.com/top-appeals-court-reverses-blasphemy-decision-against-turkish-pianist-say.aspx?pageID=517&nID=90336&NewsCatID=339 This judicial process has now lasted over two and one-half years, and shows no sign of ending soon. The threat of drawn-out legal proceedings with their worry and expense may be a more effective muzzle on those like Mr. Say who wish to express their opinions than the original conviction.

[443] *"Rules of Court"* European Court of Human Rights, accessed October 28, 2015, http://www.echr.coe.int/Documents/Rules_Court_ENG.pdf

444 *Leyla Şahin v. Turkey* [GC], no. 44774/98, ECHR (2005) 8, paragraph 35
445 *Şahin*, 45, paragraph 5, Dissenting Opinion of Judge Tulkens. The discussion here is only a brief summary of the case, leaving our many interesting details. If you'd like to read the entire 54-page opinion, it is available online at HUDOC, the search page for European Court of Human Rights opinions.
446 Arzu Çakır Morin, "Mosque for gays to open in France" *Hurriyet Daily News*, (Istanbul) November 19, 2012, accessed October 28, 2015 http://www.hurriyetdailynews.com/mosque-for-gays-to-open-in-france.aspx?pageID=238&nid=34981
447 Wendy Gillis, "Toronto mosque is gay friendly, mixed gender prayers led by a woman" *Toronto Star News*, August 25, 2013, accessed October 28, 2015 http://www.thestar.com/news/gta/2013/08/25/islamic_scholars_experience_d iversity_of_muslim_practices_at_u_of_t_summer_program.html
448 Nuray Mert, "An open letter to some 'Western liberals and leftists, '" *Hurriyet Daily News*, (Istanbul) January 26, 2015, accessed October 28, 2015, http://www.hurriyetdailynews.com/an-open-letter-to-some-western-liberals-and-leftists.aspx?pageID=449&nID=77419&NewsCatID=406
449 Cairo – AP, "Saudi woman sentence to 10 lashes for driving car", *Hurriyet Daily News*, (Istanbul) September 28, 2011, accessed October 28, 2015 http://www.hurriyetdailynews.com/default.aspx?pageid=438&n=saudi-woman-sentenced-to-10-lashes-for-driving-car-2011-09-28
450 Hassan Rouhani, "Iran 'happy' dancers get suspended sentences", *Al-Jazeera*, September 19, 2014, accessed October 28, 2015, http://www.aljazeera.com/news/middleeast/2014/09/iran-happy-dancers-get-suspended-sentences-201491913331993392.html
451 Mark LeVine, *Heavy Metal Islam: Rock, Resistance, and the Struggle for the Soul of Islam*, (New York: Three Rivers Press, 2008) 157-158
452 Ankara - Anatolia News Agency, "Religious leaders mull conditions for 'breast milk bank'" *Hurriyet Daily News*, (Istanbul) February 27, 2013, accessed October 28, 2015, http://www.hurriyetdailynews.com/religious-leaders-mull-conditions-for-breast-milk-bank.aspx?pageID=238&nID=41942&NewsCatID=341
453 Belgin Akaltan, "We are like the cop shot on the pavement", *Hurriyet Daily News*, (Istanbul) January 17, 2015, accessed October 28, 2015, http://www.hurriyetdailynews.com/we-are-like-the-cop-shot-on-the-pavement.aspx?pageID=238&nID=77045&NewsCatID=469
454 Sabir Nazar, "Principle political standpoints in Al-Absurdistan", *Dawn.com*, (Pakistan) August 29, 2012, accessed October 28, 2015,

http://www.dawn.com/news/745445/principle-political-standpoints-in-al-absurdistan
LeVine, 286

Chapter 12

456 "Former Imam Of Mecca's Grand Mosque: There Is No Escaping Reform To Bring Islam Back To Its Path Of Tolerance", *MEMRI*, Special Dispatch No.6063, June 2, 2015, accessed October 28, 2015, http://www.memri.org/report/en/0/0/0/0/0/0/8593.htm This report notes his article on February 22, 2015, in the Saudi daily Al-Riyadh, which together with earlier articles in the Fall of 2014, set out his call for reform.
457 "Qatari Religious Scholar Calls for A Moderate and Modern Islam" *MEMRI*, Special Dispatch No. 885, March 25, 2005, accessed October 28, 2015, http://www.memri.org/report/en/0/0/0/0/0/0/1345.htm
458 Steven Stalinsky, "A Muslim Friend of America", *New York Sun*, May 23, 2007, accessed October 28, 2015 http://www.nysun.com/foreign/muslim-friend-of-america/55011/
459 "Saudi Intellectual: Western Civilization Has Liberated Mankind", *MEMRI*, Special Dispatch No.2332, April 29, 2009, accessed October 28, 2015, http://www.memri.org/report/en/print3264.htm
460 "In Open Letter To Muslim World, French Muslim Philosopher Says Islam Has Given Birth To Monsters, Needs Reform", *MEMRI*, Special Dispatch No.5873, November 5, 2014, accessed October 28, 2015, http://www.memri.org/report/en/print8206.htm
461 Mustafa Akyol, *Islam Without Extremes: A Muslim Case for Liberty*, (New York: W.W. Norton & Company, 2011) 205
462 Ibid. 261
463 Nimrod Raphaeli, "Sayyed Ayad Jamal Al-Din – Liberal Shi'ite Cleric and Foe of Iran" *MEMRI*, Inquiry & Analysis Series Report No.582, January 21, 2010, accessed October 28, 2015 http://www.memri.org/report/en/print3920.htm
464 Yotam Feltner, "Liberal Iraqi Shi'ite Scholar Sayyed Ahmad Al-Qabbanji Calls For Reason In Islamic Discourse and Jurisprudence", *MEMRI*, Inquiry and Analysis Series Report No. 937, February 21, 2013, accessed October 28, 2015, http://www.memri.org/report/en/print7015.htm
465 See, e.g., Noha El-Hennawy, "Gamal al-Banna leaves behind a legacy of controversial views on Islam" *Egypt Independent*, February 17, 2003, accessed October 28, 2015, http://www.egyptindependent.com/news/gamal-al-banna-leaves-behind-legacy-controversial-views-islam, Michael A.

Page 356

Slackman, "A voice for 'new understanding' of Islam," *Africa & Middle East - International Herald Tribune*, in *New York Times*, October 20, 2006, accessed October 28, 2015, http://www.nytimes.com/2006/10/20/world/africa/20iht-profile.3237674.html?_r=1& See as well any bookseller for the many published works by al-Banna.

[466] Gamal Al-Banna, "The Muslim Brotherhood is strong, but weak to lead Egypt" *Oasis*, December 5, 2012, accessed October 28, 2015, http://www.oasiscenter.eu/articles/arab-revolutions/2012/12/05/gamal-al-banna-the-muslim-brotherhood-is-strong-but-weak-to-lead-egypt

[467] See the website for the documentary on the Morchidat: http://www.casablancacalling.com/, accessed October 28, 2015; also, Emma Batha, "Morocco's Islamic women preachers lead social revolution" *Reuters*, May 19, 2015, accessed October 28, 2015, http://www.reuters.com/article/2015/05/19/us-morocco-women-morchidat-idUSKBN0O40MG20150519

[468] Ayaan Hirsi Ali, *Heretic: Why Islam Needs a Reformation Now*, (New York: HarperCollins Publishers, 2015) 50-55

[469] Ibid. 7

[470] Ibid. 24 *ff*

[471] "Muslim Intellectual Calls for 'Protestant Islam'", *MEMRI*, Special Dispatch No.1198, July 6, 2006, accessed October 28, 2015, http://www.memri.org/report/en/0/0/0/0/0/0/1734.htm

[472] "Egyptian Philosopher Murad Wahba: Secularism Is the Only Way to Emerge from Our Crisis of Lack of Rationality" *MEMRI*, Special Dispatch No. 3446, December 14, 2010, accessed October 28, 2015, http://www.memri.org/report/en/print4841.htm

[473] "Reformist Author Dr. Shaker Al-Nabulsi: Recent Attacks by Islamists on Arab Liberals – A Sign of Distress and Imminent Defeat" *MEMRI*, Special Dispatch No.1163, May 12, 2006, accessed October 28, 2015, http://www.memri.org/report/en/0/0/0/0/0/804/1688.htm,

[474] Lafif *Lakhdar, "Why the Reversion to Islamic Archaism?"* Forbidden *Agendas* from the Journal *Khamseen*, (*1984*) 276, also online, accessed October 28, 2015, https://libcom.org/book/export/html/51691

[475] Ibid. *passim*

[476] Ibid. *passim*

[477] Lafif Lakhdar, "Moving from Salafi to Rationalist Education," *Middle East Review of International Affairs* 9:1 (2005) 30

[478] M. Zuhdi Jasser, *A Battle for the Soul of Islam: An American Muslim Patriot's Fight to Save His Faith* (New York: Threshold Editions/Simon & Schuster, Inc., 2012) 5

[479] Ibid. 21

[480] Ibid. 115

[481] Abdullahi Ahmed An-Na'im, *Islam and the Secular State: Negotiating the Future of Shari'a*, (Cambridge, Massachusetts and London: Harvard University Press, 2008), preface, at p. vii

[482] Ibid. 1

[483] Ibid. 7

[484] Ibid. 84

[485] Ibid. 104

[486] Ibid. 13

[487] Ibid. 135

[488] Raymond Ibrahim, "Egypt's Sisi: Islamic 'Thinking' Is 'Antagonizing the Entire World'", *Arab World*, translation by Michele Antaki, January 1, 2015, accessed October 28, 2015, http://www.raymondibrahim.com/from-the-arab-world/egypts-sisi-islamic-thinking-is-antagonizing-the-entire-world/

[489] Dieter Bednarz and Klaus Brinkbäumer, "Interview with Egyptian President Sisi: 'Extremists Offend the Image of God'" *Spiegel online International*, February 9, 2015, accessed October 28, 2015, http://www.spiegel.de/international/world/islamic-state-egyptian-president-sisi-calls-for-help-in-is-fight-a-1017434.html

[490] Dale F. Eickelman, "The Coming Transformation of the Muslim-Majority World," *The Review of Faith & International Affairs* 7:2 (2009) 23

[491] Charles Kurzman, editor, *Liberal Islam: a Sourcebook*, (New York: Oxford University Press, 1998) 4

[492] Ibid. 13-16

[493] Menahem Milson, "Reform vs. Islamism in the Arab World Today" *MEMRI* Special Report No. 34, September 15, 2004, accessed October 28, 2015, http://www.memri.org/report/en/0/0/0/0/0/855/1220.htm

[494] "Liberal Writer Mansour Al-Hadj Proposes Founding An Independent Islamic Organization To Address Root Causes Of Violent Extremism, Promote Peaceful Aspects Of Islam" *MEMRI*, Special Dispatch No. 6118, July 30, 2015, accessed October 28, 2015, http://www.memri.org/report/en/0/0/0/0/0/804)/8681.htm

Chapter 13

[495] Lafif Lakhdar, *"Vatican II as a model for Islamic reform"*, Almuslih.org, accessed November 6, 2015, http://almuslih.org/index.php?option=com_content&view=article&id=228:va tican-ii-as-a-model-for-islamic-reform&catid=38:obstacles-to-reform&Itemid=207

[496] Abdullahi Ahmed An-Na'im, *Islam and the Secular State: Negotiating the Future of Shari'a*, (Cambridge, Massachusetts and London: Harvard University Press, 2008) *passim*

[497] W. Montgomery Watt, *Islam and the Integration of Society*, (London: Routledge & Kegan Paul, 1961) 283

[498] Taha Akyol, *"The founding of an Islamic university in Turkey"* Hurriyet Daily News, October 2, 2014, accessed November 8, 2015, http://www.hurriyetdailynews.com/the-founding-of-an-islamic-university-in-turkey-.aspx?pageID=449&nID=72424&NewsCatID=458

[499] Khaled Abou El Fadl, "Constitutionalism and the Islamic Sunni Legacy," *UCLA Journal of Islamic & Near Eastern Law* 1, no. 67 (2001-2002) 67

[500] El Fadl, 93

[501] Peter Beyer, "The Religious System of Global Society: A Sociological Look at Contemporary Religion and Religions" *Numen* 45, no. 1 (1998) 20

[502] Selma Tatli, *"AKP is secularizing religious people"* Today's Zaman, June 9, 2014, accessed November 8, 2015, http://www.todayszaman.com/anasayfa_akp-is-secularizing-religious-people_349917.html

[503] Barçın Yinanç, *"I worship so I can do anything I like' is Turks' lifestyle: Scholar"* Hürriyet Daily News, June 16, 2012, accessed November 8, 2015, http://www.hurriyetdailynews.com/i-worship-so-i-can-do-anything-i-like-is-turks-lifestyle-scholar.aspx?pageID=238&nID=23284&NewsCatID=338

[504] Patricia Crone, *Slaves on Horses: The Evolution of the Islamic Polity*, (Cambridge: Cambridge University Press, 2003)87

[505] Richard W. Bulliet, *The Case for Islamo-Christian Civilization*, (New York: Columbia University Press, 2004) 73

[506] W. Montgomery Watt, *Islamic Political Thought, the Basic Concepts*, (Edinburgh: Edinburgh University Press, 1968) 123

[507] Muhammad Qasim Zaman, *The Ulama in Contemporary Islam: Custodians of Change*, (Princeton: Princeton University Press, 2002) While this book shows some innovators within the ranks of today's *ulama*, it is without question that they are, and remain, a minority among their brothers.

Afterword

[508] Christopher Melchert, *Makers of the Muslim World: Ahmad Ibn Hanbal*, (Oxford: Oneworld Publications, 2006) 85

Made in United States
North Haven, CT
05 May 2024

52145256R00202